Mindful Jewish Living

Compassionate Practice

Jonathan P. Slater

AVIV PRESS

NEW YORK

Library of Congress Cataloging-in-Publication Data
Slater, Jonathan P., 1952–
    Mindful Jewish living : compassionate practice / Jonathan P. Slater.
      p. cm.
    Includes bibliographical references.
    ISBN 0-916219-23-2 (alk. paper)
    1. Meditation–Judaism.   2. Spiritual life—Judaism.   3. Compassion
—Religious aspects—Judaism.   4. Ethics, Jewish.   I. Title.

BM723.S6 2004
296.7—dc22   2004047631

Grateful acknowledgment is given to Farrar, Straus and Giroux for permission to
reprint "ABC" by Robert Pinsky, from Jersey Rain © 2000, reprinted by permission of
Farrar, Straus and Giroux, Inc.

Published by Aviv Press
An Imprint of the Rabbinical Assembly
3080 Broadway
New York, NY 10027

Jacket design by Adrienne Weiss
Printed in the United States of America

To Martin S. Cohen, my friend and my teacher
To Sylvia Boorstein, my teacher and my friend

Table of Contents

Foreword

"**L**ook with your own eyes and you'll see," my mother would say when I, as a child, protested that I couldn't find something that she'd asked for, something in plain view. I always laughed. Who else's eyes, after all, could I have looked with? Or, indeed, what *other* than eyes (nose? ears?) could I have looked with? I did not know—and neither did my mother, I'm sure—that "Look with your own eyes and you'll see" is from Psalm 91:8, *rak b'einekha tabit,* and that, in context, it introduces the fundamental truth that actions create consequences. Even without knowing the particular teaching, or its source, I got the larger sense of the phrase: It is possible to walk around in a life, eyes open as if awake, and still miss what most needs to be seen and what is in plain view. This is a book about looking with your own eyes— looking with *all* the organs of physical sensation as well as with the mind and heart—looking with full attention at every moment so that life is continually revealed as sacred, inspiring a just and compassionate response. And it is most particularly a book that celebrates looking with eyes that are directed, supported, nourished, encouraged, and informed by Judaism.

Paying close and careful attention—being mindful—is a universal human possibility. Apart from any religious or cultural context, paying attention reveals basic truths of existence: things keep changing so everything in form is temporal and fragile; the mind suffers pain in excess of the situation when it is unable to accommodate to situations it cannot change; everything that exists is in relationship, the result of complex causes and a factor in the yet-to-unfold future. It's enormously inspiring to me to think that human beings are naturally endowed with the capacity for mindfulness that establishes wisdom and I trust that wisdom sustains compassion.

My own experience is that paying attention makes me grateful and intentional and careful and inspired about living. If, when I get up in the morning, I notice that the continuing cycle of in-and-out breaths that has kept my body alive all these years is still comfortably operating and realize that it could have been otherwise, I'll feel grateful. Any gratitude I feel will help me keep my mind from grumbling if, as I get out of bed and do my morning stretching exercises, the room is too cold, or my body is too stiff, or worse, the things I'd hoped would be happening in my life are not turning out the way I wanted them to. If I am able to acknowledge what is true for me and just stretch, my mind will not suffer. It will intend, instinctively, toward compassion. The more I realize how my best intentions are challenged by even the smallest of difficulties and how easily I fall into unhappiness and then cause unhappiness, the more I am motivated to choose my response carefully. And anytime I stop telling myself the story of *what* is happening and allow my mind to shift, as it will naturally, to the awareness *that* it is happening, I am amazed. I fall in love, again, with the miracle of life itself. The fundamental truths of life experience aren't parochial. I think it's the same for everyone, regardless of context.

And, I am glad for my context. I am glad to have a blessing for saying, "Thank you . . ." when I wake up in the morning and a liturgy that keeps my mind hopeful—"With an abounding love You have loved us"—as it demands that I affirm that what I want most of all is for my heart to connect with goodness. I experience all of the particulars of my life as a Jew—Scripture, prayer, Sabbath, holidays, family, life-cycle awareness, commandments—as reminders of the truths I need to know, as focusing tools that direct my attention to the truths I need to know, and as ways to talk about and sing about and manifest in the world the truths I need to remember.

It's possible to see what is true with plain eyes, but this book says, "Look with your own Jewish eyes. . . ." It promises, and demonstrates through personal example, how looking through those eyes can discover that accommodating to the reality of any moment ends suffering in the heart. It shows, again through personal example, how the forms and practices of Jewish life evoke the absolute, direct knowledge that the non-suffering heart is gracious and compassionate, patient and honest. You'll recognize yourself in this book, and as you read you will rejoice in your own goodness and celebrate your connection to all Creation. You will know that God is real.

You could look with plain eyes, but here in this book are the extra eyes of the many perspectives of a Jewish life that facilitate clear seeing. And, as a bonus, you get to look through the eyes of mystics whose minds were so full of the words and images of Jewish tradition that they could not help but see import and meaning and direction—the presence of God—in everything. You'll find, I think, as I did, that the central message, "Look! It's right there!" builds as the book adds—one after another—yet another aspect of Judaism as an incliner of the mind in the direction of truth.

And, you get to look through the eyes of my good friend Jonathan, my colleague and my teacher and my spiritual companion whose own ability to see the Divine all around has written its way into the confidence behind his words. Reading what he has written is like having someone stand next to you as you try to see the hidden picture in a puzzle book. "Look!" he keeps saying. "It's right there! Look with your own Jewish eyes!"

Sylvia Boorstein

Preface

*T*here is an old story from the *shtetl*. The rabbi of the town has served in his position for many years, a little bit longer than even the gentile town constable. Every morning the rabbi leaves his home to cross the town square to go to services. Every morning on his way he crosses paths with the constable. One day, the latter was in a foul mood, and when he saw the rabbi rushing to the synagogue, out of habit in such situations he yelled, "Where do you think you're going?" The rabbi, startled at this unusual and unexpected question replied, "Who knows?" The constable, somewhat embarrassed by his own brusque challenge, found this response curious, but also irritating. "What do you mean you don't know? Where are you going?" The rabbi, again, responded, "Who knows?" With this, the constable flew into a rage, cuffing the rabbi about the head, grabbing him by the collar, dragging him to the police station, and throwing him in a cell. "Now you're not going anywhere!" the constable yelled. To which the rabbi replied, "You see, I set out this morning to go the synagogue, but, who knows when they set out where they will wind up?"

How far back should I look to find the point in my life from which this book emerges? Where do its origins lie? How have I moved from "Who knows?" to "Here I am"? Now, having concluded the process of writing it, I sense that there is nothing else I could have done instead—and that is true, because, in fact, I have done that very thing. Perhaps, at some moment in the past, at some point along the road to this moment I could have decided otherwise, or exigencies of health, expectations of family, flagging interest, or other conditions could have distracted me from this enterprise—but they did not. I have arrived at this moment, book in hand, with gratitude and wonder.

I am grateful to my father, the son of immigrants, whose love of Hebrew, Judaism, and synagogue prayer helped me to be one of those (apparently) rare children who liked Hebrew School. His inner prayer life (of which we learned only as he was dying), his trust in the goodness of the world despite his experiences in the Second World War, and his personal integrity have all shaped my own experience of my life.

I am grateful to my mother, a third-generation American, whose scientific interest in the physical world and curiosity about all people have helped me to find pleasure in the everyday. She has undertaken her own course of study of Jewish texts and meaning, and shared that with me—even as she has pursued her own ongoing personal spiritual quest, shaped by her scientist's skeptical eye but motivated by her caring heart. I thank her for her company, and for her example.

I am grateful for the fact that I have had the opportunity to serve as a congregational rabbi. In particular, I want to thank the members of Congregation Beth Ami in Santa Rosa, CA, and the broader Jewish community of Northern California. Over the course of my nineteen years in that congregation I grew and changed, as I studied different texts and investigated their teachings. And those loving people willingly joined in and supported me, growing themselves, learning who they were to be as Jews. I learned much of what I have written about living my life with them.

I am grateful to have had exceptional teachers and guides on my path. Rabbi Levi Weiman-Kelman was a friend in high school and a roommate during rabbinical school. From him, I learned about the spirit behind the texts we studied together. Rabbi Shelly Lewis taught hasidic texts to the Conservative rabbis of Northern California when we met on retreat. While I did not quite understand them then, he helped to place them in the realm of "legitimate" Jewish texts for me. Rabbi Amy Eilberg cited hasidic texts in many of her Torah commentaries in the *Northern California Jewish Bulletin,* and opened my heart to their message of compassion and truthful living.

I am grateful to the vision of the Nathan Cummings Foundation, and particularly to Rabbi Rachel Cowan, its Director of Jewish Programs for many years. The Foundation supported two programs that have contributed significantly to my own spiritual growth: the Mindfulness Leaders Training Program and the Spirituality Institute. Through those programs I have met many wonderful fellow seekers and found support for my own spiritual quest; I have also had the opportunity to learn with Rabbi Jeff Roth. More important, the programs provided the context in which I have become friends and co-workers with Rabbis Cowan, Nancy Flam, Sheila Peltz Weinberg, and Nehemia Polen. Their friendship, open-hearted companionship, and mindful approach to work have helped to transform my life. How we work together, how we speak together, how we endeavor to see, know, and act the truth help me to experience the reality of what I have written about.

Through the Spirituality Institute I met, again, Dr. Arthur Green. Our paths crossed when I was in college and he was at Havurat Shalom. His book *Seek My Face, Speak My Name* challenged me deeply when it first appeared in 1992. By the time I met Art again in the rabbinic program of the Spirituality Institute, I had come to embrace the theology he presented in his book. In this program, Art introduced me to the power of hasidic thinking and the beauty of hasidic texts. His passionate teaching and his love for these texts inspired me, in part, to write this book. I hope that it is worthy of one of his students. Any flaws, of course, are only my own.

I am grateful to Aviv Press and the Publications Committee of the Rabbinical Assembly, chaired by Rabbi Ira Stone, for having given me the opportunity to present what I have learned, and what I live, to a larger community of seekers. It is an honor, and a great responsibility, as a new writer, to be featured so early in the life of a publishing imprint. May my work support those who come after me. If I succeed in that way, it will be largely due to the helpful, sustained and friendly support of Ms. Amy Gottlieb, the editorial director at Aviv Press, and my copyeditor, Ms. Michelle Kwitkin-Close. I am grateful for every question they raised, every challenge they posed and every suggestion they offered to improve the text. The final decisions were mine, but I never made them without recognizing how much care they brought to their work.

I am grateful to my sons Joshua and Derek. They helped me, and allowed me, to become a father in the only meaningful sense of that word. They both, in their own ways, live mindfully and they open my eyes again and again to the truth of my life and of theirs. I could not be prouder of them.

I am grateful to my wife, Barbara. Her love and support have made this book possible. My awareness of how wide a heart can open and how powerful a source of strength it can be flows from the depth of trust we have found together. The preciousness of each day and moment is epitomized in the joy we have found in each other.

I am grateful to my friend Rabbi Martin S. Cohen. He has been an ongoing presence in my life. Irregular letter exchanges, followed by more regular emails and phone calls, have accompanied me from rabbinical school to this day. His humor, his boundless curiosity, his compendious knowledge, and his dedication to helping Jews live their Jewish lives to the fullest are the cause of both joy and admiration. In addition, he was the one who initially encouraged me to even consider writing a book. His regular prompting, "Someone has to write this book, and no one will do it better than you. I'll be right behind you!" actually was an inspiration. As with any good student challenged by his teacher, I took on this project to make him proud of me, and in the end came to realize it was to my own benefit.

I am grateful to my teacher and friend, Sylvia Boorstein. Sylvia and her husband Seymour opened their home and their lives to Barbara and me, and to our families. I have cooked in Sylvia's kitchen. They have eaten at our table. We share such joy in the sense that we have become family to each other.

Sylvia and I met at Congregation Beth Ami, connected by happenstance through Levi Weiman-Kelman. Having Sylvia in the pews on Shabbat inspired me to speak more directly about the experiential spiritual meaning of the Torah, its challenge to wake up and live fully in our lives. I was soon her student in meditation in both the Mindfulness Leadership Training Program and the Spirituality Institute rabbinic program. Over time, I became her teacher as we studied hasidic texts together. More profound than our relationship as students-teachers, however, is the connection we have found in our spiritual lives. We speak the same language. With each other we can say the truth, and we encourage each other in that endeavor. Sylvia read each version of this book and helped me to hear clearly what it is I was trying to say, teaching with every comment. As her student, I sense how much her teaching is in this book. Wherever it falls short in presenting the power, importance, and meaning of mindfulness, I have fallen short.

Martin and Sylvia are my closest friends, and my truest teachers. Together, they officiated at my marriage to Barbara. It is with great love and gratitude that I dedicate this book to them.

JONATHAN P. SLATER
9 JANUARY 2004
15 SHEVAT 5764

Author's Note

*M*y intention in writing this book is to demonstrate the depth of Jewish spiritual life and thought, particularly as reflected in classical hasidic writings. Very little of this corpus has been translated and made accessible to the broader Jewish public. (One central exception is Dr. Arthur Green's work in *Menahem Nahum of Chernobyl: Upright Practices, The Light of the Eyes* and *The Language of Truth: The Torah Commentary of Sefat Emet.*) All of the translations of hasidic texts are my own.

When I cite texts from the Bible, I have used the *JPS Hebrew-English Tanakh* (1999), but regularly change those passages to meet the needs of this work. Similarly, I have consulted the Soncino translation of the Talmud, Midrash Rabbah, and the Zohar, but have offered my own translations.

An ongoing problem in bringing texts from antiquity (even just a pre-modern antiquity) to a modern audience is that of gender. The Hebrew language is gendered, and it addresses the collective in the masculine. But, the Hebrew mind, and the Jewish mind up to the (post-)modern period, is also masculine—thinking primarily in terms of men's experiences, men's perspectives, and men's roles in Jewish society. God, too, is gendered in language and, as a consequence and cause, in thought.

While God is not male in any sense, God yet remains masculine. That is part of the contemporary Jewish project: how to speak of and to God without any gender concept. I have not yet found a way to do this consistently. In this book, at times I have been able to avoid addressing God in the third person masculine, and at other times, not. In some translations I have succeeded by shifting the address to a neutral collective—"we"—while in others I have left the text referring to the male actor—"he." Perhaps this is a failure on my part. I mean no harm or disrespect to any reader, and I do not intend to communicate any gender inference about God or spiritual seekers. I hope that we will all be able to "read through" these texts to the inner message addressed to the hearts and souls of all those who are prepared to wake up and see clearly, to know the truth in their hearts, and to act with compassion.

JONATHAN P. SLATER

Introduction

*O*ver my desk hangs a whimsical, cartoon-like print called "Angels of Mercy." It depicts a winged angel prancing behind a man turned over on his head. The caption reads: "Most people don't know that there are angels whose only job is to make sure you don't get too comfortable & fall asleep & miss your life." At times in my life I have been like "most people," mistaking the angels for the gremlins we think plague our lives, tripping us up and causing us grief and loss. After all, isn't it a gremlin who hides our car keys to make us late? Wasn't it some demon who hid that car from me when I almost sideswiped it? I have learned, over time, to see that they were not imps but angels. They remind me to slow down and pay attention to where I put the keys; they keep me awake and alert when I drive, even if they sometimes scare me. Thanks to those angels, I have woken up to the whole of my life. I am more alive to each moment, grateful for God's blessings announced by these messengers: I can be alive to the whole of my life and not sleep through it.

This is mindfulness: the capacity to see clearly, with calm and awakened mind and heart, the truth of each moment of our lives. As a congregational rabbi I have sat with the dying and their families. There was nothing that I could do to prevent the end of life, nor to lessen the weight of sorrow. That was all true. But, angels of mercy accompanied us, and the truth of death and loss did not prevent us from also seeing the beauty of a life lived with love and respect, of family drawn together in reverential vigil. When I see my life with the greatest clarity, I experience the presence of God in each moment, even in pain and failure. I feel joy in being an expression of God's intent in Creation. Mindful attention to all of life has helped me know great compassion for other people, for their suffering, and also an expansive love for other people, for their dogged will to make a meaningful life. My heart has been wrenched open at the courage of the recovering alcoholic who knows with every fiber of his body that he must focus on "one more breath," "one day at a time," to survive grief and terror, to resist the siren call of drink. At such times, even my sense of "self" as an independent entity and consciousness has dissolved, leaving nothing but love and awe of God.

Mindfulness is not a state; it is a practice. We do not achieve mindfulness once and for all. Rather, we train ourselves to more finely sense and name all aspects of our feelings—physical, emotional, psychological, and spiritual. We make ourselves aware that "this hurts," "this is fun," "this is scary," or "this makes me high." That awareness may then help us to wake up to the manifold ways that we also hide from our feelings, project our anxieties onto others, let our fears control us, and otherwise "miss our lives." When we are blind to the angels who are constantly trying to wake us up, we are also ignorant of the fullness of the lives of others around us. We are blind to their needs, their fears, their struggles. My teacher, Rabbi Saul White *z"l*, loved to talk about "a tzadik in a *peltz*" (a fur coat). The story revealed how hard it is for a person in a fur coat to act compassionately toward others, since he doesn't feel the cold and consequently doesn't sense their suffering. Constricted hearts limit our capacity to see beyond ourselves and diminish our ability to honor the full human dignity of others.

The practice of mindfulness, then, helps us to wake up both to the glory of human existence (of all existence!) and to its pain. When we really pay attention, we come to realize that whatever it is we see in the moment is seen only for that moment. This particular breath lasts only as long as a breath. This itch lasts only until it is scratched or until we are distracted by the mosquito that caused it. Even the pain of loss or flight of ecstasy has a terminus, a limit. Nothing lasts—not even our grudges, not even our loves. Sad as this might sound, it is also liberating. When you step on my toe, I register and recognize pain. I can wince, cry out, and perhaps even react, startled, pushing you away. But, if I can remember that the pain will pass, that it is only my toe, that I have not been attacked by an enemy, I will more quickly calm down from my alarm. I might then also hold back from calling you a clumsy oaf, reminding you of all the mistakes you have ever made in your life, and declaring that I never want to see you again. And, I can even remember to apologize for having pushed you so hard.

We can experience each moment filled with the joy, excitement, grief, or grudge that arises and yet also be set free of attachment to those feelings, since they will pass in the end, anyway. The feelings don't go away immediately, but we are not compelled by them to act in any particular manner. We can choose how to respond. We need not be caught up in our conflicts and struggles. We need not cause ourselves even greater suffering by clinging to the happiness or contentment we may experience in this moment. We feel all of life, but we need not suffer because of it.

When we realize that our feelings are passing phenomena, and we learn thereby to let them pass, we are liberated again from endless conflict with others. What we might consider to be our rightful resentment of another's inattention or impoliteness need not become a righteous vendetta. It need only point us to a clear understanding of the source of our hurt, and the capacity to express that hurt calmly, without projecting motive or moral imperfection onto the other. Further, when we step back to observe our feelings, we may even develop a deeper understanding of how other people, in their complicated inner lives, may inadvertently or unconsciously hurt others. This inclines us to forgive them for having caused us pain. We do not need to cause them pain in turn, and we can help them to make amends by offering them the space to acknowledge our hurt and to reflect on their role in it. The spaciousness in our heart provides room for their change of heart.

And, when we hurt other people, a spacious mind expands our capacity to respond to their pain without lashing out again, resisting the possibility of our having done wrong, avoiding the shame of having hurt another person. When I first entered rabbinical school I remember sitting in the cafeteria. I saw a man come in, his jacket askew, his hair awry—and his gait uneven, labored, jerky. My first thought was, "That drunk, what is he doing here?" Later, when I found out he was a brilliant professor of Bible suffering from a degenerative muscle disease, I thought, "What a fool I am." That thought could have led me to avoid taking any classes with him, to avoid confronting my inner shame again. Had I done so, I would have closed my eyes to an angel of mercy. Instead, I opened my eyes to the truth: I was insensitive, I jumped to conclusions, he suffers from this illness, he is nonetheless able, I am still a student, I can change—and I opened my heart to his teaching. His classes were among the best I took in rabbinical school.

Mindfulness, then, is a practice that helps us to look beyond our particular lives to see the reality of all life—and respond more fully to it. It is not introspection or navel gazing simply for the sake of "self-awareness." It is a path toward a peaceful heart, loving relationships, and a joyful embrace of all of life. It is an invitation to acknowledge the likelihood of making mistakes and the reassurance that it is possible over time to make fewer and repair those we make faster. It is a path of *teshuvah,* return—to the truth, to the reality of our lives, and to God. For in those moments that we are most clearly aware of living the truth of existence, we are most alive and we live most clearly in the presence of God.

Judaism demands that we pay attention to what we are doing, and it is also a path that helps to wake us up to our lives, to remain attentive to what we are doing. The *mitzvot* (and not only the ritual commandments) are not generally acts that we would do naturally. The commandments direct us to do things that refocus our attention away from our "natural" inclinations and toward those values that lie behind the commandments. They also point us toward God. For example, while we may light candles to illuminate a dark dinner table, doing so may not illuminate our hearts or minds to the joy of existence, nor show us how the darkness of sorrow may lighten toward healing. However, when we light those candles at a particular time with a particular prayer formulation, we are taken out of our "normal" routine and directed to pay attention. Reciting the blessing over the candles brings our attention to the presence of holiness in time, helping us to acknowledge our intention to observe Shabbat. In that same moment, we may also wake up to the sadness at the absence of a loved one at the table, the connection to those departed whose traditions we keep, the healing power of light.

In any moment of ritual associated with these natural acts we might wake up to the wonder of our existence. Eating and defecating are natural acts, necessary to sustain life. Marking those acts with blessings lifts them up, demanding that we not take them for granted. Moreover, when we are ill and eating or defecating no longer feel "normal," reciting blessings helps us to maintain a certain trusting calm in the possibility of healing, and again we are awakened to the wonder of our existence.

Judaism as a whole seeks to interrupt the "natural" course of our human existence to point us toward the possibility of a deeper experience of human life. Commandments continually call us to attention. We cannot sleep the day away since we are charged (to the best of our abilities) to engage in productive work. We cannot spend all of our time at work, however, since we must also stop to pray, to study, to procreate, to observe Shabbat and the holidays. We may consider the world to be at our disposal, but the tradition demands that we limit our use of the world's resources. We cannot eat everything that we see; we cannot destroy things wantonly; we cannot take what is not ours. When we work, we rightly expect to earn a fair wage for our work. When we employ others, we must compensate them fairly for their work. The money that we earn is ours to use, but not in its entirety. We are also obligated to give money to the poor and pay for the upkeep of communal religious institutions. In every instance, Judaism intervenes to wake us up, to remind us that we are alive in this world, connected to other people and responsible for our actions.

A central moment in my spiritual development took place in the spring of my senior year of high school. I attended the annual national retreat of my youth group. The topic of study for the weekend was *kashrut*. To help us understand the laws of kosher slaughter in a concrete manner, a *shohet* (ritual slaughterer) had been invited to demonstrate his work. He explained the importance of his intention in the act, and taught us the blessing he recited before cutting. He demonstrated how he sharpened his blade and tested it each time he cut. He taught us some of the details regarding what blemishes might disqualify an animal from being kosher. He had brought a number of chickens, and proceeded to slaughter them. He held each one under his arm, using one thumb to push back the feathers on the neck to reveal the skin. He quickly passed the other hand and blade over the neck of the chicken and then placed it in a large container for its last moments. Some of the other kids at the retreat were grossed out. Others were reverential, deeply invested in the power of tradition and committed to seeing the painlessness of kosher slaughter. I was awestruck, riveted to my place. This was my first direct experience of death. But more, it was my first experience of life-and-death. For all that the chicken flapped about in the container, suggesting some sort of vitality, I knew it was dead. I had so clearly witnessed the instant that the chicken ceased being "alive" and began being "dead" under the knife of the *shohet*. Alive. Dead. Alive. Dead. I was overwhelmed by how fragile life seemed at that moment. I realized how tenuous our hold is on this thing we call "our life." With each breath, I sensed myself the next chicken. It, too, was in the world. It, too, was breathing the air. It, too, felt the spring sunshine. And, then, it was dead and I was alive. From that moment on I have sensed how intimately connected I am to all other beings, to all life. At any moment I am alive or I am dead, just like the chickens. So far, I am still alive, and many other people—including my sister and my father, beloved congregants, and millions of other people—are dead. With each breath: alive, dead, alive, dead. My life is measured along with all other lives. I cannot take my life for granted, nor can I take anyone else's for granted. I cannot deny the inevitability of my death, nor can I prevent or deny the inevitable death of anyone else. But, for each moment that I am alive, I will cherish each breath and do all that I can to sustain and benefit the lives of all those around me.

This is mindfulness: the capacity to experience deeply, with calm and awakened mind and heart, the truth of each moment of our lives. Alive. Dead. Alive. Dead. When we open our hearts and minds to this awareness, we create the possibility that we will make our lives meaningful through love and reverence for other people, and so also for God. This is Judaism: following a religious practice to open our hearts and minds toward others and to God. I have written this book to present mindfulness as a practice in its expression through Jewish life. I have written this book to present Jewish living as a form of mindfulness practice. For me, the two are inter-connected, mutually reinforcing, each pointing to the same ulti-mate goal: a life of truth and joy in the presence of God.

One way to develop mindful attention is through meditation. Meditation is not alien to Judaism. It has been manifest in many different forms in various contexts, shaped by diverse spiritual approaches to Jewish life. It is valuable as a tool. I have practiced meditation as an ongoing exercise only sporadically in my life. Still, I have found that through meditation I have been able to make clearer to myself what wakes me up, what keeps me from missing my life and trampling on others along the way. I will review some of that in the first chapter by way of introduction, to establish a com-mon starting point, a language, a set of values.

Since Judaism is a form of mindfulness practice, I don't really need to find a new way to present Judaism or Jewish practice to speak about mindfulness. Jewish tradition speaks for itself. In that sense, the popular teaching of Shimon Hatzadik rightly can serve as my organizing rubric: "The world rests on three principles: Torah, worship, and lovingkindness" (Pirkei Avot 1:2). In section two of this book (Torah) I will address three subjects. I will first lay out my understanding of Torah and the commandments as a dynamic system that is generated by the willing, mindful interac-tion of Jews with the tradition (chapter two). They meet God in that interaction, and I will talk about the God we can know through mindfulness. We call God *elohim ḥayim,* a living God, a God of life. But, God must also be God in death, and in chapter three I will present awareness of the tension of life-and-death as a powerful source of spiritual growth. The last chapter (four) in this second section will lead us to understand how we interconnect with Torah and God in our relations with others.

Section three deals with *avodah* (worship), the service of God. When we are awake to our lives we can embrace all of life with all of its attendant moments of frustration, loss, and struggle—as well as its moments of satisfaction, love, and joy—with a balanced heart. Returning to the truth of the moment over and over, we learn to see more clearly. As our hearts become more open, more "transparent," we realize that our deepest intentions are for the good of all. Our prayers become confessions. We will consider the connection between the rabbinic concept of *kavanah* (intention) and mindfulness, and look at ways that close attention to the siddur and the form of Jewish prayer can open our hearts to God (chapter five). The siddur is a text whose words may stimulate us to greater awareness; they may wake us up. But the act of prayer is a different phenomenon. We will also, then, pay attention to prayer as a mode of service of God. When we fully engage our hearts and minds and souls in prayer there is nothing left but to love God, and that love is joy (chapter six). To limit the sense of worship to prayer would misrepresent the whole of Jewish religious practice, and we will give attention to ways in which the Jewish holidays open our hearts as well (chapter seven).

Much of Jewish religious and communal life has come to be organized around *tikkun olam* (repairing the world) and *gemilut ḥasadim* (deeds of lovingkindness). Our moral obligations to others, expressed through these activities, are of central importance to any spiritually meaningful life. When they are rooted simply in a sense of obligation, or expressed as a moral imperative without connection to an experience of God, they may fail to sustain that spiritual life. In section four we will consider "deeds of lovingkindness" first from the perspective of the source of all lovingkindness, which is God. This will help us to see more clearly why it is that we must care for others (chapter eight). The ebb and flow of our experience of God's love is sometimes confusing. It may appear that God does not always show us favor, or that God's love is somehow stopped up, unable to reach us. We will consider a different way of viewing the flow of God's love, seeing it even in our needs and deficiencies.

We can be whole even when we lack. We can be full even when we are deficient. Our possession or ownership of things takes on a different meaning when we see that we are truly possessed, owned by God. In that light we will see what a blessing it is to have anything at all and we will have a different sense of what it means to do *tzedakah* (chapter nine). God's love does not flow in a pure form. It is filtered through justice. And it is sometimes perverted through our deeds. We have an obligation to make God's love manifest in its fullest form. That requires us to do the work of justice, which will result in peace. We, then, must seek the balance between love and justice; we must do both righteousness and justice. This endeavor will truly repair the world and bring the Messiah (chapter ten).

I have already suggested that mindfulness as a practice leads to a life of constant *teshuvah*—return to the truth of the moment. This is the movement of: "Alive. Dead. Alive. Dead." Our capacity to wake up again and again to the wonder of being alive is a process of *teshuvah,* since it brings us back to an awareness of God. Our willingness to look carefully at the working of our hearts and minds, to know fully the depths of our pain or the heights of our pride, offers us the possibility of overcoming grief and seeing all others as ourselves. This, too, is *teshuvah,* since it helps us to reconnect with people and it prevents us from hurting them. When we try to live with a full awareness of the moment, we will always be turning toward the truth, and so toward God. Chapter eleven will address the experience of *teshuvah,* and conclude the book.

I believe that mindfulness practice is a way of acting in the world that is enlivening. It is a way of thinking about Judaism and Jewish practice that gives renewed meaning to ritual practice. As a rabbi I am committed to teaching Judaism as a religious, spiritual system—one that takes God seriously. As a Jew, I need Judaism to be a system that leads me to an experience of God. It has been my experience that mindfulness can serve as a path to God. The reality to which the heart wakes up through mindfulness practice is God. We can liberate our hearts to know that truth and to experience the joy that attends its realization. It is that which I hope to share with you.

Section One

Meditation

Chapter One

Waking Up to Compassion

*P*aying attention is not difficult. We do it all the time.

◇   At leisure on the grass we may notice a trail of ants, moving back and forth with great purpose, carrying food to and detritus away from their nest. They work with such determination, with such unity of will, and we sense how satisfying it would be to work together with other people with such a will. It would feel good to be so motivated, so committed to a common task.

◇   At the end of a pleasant dinner, filled with good conversation and satisfying food, we are presented with a sumptuous dessert. The colors of the drizzled sauces dazzle our eyes; the flower garnish sets off the cake, making it come alive. We smell the scent of chocolate, coffee, and cinnamon and our mouths water. We take a small piece on the fork, bring it slowly to our mouths, and taste it carefully, striving to sense each element of its make-up, to take it all in at the same time. The parts make up the whole and the whole transcends our preconceptions. We eat slowly, both to make the experience last and also to enter ever more deeply into its wonderful complexity.

◈ We have taken up a new project at work, one that we had hoped would finally come our way. It is intellectually challenging, requires us to involve a number of interesting and talented people, and will call upon us to use every lesson we have learned up to this point. With each step along the way, we can hardly hold in our excitement, rehearsing for partners and friends what we've learned and what is yet to be done. Our thoughts stay focused on the project—in the shower, eating breakfast, commuting, at the gym, even as we fall asleep. The chance to bring the project to fullness is engaging and enlivening.

◈ We are at the gym for our regular workout. We haven't planned to do anything more than usual, but after warming up we sense that something is different. We feel a surge of energy. Each exercise, in turn, challenges different parts of our bodies and we feel every sinew, each ligament, every surge of blood in our muscles. We breathe deeply, and find that we can do more than ever before. When we are through our bodies are tingling, alive. We sense the wonder of our physical selves, and a connection to all life.

◈ We are at lunch with a friend, at dinner with a child, having coffee with a loved one. Suddenly we realize that the conversation has turned, that we are hearing a tone of voice that means, "I need you." We lower our fork, put aside the dishes, and turn to face the other person. All other sounds disappear, leaving only the voice. The world in the background grows blurry as we concentrate our attention on the other's face. Our hearts and minds are fully open; we are ready for anything. Without fear, without prejudice, without any other intention, we prepare to listen and to respond with love, wholeheartedly.

◈ We are at Shabbat services. The leader reads the list of those who are ill in the congregation in preparation for reciting the *Mi Sheberakh* prayer for healing. We hear the name of a friend, someone who has been ill for some time. Our minds turn to them, and we realize how deeply we fear for their life, and how much that has made us fear for our own. In fact, that fear has kept us from visiting—we cannot stand to see ourselves mirrored in their yellowing face, we cannot tolerate the thought that we, too, might wither away. Our hearts are broken for our friends, and for ourselves—that we find ourselves so scared, and that this previously unnamed fear had kept us from paying a visit to a sick friend. We recite the prayer for healing for our friends, and for ourselves, with tears of guilt, relief, sadness, and joy in our eyes. We are prepared to pay a call, and perhaps to care for others, as well.

We pay attention all the time—but not always with intention, and rarely with awareness of the lesson of the moment. We might decide to slow down and consciously remind ourselves to look carefully at what is about us: the natural world, our bodies and how they work, our relationships and the people who fill our lives. Even then, however, our awareness might be fleeting, and may not help us to connect with the fullness of our lives or to those around us. Mindfulness is a practice that helps us to pay attention with both intention and awareness. It provides a method by which we can invite mindful awareness into every moment of our lives, as well as a means to sustain this effort. Practice and discipline, rehearsal and repetition, breaking bad habits and developing new skills and understanding are the ways that we learn anything new, that we learn to change. Adopting mindfulness as a practice will demand these same actions.

One of the more effective means for training and sustaining a mindful awareness of our lives and the world is meditation. The goal of meditation in this instance is not to empty one's mind or to remove oneself from the world. Rather, it is to help one to pay attention by practicing paying attention. Meditation provides both the technique by which we can learn to see clearly, through which we might wake up, as well as an opportunity to experience this in the moment. The experience we have in meditation is for the sake of how we should live when we are not meditating; it is practice and preparation for life in the midst of our life.

Here is one way in which you can begin meditating. Find a relaxed but attentive position, such as sitting in a chair. You should be able to sit without discomfort, but also in such a manner that you will be able to remain alert to your experience. Once you have found this position, it is customary (though not required) to close your eyes. This is helpful, since it limits one of the more powerful (and distracting) sources of mental stimulation. You do not want to be so calm or cut off from the world that you will fall asleep, but you do want to be able to focus your attention on a limited field.

Where should you place your attention? Although any one phenomenon would do, mindfulness meditation identifies the breath as the point of focus. At the same time, you could also pay attention to any other phenomenon or physical entity. That is, you could pay attention to the sensations in your body as you sit, the sounds of the room, a point on the wall, or a candle-flame or flower before you. But the breath has the advantage of being something that is always present, regular and dependable, and that doesn't demand special equipment or finding the "right" place.

So, now, let your attention rest in the easy, unaffected in-and-out of your breath. You need not control your breath—it will work fine on its own, just as it does at all other times. At first it may be difficult to breathe without conscious interference, but after a few moments, you will find that you can let go, and just breathe. When your breathing is easy and calm, notice where the sensation of the breath is most prominent—where you sense it most clearly. This may be at the tip of your nose, or at the top of your lungs, or in the rise-and-fall of your chest or belly. When you sense this most clearly, allow your attention to rest in that part of the breath.

After a time, you may sense that your action draws the breath in as much as the air moves itself into your body. The process happens by itself; as others have described it, you are "breathed." When you notice this, try not to take over again, but allow the process to proceed. Attend to the rising and falling of your abdomen, the shape of your chest, the sensations of the air going in and out. These are the sensations of breathing; this is what you are attending to. We depend on our bodies to breathe, and we take it for granted (in normal circumstances). But with even the slightest attention we can discover so many interesting aspects of our breath that we had never discerned before.

Until, that is, our minds wander, which they undoubtedly will. We rely on our minds to be active, inquisitive, curious, analytical, creative. We are used to taking in a plethora of stimuli, information of all sorts. Our minds are surfeited in the course of our normal waking life. But when we close off sources of stimulation and try to limit the focus, our minds tend to jump about even more. They reach out for something new to pay attention to, to latch onto, to investigate. This is quite normal, but it is also part of what we want to watch, to notice and to make part of our mindful awareness of our inner workings.

When in the course of sitting and paying attention to your breath you find that instead your mind has wandered down another path—stop for a moment and pay attention to that fact: "Hah, my mind has wandered." The moment of realization that your mind has wandered is a moment of waking up. Before that instant, you had followed whatever train of thought came up, perhaps even retaining some sense of the ongoing movement of your breath. But you were not paying attention specifically to your breath. You were not being mindful. So, when you recognize that fact, you have once again become mindful of your state, and you can once again set out to follow your intention. Do not berate yourself. Many of us are used to succeeding in our daily endeavors, our jobs and work; it is hard for us when we find something difficult. And, after all, how hard could it be to pay attention to one's breath? But it *is* hard. It is a new discipline, a new exercise or practice. And, just as we need to work up to any form of physical exercise, both in warming up as well as in stages increasing our capacity, so too do we need to work up to paying attention.

In a sense, that moment of waking up is a moment of grace. Your awareness is most open, the consciousness of your intention is most clear, and your capacity to combine them in action is most powerful. My clear sense is: not only do I wake up in consciousness in that moment, but my breath returns to a long easy cycle, I straighten up and feel at ease, and my mind feels clearer. When I wake up in my wandering mind, I am liberated from mindlessness and am given again the opportunity to choose where I wish to place my attention. I become more fully myself. I am happy.

Over time, this practice can lead to deeper levels of awareness and to various physical and psychic sensations. We will leave that for others to teach. Even this brief introduction to meditation practice can offer us a great deal of insight into our own lives, and it can lead us to a new understanding of Jewish spiritual practice. The basic elements of this exercise—pay attention, sense changes, note resistances, rededicate oneself to pursue an intention, etc.— are the same elements that mark a mindful life in general. Let's look at ways in which the practice of mindful meditation connects to the practice of mindfulness: an awakened, attentive life.

To be fully present in our lives we must have the capacity to bring a calm, focused attention to all of the ways that we exist in the world—physically, emotionally, psychologically, and spiritually. The practice of paying attention to our breath helps us to develop an awareness of how our breath reflects our inner experience: rapid breath expressing fear or anxiety, slow regular breath corresponding to ease, somnolence, the effort to calm oneself, etc. In particular, the experience of paying attention to our breath helps us to learn how to calm down in most circumstances. Taking a long, calm breath creates the inner space (and, to an extent, even the physical space) from which we can assess and evaluate whatever it is that affects us, and then decide how to respond.

This would be true, as well, if we had chosen to pay attention to any of our other bodily sensations. Paying attention to our posture, or to the feelings of pressure on various parts of our bodies, our minds may also wander. When we wake up to that fact, we sense our bodies anew. We find that we relax in that moment, and sense how our bodies function and respond to different stimuli. We learn the signs that our bodies give us to tell us how we are feeling. When we notice particular sensations—cramp, ache, ease, strength—we can build up a library of experiences to use in the future to help us understand what it is that we are feeling. This, again, can provide the platform from which we can assess and evaluate whatever it is that affects us, and then decide how to respond.

Mindfulness practice helps us to create a more spacious field in which to move through the world. One student noted that when she woke up to the fact that her mind had wandered, she noticed that her breath had shortened, and this was what her breath was like during the frenetic pace of her workday. When she realized that and then brought her attention back to her breath, her respiration rate slowed, each breath lengthening, and she felt more at ease. Often our spontaneous response to stimuli is to shorten our breaths, to pull into ourselves, and to retreat somewhat from the world. When we bring attention to our breath, we then often take deeper, longer breaths. Our chests expand, and we take up more space. When we begin to exhale, the sensation of inhabiting a larger field remains, and we sense a "buffer" around us, so we feel less threatened. We can relax a bit. We have time, and "space," in which to look carefully at what is happening, how we feel, what we expect, what is true. Paying attention to our breaths (or bodies) provides us with room to maneuver in wisdom through our lives.

As we pay attention to the basic physical phenomena of our lives—our breaths, the immediate sensations of the moment—we develop the capacity to notice and identify other feelings and sensations. We learn to note where they exist, where they "come from," what causes them, and what mitigates them. This is part of an important, dynamic process. As we learn to wake up in the moment and not run away from the fact of our inattention, we develop the capacity to tolerate other surprising or embarrassing moments in our lives. As we pay attention to the movement of our breath and to the diversity of our feelings as they spontaneously arise, we become more expert in identifying them when they appear at other moments. In this manner, we will be able to tolerate and hold them, and we will be less surprised by (and more curious about) whatever may come our way. Mindfulness, then, helps us to open up the field we inhabit, and in turn we open our hearts, bodies, and minds to embrace more of the world. Mindfulness practice can help us to be more openhearted and more at ease in our lives.

One of the reasons that we are more able to tolerate and hold whatever may arise in our hearts or minds (or in the world around us) is that as we pay attention, we become aware of the spontaneous nature of thoughts and feelings: they just happen. When we sit to meditate, our minds may be calm and our attention may rest in our breath. And then, without any warning, our minds are running away with this thought and that. Or, our hearts return to this feeling or that. As we sit, our bodies experience sensations: an itch, an ache, a twinge, a gurgle, a flutter. For a moment this feeling may become fascinating. But it also passes as another arises to take its place. The arising and passing away of thoughts and feelings are like the rising and passing away of each breath. It is there for a moment, it has its temporary place, but then it is gone. As we witness this, we learn a new truth about thoughts and feelings: they rise and pass away.

How much attention should we pay to sensations, thoughts, and feelings that are fleeting, ephemeral? Perhaps, a lot; perhaps, none at all. When we are meditating, it may well be that the latter is true. That is, the sensations, thoughts, and feelings may simply be the static of our daily affairs that can be dealt with later. Or they may be the product of our minds, generated to give us something "exciting" to attend to, rather than simply watching our breath. It is well and good to say that these sensations and thoughts do not merit our attention, but often it does not feel that way in the moment. Whatever arises seems important, because we are habituated to think so, to pay attention to thoughts or sensations instead of letting them go. Moreover, what often arises in these moments of relative calm and ease is some aspect of our lives—whether of the moment or from some deeper reservoir of unfinished business—about which there is a particular attraction, a "charge" that draws our attention.

That charge often comes in the form of a story, accompanied by or communicating an aspect of self-assessment or self-judgment. Again, we are used to doing well, to succeeding in all that we set out to do. How frustrating it might be, then, to find that we can't keep our minds on a simple little thing like our breath! "What's wrong with me? Am I so scatterbrained that I can't keep my mind on my breath?" we might find ourselves saying inside. Alternatively, as we think about things that are pressing—work, family, personal health

—we might question the whole of the enterprise: "What am I doing here watching my breath when I have so much to do, when I have to accomplish X?" Our bodies may present us with distractions: aching backs or legs, itches, or cramps. And so, we tell a story about it: "I wish I were in better shape," or "The meditation leader is a tor-turer—when will he finish this session?" or "If I don't scratch my nose I'll scream!" Each one of these is a story—of self-judgment, of deflected emotions, of distraction. We stay in the story because it carries a charge, it gives us something to think about, it fills our hearts and minds. But the story is often untrue. Relief is frequently a breath away. The transitory nature of the phenomenon and our awareness of it will be revealed when we awake to the awareness of having been distracted, and when we return our attention to our breath.

Telling stories about our lives rather than seeing the truth is a common habit. Mindfulness practice helps us to see the truth more clearly and avoid being caught up in distracting stories. Let's examine each of the stories above. To the wandering mind we might say, "What's wrong with me? Am I so scatterbrained that I can't keep my mind on my breath?" But what is actually the case? The truth is that in this exercise, something new, unusual, and unfamiliar, you have actually experienced what everyone experiences: a mind at work. You might just as easily have responded by saying, "Wow, what a fertile and creative mind I have! It's really working overtime now. But I would like to keep trying this medita-tion stuff, so let me put those thoughts aside for the moment." Without judging the situation you would have acknowledged the truth (that your mind wandered) and testified to your true intention (to practice meditation) and, without engaging in a whole drama, returned to your breath. Without making your mind your adversary, you woke up to its wandering and chose, clearly and intentionally, to return to your breath.

To the wandering mind that elicits, "What am I doing here watching my breath when I have so much to do, when I have to accomplish X?" we might alternatively respond: "I feel burdened by my work and life. It takes up so much of my attention. But I've chosen to try meditation, and for now, I would like to pay attention to my breath. I will catch up with my work later." The story, which set up a competition between the activity at hand and other work, is unnecessary and untrue. After all, if indeed the work were more pressing, if it needed to be finished before the meditation session concluded, a wise choice would be to leave the meditating to some other time. Attending meditation sessions, or paying attention to one's life, is a matter of choice. One is present intentionally—or not —and knowing that is an important piece of information that mindfulness practice may help to reveal.

What about the physical matters—aches and cramps and itches? The response, "I wish I were in better shape" need not be evaluative—it may be true! But when it comes connected to an aching body it frequently expresses a judgment. This thought then compounds the moment of distraction by generating a long discursive report on how and why you are not in better shape, for that is where the evaluation comes up. An alternative way of acknowledging that truth without judgment and without the story might be: "It is hard to sit still for so long. I will have to pay attention to getting in better shape to do this. For now, let me shift positions." A similar response would work, as well, for one who chooses to blame the meditation leader for his discomfort. After all, one is engaged in the practice by choice. It may be difficult, and that may express itself in discomfort. But that will pass. Paying too much attention to discomfort may both exacerbate it and introduce conflict and criticism where it is inappropriate.

Itches are interesting phenomena. They seem to arise suddenly and then demand immediate attention. One response is simply to scratch them. But in the larger enterprise of practicing meditation, that response skips over observing the phenomenon and understanding it as a distraction from paying attention. The truth is that we don't die from itching. What we have here is a mind grabbing onto a distraction, an attractive focus away from the breath. A whole drama evolves around the itch, and the mind sets to examining it with great intensity. When we seek to bring the mind back to the breath, the itch rises up in competition—"No, no, pay attention to me!" Often, however, when we turn our minds to the itch with a more dispassionate awareness, without scratching but also without engaging it, we find that its intensity diminishes, and it often goes away on its own.

An orientation of mind that underlies most of this discussion is compassion. Although our intention is to learn to pay close attention to the whole of our lives, we have compassion for ourselves when we find that we cannot do so at once. We realize that we will have to work to train our minds to follow our intentions. So when our minds wander, as they will, and we wake up to that fact, we respond with compassion. Rather than blaming ourselves (or others), rather than creating a story that reinforces resistance to focused attention or that justifies our distraction, compassion allows us to acknowledge the truth of the moment: our minds have wandered.

Compassion allows us to approach the moment from a position of calmness and openness. We accept the truth that our minds have wandered, but we do not add on the judgment that we have done something wrong. We learn that we are not inept. We see that when in pain, when uncertain, when startled, when embarrassed, we tell stories about ourselves rather than simply admitting the truth. We run away from or push away difficult feelings. However, we find also that in the moment of awakened attention, we can hold those feelings with compassion. They need not take us over, and we need not banish them. We realize that these difficult feelings are neither right nor wrong—not even shame, arrogance, and anger. However, when we hold them with compassion, we have more inner space in which to examine the roots of these feelings, and we can discern the deeper truth that lies behind them: we were startled, uncertain, in pain. Just as paying attention to our breath can open up the field in which we move through the world, so too compassion expands the space in which we hold our feelings. We then have more space in which to maneuver with wisdom through our inner lives.

The dynamic play of attention-inattention-awakening-return is the first lesson we learn when we practice paying attention. We gradually come to see that it leads us to an awareness of our inner lives, where the same cycle is at work as well. The process that we use to learn *how* to pay attention is the process by which we *come* to pay attention. The mechanism of the breath becomes both a tool for deepening our capacity to pay attention and a metaphor for the process itself. The out and in of the breath is the falling away from attention and the return to attention. In the moment before we begin the cycle, in that instant when we are not yet inhaling, we are at the peak of our intention to live an awakened life. By the time we approach the fullness of the breath, our intention has waned, we have lost our focus. As we exhale, we awake to the awareness that we have strayed from our intention and we then renew our intention. The start of the next breath is the expression of our restored, wholehearted intention, again full of promise.

This is the inner dynamic of the religious process we know as *teshuvah,* return. Often the word is translated as "repentance." To the extent that the awareness to which we come is that we have sinned, that we have acted offensively toward God or others, then indeed our return to proper behavior must include the work of repentance, including acts of atonement and changed behavior. But *teshuvah* also is simply: return—to the truth. Over and over, as we practice meditation and bring mindful attention to our lives, we return to our breath, to our point of focus. When we do this, we experience a return from the grip of a distracting feeling, an engrossing thought; a return from thoughtlessness to self-control and mindfulness. We return with a sense of regret with and a heart full of compassion. With awakened minds and compassionate hearts we rededicate ourselves to living lives of intention and responsibility, and in response experience an opening of horizons and a deep welcome to the world. This is the meaning of *teshuvah* as return: the constant course correction, the ongoing reaffirmation of our intention to acknowledge and accept the truth.

The ongoing process of return that entails holding compassion toward ourselves soon leads us to compassion toward others. When we have learned to recognize our inner habits—of blaming ourselves, of projecting malicious intent onto others, of denying responsibility—and when we can hold them in a calm, open heart, we are better able to realize that everyone else struggles with the same issues. Other people confront their own inner habits, and they struggle with their own versions of the same uncertainties. When we learn to direct the same sense of compassion toward other people, we find that every day our hearts expand wider and wider. We see the enormity of the struggle of life all around us, and we are moved to offer succor to all whom we touch.

Using the breath as our point of focus is also a path to God. According to the biblical story, that which animates the first human, what makes him a living being, is the breath of God: "He blew into his nostrils the breath of life, and man became a living being" (Genesis 2:7). Since that very moment, the autonomous system of respiration has been the constant presence of God's sustaining power in each and every human being. It is dependable (when not impeded by illness) and reflects God's faithfulness. Close attention to each breath, and to each minute detail of that breath, leads us to perceive the unique nature of each moment, and each fragment of a moment. We are breathed, and when we recognize the constancy of our breath we are led to awe and amazement at the fact of life at all.

Mindfulness practice is not only paying attention to our breath. Rather, the breath is the path to a deeper awareness of every aspect of our lives. In the same manner that our breath is complex, so is the whole of Creation complex. The air that I breathe has been breathed by all of Creation. My exhalation sustains the trees and grasses, and they depend on me for their life. The oxygen they offer me is offered to all other beings as well. What I leave over in my breath is breathed by my neighbor. The winds blow the breath of my distant neighbors to me, and I share their breath as well. But we do not compete for each breath. The air is there for all of us, whether we live in smog-filled valleys or on crystal-clear mountaintops. My need for clean air cannot be fulfilled for me alone, and I cannot deny others fresh air without harming myself as well. When I breathe, all of Creation breathes as well, and we are all sustained by the breath of God.

The longer we sit, paying attention to our breaths, the more fully and unconditionally we open our hearts to the truth of existence, and the more deeply aware we become of how miraculous each moment is. Rather than leading us inward and away from the world, mindfulness practice leads us wholeheartedly into a loving connection to all of Creation. As we slowly uncover the truth of our experience, we realize that no experience—not on its own, not in memory, and not as we sense it in our bodies—has happened to us alone. Nothing happens outside of a context of relationships and connections. We become aware of how many different interactions had to take place to bring us to this particular moment, to this particular breath. We did not get here alone, and we did not get here solely through our own power or on the basis of our own decisions. We discover that we are not all-powerful, that we are not the center of the universe—and we offer ourselves compassion for having thought that it was true, and for discovering (with a twinge of embarrassment) that it is not. Compassion for ourselves makes us aware of the myriad contingencies that conspire to bring about any moment, act, or word.

The space that we create with each breath, affording us room to hold experience without being overwhelmed or confused, expands the heart. We learn compassion for ourselves, and then for others. We become aware of how many other events had to occur to bring about any one interaction or communication, how many other people had to do just this one thing to make everything else happen. How much more complex must the whole system be for all of existence to be going on, for all people to be just where they are, doing what they are doing: being born and dying, loving and fighting, sleeping and waking, gaining and losing. The further we follow the course of mindful awareness, the more we find that we must push out the edges of our hearts to take in the world. Over and over we find that some feeling or thought constricts our hearts, and over and over we take a breath and make room for greater compassion. The experience, as we push farther and farther out against the limits of our current awareness, is that our hearts begin to break. We are overwhelmed by the need of the entire world for compassion. In seeking to embrace the whole world, we must transcend all boundaries of heart and mind.

When we sense that our hearts have reached their limits, when we fear our hearts may break, we are at the doorstep of the Holy One: "The Lord is close to the brokenhearted; those crushed in spirit He delivers" (Psalm 34:19). In the movement from self-awareness and self-protection to openness to the whole world and compassion for all beings, we open our hearts to the presence of God. When in the course of our practice we realize that distracting thoughts are often "just a story," a way that we distract ourselves from that which we find difficult, we find that we can let go and return to a more open, more compassionate awareness of our lives. Eventually, we can let go of all stories and extend our hearts and minds to hold all of life. "I," "me," and "mine" all fall away and all that is left is the Everything, the One, God.

The return to the truth, which is *teshuvah,* is, fundamentally, a return to God. Our tradition teaches us that God's seal is Truth. It makes sense that the awareness that motivates us to return to God is the experience of compassion for ourselves and for others. It reflects the fundamental spiritual yearning of our souls for compassion—to be known, accepted, and loved by God. When we experience this, then we, too, can bring it into the lives of all other beings. It is no longer our wills that count, our stories that need to be told. Rather, we sense that what is necessary is to make our choices come closest to expressing the wholeness, the closeness, and the lovingkindness that are the Being and Becoming of God. Every time that we lift our awareness out of our particular story and see how much love, compassion, righteousness, and justice must be done for the sake of all beings, we are inspired to act for that good. Our will becomes God's will.

Mindfulness is the practice of paying attention to the truth of our experience. Requiring constant attention, it is accomplished through the ongoing process of "waking up" from distraction, and returning our attention to our original intention—*teshuvah.* Full *teshuvah* can only be achieved by continuous, complete candor, and it requires self-compassion. And compassion for ourselves would be false if it did not lead us to a deep awareness of the needs and concerns of other people and Creation. Thus, *teshuvah* leads us to express compassion for others, a process that ultimately breaks our hearts. We give up our personal stories, we relinquish our self-centered orientation, and we open up to the All, to God. In the end, we learn the deep meaning of the verse: "Know therefore this day and return to it over and over to your heart that Adonai alone is God in heaven above and on earth below; there is no other" (Deuteronomy 4:39). Pay attention, now and again, and again and always. All that exists and all that goes on in the heavens above and on the earth below is God. There is no other; there is nothing else.

Section Two

Torah

Chapter Two

Mindfulness, Torah, and Commandment

*W*hen we sit quietly, letting our mind rest in calm attention to our breath, we set out on a path toward becoming more awake in our lives. Yet, after the first few moments of sitting we may find that our minds have wandered; we have strayed from the path. The instant we wake up to that fact, however, is enlivening. We are more aware of the truth of the moment, where we are and what our intention is. We are also more aware of the nature of our minds: what it is that distracts us, what attracts our attention, what calls us away from our chosen path. And in that moment, even having wandered from the path, we find that we are on it. The goal of the journey is not a point or place; it is the experience. We attain that goal in moments of awakened attention, both when we set out and when we return.

Over and over, we set out on our path. Over and over, we wake up to the truth of the present moment. Sometimes we wake up when we sense that our minds have wandered, but that is not the only way that our hearts and minds may open. In our struggle with difficult thoughts, in the arising of unexpected stories or thought-associations, we may become aware of the source of our resistance to practice, or our attachment to a particular character trait. In the falling away of the sensation of our bodies, we may awaken to the oneness of Creation. In the rising and falling away of the breath, in the deep awareness of the transitory nature of all things, we may experience a deeper compassion for other people who struggle with their own loss, their own intuition of death. In these and all other experiences that may arise in the moment, we are both on the path to greater awareness of our hearts and minds, and also at its end and at its beginning. There is always the next breath to feel, the next moment to experience, the next instant of waking up.

Mindfulness meditation, as a contemplative practice, can seem "boring." Nothing happens. We just sit there, paying attention. No visions, per se. No lights or colors. No trembling or levitating. Just sitting, paying attention. We attend our breath, we undertake yet again to stay awake, only to find that, in time, our minds again have wandered, that we have met a resistance or an impediment. Still, we come back to awakened awareness, over and over. And it is the same, over and over. We don't "get anywhere," and it doesn't "do" anything for us—unless, of course, we consider developing the capacity to live more fully awake "doing" something. The end product—a broken heart that opens us up, helping us to be more compassionate, more truthful with ourselves and others—is difficult to attain, and it may not be "fun" to do. But, it is worth the effort. To be transformed is a worthy goal; attaining it is hard work.

I have described the moment of realization that one's mind has wandered as a moment of waking up. In a sense, it is a form of revelation. In that moment we experience being alive anew. We experience, in a very deep way, that following the natural course of life without awareness will ultimately hide the truth of life from us. The natural course of our minds' activity is to grasp something interesting to analyze, to compare, to judge. The process is exciting, engaging. That is partly why we follow it away into reverie, list-making, discursive story, or judging, evaluative thoughts. But when we do that, we lose touch with our intention, and with the immediate reality of our existence in this place, in this moment. The truth of the moment is hidden from us. God, life, experience are obscured from view. But, in the moment of waking up, such power! Such clarity of sensation, of being in our bodies, of the flow of our breath and the pounding of our pulse! In that moment, I want nothing else but to be fully attentive to every detail of existence.

Mindfulness practice is not only meditation, and it is not limited to our time in the meditation hall or on our cushion or seat. If it is to mean anything, meditation must provide tools for living mindfully in the fullness of our lives. That we come to see our lives in truth while meditating helps us to recognize the truth when we are not meditating. Through meditation we seek to develop the capacity to sense, at any moment, when we are running away from the truth, when we are telling a story to hide from our own feelings. In meditation we develop a sensitivity to how distraction, avoidance, resistance, fear, attachment, avarice feel in our bodies, and we can later bring this sensitivity to the rest of our lives as well. With these tools we can hope to be able to wake up in the midst of breakfast, a business meeting, speaking with our child, or making love—and so know fully the truth of that moment, and be wholly present.

Over time, waking up in the midst of our lives leads us to realize that there are rules by which we must live if we are to live in consonance with the truth. The repeated straying from and return to the moment makes us mindful of how easily we stop paying attention. This leads us to realize that we must always be watching for mistakes. We seek ways to keep coming back to what we know is proper behavior. The movement of our hearts from compassion for ourselves to compassion for all others makes us especially aware of our responsibilities toward those others. Being awake leaves no room for "not today" or "I don't feel like it." The demands of compassion and justice are unavoidable when our eyes, hearts, and minds are open and attentive. Mindfulness ultimately leads us to a sense of obligation, of responsibility—of being commanded to act with compassion and justice.

The goal and product of mindfulness meditation, the discipline of mindfulness practice as described above, is easily expressed in Jewish terms. "Rabbi Ḥanina taught: Truth is the seal of the Holy One" (Shabbat 55a); "Know the God of your father and serve Him" (1 Chronicles 28:9). If we wish to know that which signifies God's presence in the world and in our lives, we must seek to know the truth. This is hard work—emotionally, spiritually, and physically demanding—and it challenges us to respond in every moment. Mindfulness practice demands that we constantly seek to be aware of the truth of our very existence, to know God. Whenever we awaken to that truth, we experience Revelation, the appearance of God in our lives. What we learn in the moment of awareness is how we are to act, how we must behave for our own sake and for the sake of all others. This knowledge is Torah, divine instruction. Through this knowledge, as our hearts break open in the awareness of our own suffering and the suffering of others, as we offer ourselves compassion and seek to extend it to others, we sense that we must respond out of compassion for ourselves as well as for others. The product of God's Revelation, the purpose of Torah, is commandment.

God, Torah, commandment—fundamentals of Jewish spiritual life, meet in the experience of mindfulness practice. This is not surprising. In a way, this is close to a normative Jewish understanding of what Torah is, and how its teachings become commandments. That is, God addresses people—Adam, Noah, Abraham, Moses, the People of Israel—in a manner that they experience as communication. They sense that their understanding of God's will, God's intention, God's truth came to them as divine speech. This is Revelation. The collected reports of the stories of these communications and their specific subject matter, narrated, edited, redacted, retold over time, is the content of the Torah, the Five Books of Moses. Inasmuch as this process continued and extended beyond the life of Moses, the revelations of the prophets and other biblical writers contained in the rest of the Bible constitute a form of Torah as well.

Although Jewish tradition holds that following the destruction of the First Temple (in 586 B.C.E.) and the last of the literary prophets (Zechariah, Malachi), direct communication in the form of prophecy ceased, that does not mean that God was felt to be less present, or that it was less possible to discern God's will. The study of the Torah and the Bible, the explication and interpretation of the holy texts, opened the door to further inspiration, an extension of Revelation. The work of interpretation itself became Torah, in both law and lore. At every point, the expanding body of literature of Torah-interpretation, and the original Torah from which it flowed, served as another source of inspiration, as a means to know God, to hear God's voice, to experience Revelation.

In addition, the Torah has a particular attribute that opens yet another means of hearing God, and responding to God: the covenant. God makes pacts with individuals (Adam, Noah, Abraham) as well as with the People of Israel. In the latter case, this covenant had specific terms by which the parties fulfilled their obligations to each other. In particular, the Israelites kept the covenant by observing the laws of the Torah. When Jews keep the commandments it testifies to their commitment to affirm the covenant with God, and to respond affirmatively to God's will. Finally, maintaining the covenant and observing the commandments is both an outcome of the study of Torah and a means to know God. Observance can lead to Revelation as well.

While there are numerous books discussing the meanings of these terms, describing various ways of understanding them, justifying one or another religious form, mindful Judaism knows and understands them from experience. God is not a postulate, a philosophical idea, a Being whose Existence must be proved. God is the experience of the Truth, knowable yet inscrutable, demanding yet deniable (so long as we avoid awakening to the truth). When we awaken to the truth of our lives, God is known and present. What we learn from that experience leads us to action (unless we choose to resist, to run from our awareness, and to deny both the truth and God). When we do act, we act not on the basis of personal preference, habit, or convenience, but rather we are compelled by our awareness and energized by the truth. Our experience helps us to know God, to discern what needs to be done, and that experience generates the energy needed to act.

Further, Judaism as a spiritual practice provides us with a framework, a discipline of practice that helps to lead us to an awareness of God and, in turn, to respond to that experience in action. Through the study of Torah (in all of its manifestations) we meet God over and over. When we approach these encounters open to the possibility that they may reveal the truth to us, we avoid the distracting arguments over God's nature, God's personality, God's actions. We seek God's presence: to hear and see the truth in the teaching. When we experience God's presence through the study of Torah, it becomes again a source of Revelation. And again, we find ourselves compelled to act, to respond to the awareness of the truth.

This experience is not ours alone. Those who studied Torah, and those who created Torah in the past, also sensed God's presence and responded to that experience. Their sense of how to respond became the whole body of Jewish law. Jewish practices flow from and are based on this body of law. As we enter into these practices, we too may find that they lead us to an awareness of God's presence in our lives, a deep opening to the truth of existence. The practices themselves may then be revealed as the proper and necessary response to the moment—we will sense them to be commandments—or they may generate the awareness of what the circumstances demand, and we will respond to the commandment inherent in the moment. A mindful Jewish practice will recognize that the Torah and the commandments of tradition are means of experiencing God's presence and responding to God. This experience is kept alive through developing the capacity to see clearly, to know the truth, and to recognize the obligations that flow from that knowledge. One informs and supports the other.

How can we use Torah and *mitzvot* as ways to stay connected to God? How can we sustain our intention to awaken to the truth of existence, to make practice of the law the source of inspiration to fulfill commandments? I have found that the language of the Jewish mystical tradition, particularly the hasidic stream, has offered me profound ways of speaking about God and thinking about my relationship to God and Torah. And, I have found in it practices that help me keep my eyes open and my heart awake to the presence of God in the world. In particular, the absolute monism of hasidism, its claim that there is nothing but God, enlivens me. God is not outside the world—God is the world; the world is in God. "The whole earth is full of God's glory" (Isaiah 6:3) and "There is no place that is devoid of God" (*Tikkunei Zohar* 91b) are the hasidic teachers' constant refrains. The ultimate goal of study and practice is to see beyond all the layers of the physical world (and all other conceptions of it) to realize that there is nothing but God, not even we ourselves.

In fact, too great a focus on "nature" and the natural world may actually obscure our true vision of the oneness of God. We know the divine creative aspect as YHVH, the source of the outflowing of the vital life-force that sustains and animates all Creation. That force is the expression of God's lovingkindness: an intention to do good and be good to everything by bringing it into existence and allowing all life (people, and Jews, in particular) to know God. But the full force of that outflowing is too powerful for material beings to tolerate, so that effulgence is "stepped-down," constricted, limited, and garbed in ever grosser forms until it exists in the material realm. The divine aspect of limitation, of judgment and constraint, is *elohim.*

Since we are physical beings and human, what we know of God is largely through the material world, and so we experience God largely as *elohim.* But, "YHVH is *elohim* in the heavens above and on the earth below; there is nothing else" (Deuteronomy 4:39). There is nothing else but YHVH, the ultimate source of all things. We are invited, called—always—to look beyond the material world to see the spiritual root of all things in YHVH, in God's lovingkindness. This is echoed and deepened in a numerical pun: the numeric equivalent of the letters that spell *elohim* (86) is equal to the value of the letters that spell the word *hateva* (nature, also 86). Should we focus too heavily on the "natural," on the regular, the dependable, and the expected, we might lose sight of the miraculous, of God. The wonder is not that the world exists, but rather that it *continues* to exist, second after second, millennium after millennium. It is God's ongoing, yet daily renewed, love that sustains all Creation in every second, in each moment. The outflow of lovingkindness that is YHVH is present in all things; otherwise they would not, could not exist. That both accounts for nature—the existence of all things and their interconnectedness in that natural world—and also points us beyond it. Look beyond the natural, keep your eyes open to the miraculous: these are practices and instructions that can help us on our way.

We are urged to look past the natural—the limited, the bounded, the physical—past *elohim* to see YHVH, the source of all vitality. But, that is still not to know God fully. Even that aspect of God is itself somewhat limited. In the mystical conception of the emergence of the cosmos from God's mind and thought, there are still higher levels, processes taking place deeper inside God's being, functions of God's wisdom and knowledge. They themselves are emanations from the highest level of God's Being, the point of the first stirrings of intention, of God's anticipation of any created existence outside of God's Self. That highest level (known in the mystical system of the *sefirot* as *Keter,* Crown) is *Ayin,* Nothing. Nothing can be said about it, and it can hardly be known at all. And it still is not yet God in God's fullness. That would be *Ein Sof,* the Endless, the Infinite—beyond all description, far beyond limited, finite human conception. We might come to know God by tracing all of existence back to YHVH and God's lovingkindness—but we cannot know *Ein Sof.*

How can we speak about a God who is beyond conception? What is there to say about a God who is *ein sof,* without end, eternal and infinite and beyond description? Even if that God is all that is, we still exist with minds and egos; we think, we experience our lives through our bodies. Yet, we sense that in some way we must find a path beyond our limited existences, our sense of boundedness, to participate in and become one with the Infinite. The classical mystical tradition offers a way to enter on this path. We are invited to see that God and the Torah are one. The Torah in its supernal form arose in God's thoughts and it maps them precisely. Through Torah God created everything, and so there must be something of God in Creation as well. Moreover, human beings were created in the divine image, and in some manner they must also be one with the Holy One. The nexus of God and the world is in Torah. Human beings are the physical manifestation of the divine idea embodied in the supernal Torah. Human beings are Torah.

To illustrate this point, and others throughout the rest of this book, I will be using a variety of sources, most of them from within the classical rabbinic or hasidic traditions. The following text is taken from the work *Me'or Einayim*, by Rabbi Menaḥem Naḥum of Chernobyl, one of the students of the Baal Shem Tov, the founder of Hasidism.

> It is known that "This is the Torah: man" (Numbers 19:14). Torah derives from divine wisdom, and that wisdom is the World of Thought. The Torah itself is a complete entity, made up of 248 positive commandments and 365 negative commandments. In the same manner, human beings are entities comprised of 248 bones and 365 ligaments. Just as the [physical] Torah has its source, through many descending orders of emanation, in the completely spiritual Torah, so too human beings have their source in the spiritual realm.
>
> Think of it this way: before a craftsman sets out to produce any object, he draws a precise image of it in his mind, just as it is going to be, and only after that does he bring the image into actuality. So, too, is it first written in the Torah, "God formed *(vayitzer)* the man" (Genesis 2:7) and only then, "God made" the man, in actuality. Now, the word *vayitzer* has the connotation of image *(tziyyur)*. First did the idea (image) of man arise in God's thought, in the World of Thought as a spiritual entity, and only then did God create him in his physical form. This form was just as God had imagined in His thought as a spiritual entity.
>
> (Me'or Einayim, Toldot,
> s.v. ekev asher shama Avraham bekoli)

This text bases itself first on the traditional conception in the Talmud that there are 613 commandments, the sum of 248 and 365 (cf. Makkot 23b). On this basis stands the claim that each of the commandments has a parallel in the human body (248 limbs and 365 ligaments). What is more, each of these bones and ligaments has a parallel in the spiritual form that arose first in God's mind, just as the earthly Torah has its parallel in its spiritual source. And what man does in his physical form will affect this supernal spiritual form. This is made clear in the pun on the words *vayitzer* (formed) and *tziyyur* (image). That is to say, the thought that arose, the image of man in God's mind, was the template, the blueprint, for the physical human being. Our concrete, material beings reflect, are connected to, the supernal, spiritual image that preceded us. In the same way, Torah preceded Creation. It existed in God's mind, formed the blueprint for the emergent physical world. In that sense, Torah and Creation are connected, are one. The *Me'or Einayim* continues:

> We have to be careful not to deny the significance of having been created in this manner [the physical having its source in the spiritual] in our deeds or our thoughts by not behaving according to the Torah. Again, the Torah is that complete entity that arose in the Blessed Creator's thought at the start, as we say, "The final deed was in thought from the first." This is the image of God in which we were created: that is, Torah, which then was constricted and contracted, descending from the World of Thought so that it might be clothed in the garb of physical human beings. We, too, are made up of both form and matter so that we will have the potential to grasp the spiritual Torah. . . .
>
> (ME'OR EINAYIM, IBID.)

In this text we find the argument that God's pure thought is too powerful to be projected directly into the lower realms of Creation. Therefore it is constricted and condensed, its power stepped down, and finally it is dressed in the physical garments of Creation so that it can be perceived by human beings. We must never take the material world to be the sole expression of God's intent. Rather, it is merely the "final deed" of the original thought: Torah. The parallel between the supernal form of Torah and the physical Torah, like the original human form in thought and actual human beings, actually lead the author to connect Torah and human beings: the image in which the latter were created is actually the former. Thus, a unity of divine and human Torah exists. "This is the Torah: man" means not only that Torah has a human form, but that man, conscious man, intentional man, spiritual man, is also Torah. God, Torah, and humankind are united, are one. Our text continues:

> All Creation must contain some aspect of Torah, since the power of the Creator is present in everything. Therefore we have to relate to all existence as if it were the divine Thought, and not, by our actions, deny this original Thought. Now, we can learn from our own bodies exalted spiritual matters of the highest order, as it says, "By my flesh I see God" (Job 19:26). We will merit this capacity when we remain connected with the divine source, and thus realize the ultimate oneness of all things, and that comes from never intending any action or experience for our own benefit or enjoyment. This would only separate us from the source. Rather, we must kill off our selfhood. This is the intention of the teaching, "Torah can only be sustained by one who is willing to kill his self for it" (Berakhot 63b): Torah can only exist in someone who remains in the realm of the unitary source, attached to God, someone who is able to kill off his selfhood. If we would attain to this, we will desire only to bring joy to the Holy One. "Know Him in all of your ways" (Proverbs 6:3)—we must unite ourselves with the highest level of existence, the original idea in God's Thought, so that we might actually embody that very image.

> (ME'OR EINAYIM, IBID.)

In this text I am reminded that our bodies may cease to appear to us as substantial objects each time we realize that they can point us to the ultimate, to our Creator. In the moment of that realization, we awake to an awareness of God manifested in the unity of the physical and spiritual. Our personal needs recede in importance and God's intention for all Creation fills our consciousness. Our hearts and minds are united with God's intention in Creation. The sense of a separate "self," distinct and inviolable in our embodied identities, dissolves. Unbounded, our egos expand to touch all things at once, uniting with the source of all things, with God. In this selfless, open moment it is as if we have died—we have "killed" our separateness so that we might connect fully with God. Fulfilling the commandments with our bodies so that we might open ourselves further to "sublime spiritual matters," it is as if we have "killed ourselves for the sake of Torah." In our bodies, in everything that we do, we can come to know God, to connect with the sublime spirituality of all things, of all existence.

Once we have begun on the path toward awareness of the truth and commandment, how are we to proceed? The text above suggests that we need not look too far to begin with. We need only look to our bodies, which are formed in the divine image—that is, the form of Creation that arose in God's mind. That form was Torah. Its supernal shape, its 613 spiritual limbs and sinews, are tied to our physical limbs and sinews. Its spiritual commandments are made concrete in our realm in the 613 commandments in our Torah. When we perform any one of the positive commandments, or refrain from trespassing a negative law, we actualize the spiritual form: we connect the divine realm with the created world. We help to establish the unity of God, Torah, and Creation. The opposite, of course, is also true. Failing to fulfill a commandment or trespassing, one breaks the connection, and even impairs the divine realm.

Many of us are burdened by an image of God made most concrete and popular in the publicity poster for the musical "My Fair Lady." There, Professor Henry Higgins is depicted as if he were God, sitting above the clouds of Heaven, manipulating the strings of his poor puppet, Eliza Doolittle. That is what many of us came to imagine our tradition teaches about God's relation to human beings, how God controls all things, bringing about judgment or dispensing reward in response to observance of the commandments. God pulls the strings, executing judgment below, and we are left only to obey (like puppets) or suffer. How different is the image in our text, where it is *we* who hold the strings! Our every act can either accord with the divine will or deny both thought and deed by transgressing the Torah. Our acts determine whether the divine Torah is whole or flawed. Again, I turn to the *Me'or Einayim* to illustrate this point.

A person can become complete, a whole human being, when he is one with the (divine) image—that is, when the physical, material form is one with the spiritual form of a human being in the Torah. When this happens, if the person wiggles his material finger, the "supernal" finger or limb will also be energized and caused to move. This is what makes up a "complete human being," as we read in Psalms: "A person walks about as an image" (Psalm 39:7). That is, one who walks about with the image, that is, who is one with the image of the One, is someone who is called a "(complete) person." But, if he fails to perform (a positive) commandment or transgresses a (negative) commandment, the supernal limb or sinew connected with it will be missing, and neither (this person, nor the supernal Image) will be whole.

(Me'or Einayim, Beḥukotai,
s.v. im beḥukotai telekhu)

I am amused, but even more, I am inspired by this image. When we wiggle our fingers with full awareness and intention, we cause the spiritual form to move. Our limbs control the divine limbs. When we are in line with the divine intent, when there is congruence between our actions and the divine will, then we create a wholeness in the universe and in ourselves. Our missteps, our mistaken actions, create an internal contradiction, as it were, in God. When our service of God is flawed, the divine form becomes flawed as well. We will be a "complete person," and Creation will become whole, only when we are One with the divine intent embodied in the divine image of Torah.

What this image offers us is twofold. It roots the knowledge of God in our bodily experiences. Our limbs and sinews, our most immediate sense of "self" as an entity, are pointers to the divine: "In my own flesh I see God." How we sense our bodies, how we respond to them, how we utilize them, how we treat them, how we care for them, all have the potential to lead us to awareness of the truth and to commandment. But, more, this image tells us that we are Torah. We are the expression of both the divine intention and deed. Our primary experience may be physical, but that is only an echo of the spiritual. The greater goal is to experience in our bodies "exalted spiritual matters of the highest order." Moreover, our actions in the physical plane actually express and make concrete God's intention. As embodied Torah, our actions have the potential to create newer expressions of the fulfillment of God's intention. We now understand the radical possibilities in the teaching "This is the Torah: man": what we do when we pay full attention, how we behave when we are fully mindful, is Torah. It will be true Torah, however, it will echo and reflect the supernal image of Torah, only when it is selfless action. Our intention, in the end, must be to consciously "desire only to bring joy to the Holy One," to experience and express unity of purpose with God and Torah.

The test of our fidelity to our quest will be the degree to which we avoid denying both the intent of God and the fact of His Creation through inattention. God's intent is that we might know Him. The fact of Creation is testimony to God's invitation to relationship. Our capacity to experience in our lives and in the world around us this divine force, this intention and call, can lead us beyond our limited ego concerns. It is not for our own sake that we are here in the world. It is for God's sake. As we look deeper into the reality of our physical selves, we may actually see beyond to the divine. "Know Him in all your ways" then, so that in our very physical lives we will be united with the spiritual realm and actually become the complete image of God.

We have claimed "This is the Torah: man"—that we are the embodiment of and the expression of Torah. The test of our capacity to actually know God, to look beyond our personal needs and concerns, comes in our capacity to "kill ourselves for the sake of Torah" and act only to please the Divine. This is an important counterbalance to selfishness and self-concern. What we learn and what we do ultimately become teaching and commandment, but only if we learn to act selflessly. This is illustrated in the following text by Rabbi Levi Yitzḥak of Berdichev, student of the Maggid of Mezritch, in his book *Kedushat Levi.*

> "Thus did Moses and the Children of Israel sing this song to Adonai saying" (Exodus 15:1). Why does the (Hebrew form of) the verb "sing" appear in the future tense, when it should have been in the past? With God's help we can explain this, as did the Baal Shem Tov. He interpreted the verse from psalms, "Adonai is your shadow" (Psalm 121:5), to mean that the Holy One responds to people like a shadow: whatever a person does, so does his shadow. Thus, also, the Holy Creator responds to us, doing what it is that

we do. Thus, when Israel sang at the moment of their redemption from Egypt, the Holy One as well, as it were, sang this song. That is: the verb *yashir* (sing) has the grammatical form of causing to sing. We can understand the verse, then, in this manner: "Thus did Israel [cause to] sing"—that is, Israel made something happen with their song—"this song to the Lord"—that is, that the Holy Blessed One should sing this song as well—"and they said to say *(vayomru leimor)*"—that is, they told the Holy One that He should recite this song as well.

(Kedushat Levi, Beshallaḥ,
s.v. o yevo'ar az yashir Moshe . . . leimor)

What this text says to me is that God will echo and respond to our actions; our truest intentions can become Torah, commandment. While this transformation truly comes about in the moment of opening to God, there is the constant danger that we will make our selfish interests, our limited concerns, into commandment. This aspect of the spiritual quest has the potential to become self-serving in the worst sense of the word. The awareness of being the form, the image and expression of God's intention, the ones who have God as our shadow in the world, could move us to awe and reverence, to honest self-abnegation. That is not a given, however, and we must constantly be on guard against confusing ego needs with divine intentions.

We can know God through our bodies, our physical existence. There is a danger there, in that our bodies are demanding and may seduce us into using our power to serve our physical, emotional, and hormonal needs. There must be other ways through which we can come to know God, that can balance against self-interest, helping to keep us on the path to truth. How can we come to experience God's presence? A classical response, which may serve us well, is that we can accomplish this through the study of Torah. Rabbi Yishmael adduced thirteen principles *(middot)* of interpretation by which we analyze Torah (Sifra 1:1). These thirteen principles have an analog in the thirteen attributes *(middot)* of divine mercy expressed (according to tradition) in Exodus 34:6–7: "Adonai, Adonai, a God compassionate and gracious, slow to anger, abounding in kindness and faithfulness, extending kindness to the thousandth generation, forgiving iniquity, transgression, and sin, and remitting punishment." When we utilize the thirteen principles to study Torah, we energize and draw into our study (and our experience) these aspects of God's love and mercy. Moreover, when we study Torah, we connect with these aspects of God, and ultimately we can cleave to God. Again, we turn to Rabbi Menaḥem Naḥum in the *Me'or Einayim* to demonstrate this point.

> What is the path that the Torah instructs us to follow here? Now, it says, "Cleave to Him" (Deuteronomy 11:22; 30:20). But is God not "a consuming fire" (Deuteronomy 4:24), as it says in the Holy Zohar (that God is) "the fire that consumes all other fires of this world"? Now, if this is the case, how is it possible for humans of flesh and blood to cleave to such a God? Rather, cleave to His attributes: just as He is compassionate, so, too, you should be compassionate, etc.
>
> Let us explain how this is an answer to the initial question. While it is true that we might be able to cleave to God's attributes, the verse we quoted says to "cleave to Him"! Now, in truth the Holy One gave us the Torah so that we might actually cleave to Him, but still, how can humans, who are limited and bounded, cleave to the Holy One, who is unbounded, limitless, infinite? To that end, God gave us the Torah, and contracted Himself (as it

were) into our Holy Torah so that when we cleave to the Torah we will also attach ourselves to God, who is also present in the Torah. This is the intention of the sages' teaching "cleave to His attributes," meaning the Torah, for the Torah is interpreted by means of thirteen principles (*middot;* such as drawing inferences a fortiori, or from a similar word or phrase in two texts, etc.), and these thirteen principles are actually also the thirteen attributes (*middot*) of God, "compassionate and gracious, etc." Thus, when we cleave to the Torah, we are also attached to the Holy One, who is present in the Torah.

(ME'OR EINAYIM, NASO,
S.V. VAYEDABER H'EL MOSHE LEIMOR)

I sense that this passage affirms the goal of connecting with God, of uniting our intention with the divine intent. Rather than using our bodies and human experience we are urged here to engage in the study of Torah. Yet there is an important additional component to this teaching. Beyond the formal parallelism of the thirteen principles of Torah interpretation and the thirteen attributes of divine mercy, this passage suggests that the unity of God, Torah, and Israel is expressed through compassion and mercy. This provides us with an additional test to help us discern when our inclinations to act have legitimately become commandment, when we have died for the sake of Torah: we will then be led to express God's love toward others. The experience of God's love in our lives will be, as well, an indication to us that we have not cut ourselves off from God, but rather have united form and intention in our service of God and others.

Our hasidic teachers understood that this takes work. In the following passage from the *Me'or Einayim,* we learn that the repeated injunction to remember the Exodus from Egypt has a deeper meaning related to our intention to know the truth fully, to serve God self-lessly. In this text, we are introduced to yet another meaning of the word *middot*: modes in which God manifests in the unfolding of Creation, related to the *sefirot*. The interplay of these *middot* with the thirteen attributes of God's mercy points us to an awareness of God's love as the most significant quality of God's being.

> The Exodus from Egypt was for the purpose of bringing the awareness of God out of exile. That is, even though today we still experience our exile, nevertheless the awareness of God is not in exile—except among those who absolutely deny God's existence in any form or manner. But, for most everyone, it is God's qualities that are in exile—that is Love, Fear, Beauty, and the other attributes of God. Everyone acknowledges God's existence, each according to his own way and ability. But God's qualities are dressed in exile—in false desires and groundless fears—whenever one of God's attributes is used contrary to the Blessed Creator's will: that they be employed only in the service of the Holy One. Therefore the Torah reminds us over and over: "Remember the day you came out of Egypt" (cf. Exodus 13:3), "So that you will remember" (Deuteronomy 16:3), and the like. These adjurations are instructions for bringing the attributes of God out of exile. For if each of us were to remember that awareness has already come out of Egypt, and we each acknowledged God's existence and being, then certainly it would be easy for us to redeem God's attributes from their negative applications and bring them to the good.
>
> (Me'or Einayim, Shemot,
> s.v. vehinei aḥar yetziat mitzrayim)

This text reminds me that it is not sufficient to hold an intellectual awareness of God's reality. Many people share that awareness without also serving God in truth. That is, just as it has become common for people to say, "I am spiritual but not religious," so it would be possible to live with some consciousness of God without seeing clearly the truth of our existence. The latter demands that we acknowledge how our minds work, how we manufacture our own suffering (in the stories we tell, for instance), how we distract ourselves from the passing nature of each moment, how we trap ourselves in a perception of life as static and never-changing. Those who cannot see that truth will experience only their own needs, their own pains, their own sense of self, and they will not be able to discover in each moment, in every experience, the possibility of serving others and God. Jewish life as a mindfulness practice seeks to train us to see more clearly, to attain a greater awareness, so that we might serve God and others selflessly.

When we pay attention, from moment to moment, to the truth of our lives, we can open ourselves to the presence of God, and from that we may learn Torah and intuit clearly what we are commanded to do. This very process is recognized in classical Jewish thought. The foundation of Jewish life is the Written Torah, the Five Books of Moses. Yet, that work is insufficient in itself as either a legal code or a spiritual guide to sustain Jewish life over time. Indeed, it is only because Jews have been willing (and have seen themselves as able and empowered) to interpret the text of the Torah in new and changing situations that Jewish life has evolved to address the changing needs of Jews through the ages. This process of interpretation, adaptation, and change has been incorporated into the tradition in the form of the Oral Torah. (The thirteen principles of interpretation to which we referred above constitute part of this process.) This Oral Torah is a body of lore and law, considered equal in authority to the Written Torah. The capacity of individuals to find new meaning in the Written Torah has kept it alive. The obligation to find new meaning in the Torah may even be a necessity of spiritual vitality for a community that seeks to survive over time—just as growth and change is necessary for an individual who seeks to remain spiritually vital. We turn to *Kedushat Levi* to illustrate this point.

> This is the meaning of the phrase, "I make a covenant with you and with Israel" (Exodus 34:27): the Oral Torah changes according to the sages of each generation, where this one says, "this (is the law)" and this one says, "this (is the law)." The law behaves according to the generations. (Compare the dispute between Rashi and Rabbenu Tam, who was a generation later, regarding the order of biblical passages in the *tefillin* [Menaḥot 34b, with Rashi and Tosafot, s.v. *vehakorei korei kesidran*]). Now, in truth, the way this works is that according to the *middah* (the divine spiritual quality) by which the Holy Blessed One conducts the world (at any given time), so is the law determined. If (the *middah* is) love, then the law is according to the one who says "this" (in the spirit of love); if it is (the *middah* of) glory, then the law is according to the one who says "this" (in the spirit of glory).
>
> (Kedushat Levi, Drush Lepurim,
> s.v. od yevo'ar shalḥah lahem Esther)

In this text, I feel that I am being invited to participate in the ongoing emergence of the Oral Torah. The Oral Law is determined by the sages, and according to this text it will always be in concert with the divine will. The sages seek to align themselves with God's inner state, to discern what the character of the time is, in order to determine what the law should be at that moment. And it may also be that the sages seek to align themselves with the state of the Jews at that time, and determine the law accordingly. In the end, the law as it is established will be true and right, since (apparently) it will accord with God's inner state. In this manner, "the Oral Torah changes according to the sages of each generation."

How is it that one can discern God's inner state, particularly if it changes over time? How can anyone know if the Torah that is revealed in contemplative mindfulness is the truth, is indeed the Oral Torah? The author of *Me'or Einayim* struggled with this question as well, as we see in the following text.

> The Written Torah was given to Moses at Sinai, in its generalities and in its details, along with the Oral Torah, "even including the innovations adduced by a seasoned student in the future" (Leviticus Rabbah 22:1). Nevertheless, the Oral Torah (which is a clarification of the Written Torah) was not yet fully revealed to the Israelites so that they might clarify its hidden secrets and secret meanings. This could only come about after the husks that covered and hid the Oral Torah were removed as well. And, this is still the case today. When, in the course of study, we encounter a difficult question or a problematic interpretation, it is because one of the husks is covering over this place (in the Oral Torah), creating the difficulty for us. The appropriate response is to meditate on the divine quality (the *middah*) of *Binah* (Understanding, the source of the unfolding of Creation, the source of Revelation, but also associated with the aspect of divine contraction, limitation, and judgment), struggling with painful insights, seeking to see clearly to Understanding, clearing away the husks such that the truth might be revealed to us. In the end, we come to see that the covering that hid the Oral Torah from us is actually the product of our own, clouded vision; our own struggle with what is, standing as a curtain between us and the truth. When, through meditation (*hitbonnenut*, a play on *Binah*: concentration on Understanding), we are able to attain Understanding of the truth and can see clearly how we created those very separating curtains, we will be

able to release them in their source *(Binah).* In this manner the Oral Torah will be revealed to us.

(ME'OR EINAYIM, DEVARIM,
S.V. BAPASUK B'ERETZ MO'AV HO'IL MOSHE)

In this text we are taught that it is possible for us to reveal the Oral Torah, even if it is dependent on the changing nature of God's inner state. The effect of those changes will be no different for us, in the end, than the ongoing shifting of our own inner beings. That is, from moment to moment we are challenged by our own thoughts and feelings, by our own fears and biases, by our own willingness to see the truth as well as our resistance to it. When we cannot see the workings of our minds and hearts we are buffeted by the exigencies of the moment, reacting, responding, hiding, striking out. We suffer again in response to our desperate attempts to avoid what is painful or difficult, and the truth is curtained off from us even more completely. Yet when we stop in the midst of our lives to sit, to pay attention, to wake up to the truth of the moment, we create the possibility that we may be able to release ourselves from our habitual resistances, and see clearly. We will then understand that the curtain over our hearts and minds is insubstantial and we keep it in place hiding from the truth, but that we can wake up in our lives.

When God set out to create everything (according to Jewish mystical tradition), God had to find a mechanism by which the divine impulse (which is infinite) could be transformed into finite, physical existence. The *sefirot* represent the stages through which this divine impulse moved to effectuate Creation. *Binah* is described as the "womb," receiving the first intention of that impulse and transmitting it from the "highest," most supernal, realm into the descending aspects of the Godhead toward emergent physicality. It is, then, the source from which all Creation flows. When we confront conflict, difficulty, or challenging moments, we often see them as a defect in a perfect order, a failure. When we give our balanced, open attention to these aspects of our lives, we can learn to see that they are neither defects nor failures. They are the reality of Creation in this very moment. In the language of our texts, when we raise our awareness to that of *Binah* (Understanding), we can see that what we perceive as conflict dissolves in the unity of the divine intention and the sweetness of God's desire to do good for the world. We can be released from our struggles, and become open to an acceptance of the moment. This, in turn, allows us to discern what, indeed, it is that the Oral Torah would teach us to do in the present moment.

Our access to the Oral Torah is not only through releasing our struggles through Understanding. The previous text suggests a method for holding our minds and hearts open to the truth of the moment. When we do, we come to see the infinite wonder of all of Creation. We perceive the presence of God in all things: "the whole earth is full of God's glory" and "there is no place devoid of God." That is Revelation, as we claimed above, and it, too, is how we participate in the creation of the Oral Torah. The inter-relation of the unfolding of Creation and our actions also inspired the nineteenth-century Polish hasidic teacher Rabbi Yehudah Leib Alter of Ger, the author of *Sefat Emet,* whose teaching illustrates this very point.

> "In the beginning" (Genesis 1:1). Rashi quotes Rabbi Yitzḥak, who asked if it did not make more sense for the Torah to have begun with: "This month is the first of months for you" (Exodus 12:2, since that is where God first gives commandments to Israel). He answered by quoting, "He declared to His people the power of His acts" (Psalm 111:6).
>
> Now, how does this explain the significance of the narratives of the Torah from "In the beginning" all the way down to "This month"? While it is true that the primary purpose of the Torah is found in the commandments, which comprise the Written Torah,

the Holy Blessed One also wanted to make clear that all of the Torah, indeed all of Creation, exists by virtue of the power of Torah: God looked in the Torah and then created the universe. This then is the importance of the Oral Torah, which is ultimately dependent on our actions. That is, all of the stories of the Patriarchs are to show us how their very deeds became Torah. This is the meaning of the phrase, "the power of His acts"—the power that God placed in our deeds. That is the significance of the idiom *ma'aseh Bereshit* (the act of Creation): the world came into being by means of God's ten utterances (and, therefore, Creation's very existence is dependent on Torah). Our work in the world is to reveal that our every deed is also sustained by this same vital force. When, through our intention and awareness, all of our actions flow from a connection to this vital force of Torah, then we fulfill God's initial will, and in response God renews the light of Creation.

(SEFAT EMET I 5, BERESHIT 5631)

This text reminds me that every one of our conscious, mindful acts expresses one more teaching of the Oral Torah, revealing God's will and purpose in Creation. In this manner we become partners with God in the act of Creation. By recognizing God's power inherent in everything, every moment, every act; by acknowledging that nothing, no place, no act is devoid of God's presence—we reveal Oral Torah. We embody Torah and our deeds can testify to God's intention and deeds. When we act according to the truth, we reveal that Torah.

Meditation is a means to clarity of vision, whether of divine realms or the truth of existence—though there is no real difference between them. Judaism, as expressed through the hasidic tradition, directs us to a mindful awareness of our place in the world, including our relationships with other people and with all of Creation. It directs us to notice the ways in which our vision becomes clouded and how to see more clearly. When we wake up in our lives, when we see clearly, we experience Revelation, an intimate sense of God's presence in all things. This awareness is Torah, and our behavior in light of this awareness is Oral Torah, the ongoing uncovering of God's intention in Creation. When our hearts break, whether for our own suffering or in response to the suffering of others, we find that we must act to ease that pain. The imperative to act, the ongoing intention that moves us to act mindfully, we experience as commandment. It is this perception that lies behind the classical pun, associating the Hebrew word *mitzvah* (commandment) with the Aramaic word *tzavta,* meaning unity. When our hearts open before the truth of the moment, we feel compelled to act, and we so join in partnership with God. In this way we experience deeply the truth of the teaching of the Zohar (III 73a): God, Torah, and Israel (the Jewish people) are one.

Chapter Three

Mindfulness, Mortality, and Torah

*T*he Talmud teaches: "Resh Lakish said: How do we know that Torah can only be sustained by one who is willing to kill his self for it? We learn this from the verse (Numbers 19:14): 'This is the Torah, when a man shall die in the tent'" (Berakhot 63b). To fully enter into the meaning of Torah and to live it wholeheartedly, we need to be willing to give up our egos, to kill our selfness. That is not only difficult; it is also frightening. To give up our identities, to relinquish our sense of selfhood, suggests an end to our ability to affect our environment, to execute our will in the world. To kill our selfness would be as if we were dead. That is the source of the fear we feel when we consider this teaching. The Zohar, the classical book of Jewish mystical teaching from the thirteenth century, recognizes this fear and its power in our lives, as we see in the following text.

> *Zot hatorah: adam ki yamut*—This is the teaching: man shall die (Numbers 19:14). As Rabbi Yehudah was once walking along with Rabbi Abba, he said to him: "I should like to ask you one question. Seeing that God knew that sometimes a man might sin and so be condemned to death, why did He create him? The Torah existed two thousand years before the world was created, and still we find it already written, 'When a man dies in a tent' (Numbers 19:14), 'If a man dies' (27:8), 'and so-and-so lived so many years and then died'

(cf. Genesis 5:5 and throughout), and so forth. Why does God want man in this world, seeing that even if he strives to study Torah day and night he dies, and if he does not study Torah he also dies, all going to one end? Without exception in this world, '[the same fate is in store for all:] for the righteous and for the wicked'" (Ecclesiastes 9:2). He replied: "What business have you with the ways and the decrees of your Master? What you are permitted to know and to inquire into, ask about it; and as for what you are not permitted to know, it is written: 'Don't let your mouth bring you to sin' (Ecclesiastes 5:5). For of the ways of the Holy One, and the divine hidden secrets that are concealed and hidden, you may not inquire." He said to him: "If that is the case, then all the Torah is concealed and hidden, since it is all the Holy Name, and one who engages in the study of Torah is like one who engages in the Holy Name, and if so we have no permission to ask and inquire!" He replied: "The Torah is both hidden and revealed, and the Holy Name is also hidden and revealed, as it is written, 'The hidden things belong to Adonai our God, and the revealed things are for us and for our children' (Deuteronomy 29:28). 'The revealed things are for us,' for about these we have permission to inquire, to investigate, to ask, and to understand them. But, 'the hidden things belong to Adonai our God.' They are His, revealed to Him, but who can understand and cleave to God's deep understanding, let alone ask about it?"

(ZOHAR III 159A)

This text echoes my own inner questions: What are we doing here in this world if, in the end, we will all die? This is the question we all come to, and it is the motivation for much of our spiritual life. What is the meaning of our lives? What are we to do with our days on earth? How shall we know if what we have done with our lives has been valuable, meaningful, good, or right?

It would be helpful if the answers to these questions were straightforward, if we knew the answers at birth and had only to follow those instructions to then die fulfilled, or to choose to do otherwise and accept the consequences. But as our teachers in the Zohar relate, that information is not to be found easily. Some of it is revealed, and some of it is hidden. In the end, we seek instruction, we seek teaching, we seek a path to wholeness. That quest has one of three goals: to escape death, to embrace death, or to manage to live life despite its seeming futility in the face of death.

The way of Torah embraces the third of the options above, but this path is difficult and demanding. Rather than offering a means to transcend death, and rather than celebrating a cult of death, the Torah offers a way to live in the face of death: to accept God's sovereignty and to enter into covenant with God. The terms of that covenant are the commandments of the Torah. Although no individual will have the opportunity to observe them all, and in the end, no one will observe even those they can fully or without mistake, the way toward life is to serve God by striving to keep the commandments as fully as possible. In each one of those acts—ritual, agricultural, ethical, spiritual, ceremonial, interpersonal—one is brought over and over into relationship with God through the enactment of the covenant. Moreover, the experience of life through the commandments is deepened when they are enacted or fulfilled in the company of others, and it is the covenant that binds the whole of the Jewish people to God. Death is thus neither embraced nor denied, but in the daily embrace of the covenant and the commandments, both individual and collective, we find a whole life.

The instruction offered in the Torah is, again, both hidden and revealed—presented in narrative, codified in statute, hinted at in the very structure of the world described by it. One popular classical homily points to the very first verse of the Bible as it has appeared in many English translations, "In the beginning, God," and stops there. That is what we need to know first, and perhaps even last. Whatever our personal questions might be about how we should live our lives, about the point of our lives, it can only be answered in light of God's presence and primacy. As the biblical narrative proceeds, it becomes clear that this world was made for us human beings—that we might live and procreate and enjoy its benefits. We live in God's world, yet we are not God. We are God's guests (or tenants), and all that we will need to know is how to behave properly in that regard. A guide to help us live well during all the time that we might abide on this earth is found in the various legal codes and narrative passages throughout the Torah.

One aspect of that guidance echoes the first verse of Genesis. When God brings the Israelites out of Egypt to Sinai to receive the laws of the covenant, it is so that they should acknowledge that "I am Adonai your God" (Exodus 20:2). That fact, that truth embedded in Creation, leads to covenant and relationship. "You have seen what I did to the Egyptians, how I bore you on eagles' wings and brought you to Me. Now then, if you obey Me faithfully and keep my covenant, you shall be My treasured possession among all the peoples" (Exodus 19:4–5). The benefit of that relationship, the consequence of following the laws of the covenant, is expressed in Leviticus 18:5: "You shall keep My laws and My rules, by pursuit of which man shall live: I am the Lord." And, so that the import of the verse not be lost on its readers, the rabbis glossed the verse, "That you might live by them—and not that you should die because of them" (Yoma 85a). So urgent was the desire that the people find life through the pursuit of the covenant that the Torah pleads, "I call heaven and earth to witness against you this day: I have put before you life and death, blessing and curse. Choose life—if you and your offspring would live" (Deuteronomy 30:19).

"Choose life!"—the byword of the Torah. Death is not denied, and death is not embraced. It is present, unavoidable, but not the only option so long as one is yet alive. The promise, clearly, is not that death will not come. Rather, it is through the choice to live, to follow the path of the covenant, that whatever is given will be full, whole, and blessed.

This is clearly played out in the last book of the Torah. Moses, the great leader, the prophet, God's intimate, is told to prepare for his death. Despite his devotion and tireless service, he will not receive the expected end of his endeavors—to bring the people into the Land of Israel.

> I pleaded with Adonai at that time, saying, "O Adonai, You who let Your servant see the first works of Your greatness and Your mighty hand, You whose powerful deeds no god in heaven or on earth can equal! Let me, I pray, cross over and see the good land on the other side of the Jordan, that good hill-country, and the Lebanon." But Adonai was wrathful with me on your account and would not listen to me. Adonai said to me, "Enough! Never speak to Me of this matter again! Go up to the summit of Pisgah and gaze about, to the west, the north, the south, and the east. Look at it well, for you shall not go across yonder Jordan. Give Joshua his instructions, and imbue him with strength and courage, for he shall go across at the head of this people, and he shall allot to them the land that you may only see."
>
> (DEUTERONOMY 3:23–28)

There is no more pathetic moment in the Torah than this, and it speaks to our very own experience. "'It is an unhappy business, that which God gave men to be concerned with' (Ecclesiastes 1:13). Rabbi Yudan said in the name of Rabbi Aibu: Nobody departs from the world with even half his desire gratified" (Ecclesiastes Rabbah 1:32). We struggle to do our best. We try to love well. We try to educate ourselves, to appreciate the wonders of the world, and then to share that with later generations. We seek to achieve success in our worldly affairs. Our hope is always to see our work completed, to see the product of our endeavors: our children settled well and children born to them, our work appreciated and its benefits shared with others, our aspirations fulfilled. Yet many of us die without that blessing, and those of us who live "too long" often regret what we do witness.

In the course of the liturgical year in the synagogue, the Torah is read in full. Successive sections are read each week on the Sabbath, in sequence, from the Torah's beginning to its end. In the concluding moment, at the Simḥat Torah celebration, we read, "So Moses the servant of Adonai died there . . . before all Israel" (Deuteronomy 34:5, 12), and we then immediately return to the first verse, "In the beginning, God . . ." (Genesis 1:1). For weeks upon end, from the first mention of the infant Moses in Exodus 2:2 through to the very last verse of the Torah, Moses has held center stage. He has been the leader, he has been the prophet, he has been the face of God before the people. The whole endeavor of the Exodus and the passage to the Promised Land has been at his direction, in his presence. And, then, he is gone. Moses is not the one who brings us to the Promised Land, for he cannot enter himself. In the end, it is only God who remains, and we—our plans, our hopes, our aspirations, and our desires—fall short of complete fulfillment.

No one can expect to attain the promised land in his or her lifetime. That seems to be the message of the Torah. Life is a long journey that ultimately is completed only in death. The goal of the journey, the final fulfillment of aspiration, may never be achieved. Therefore, if satisfaction is to come in life, it must be in the course of living, in the choosing of life. There can be no other hope. It is only in the connection to God, achieved through the observance of the commandments and the fulfillment of the covenant, that we truly experience being alive. More than that, such as reward for action or ultimate accomplishment in life's work, cannot be expected.

Unless that reward is in the moment itself, in the act itself. Pursuing the *mitzvot*, living fully in God's presence, may actually be the way home. Life itself, each moment, for however long we may live, may be the "rest and inheritance" (Deuteronomy 12:9) that we yearn for. We will miss it when we place our personal needs, interests, expectations, and assumptions before our attention to God's life and will. We see this clearly in the teaching of Rabbi Yisrael, the Koznitzer Maggid (late eighteenth century), below.

> "This is the instruction regarding a person who dies in a tent" (Numbers 19:14). We can understand this in light of the teaching from the Talmud that the Torah is only sustained by those who give up their own lives over it (cf. Berakhot 63b). That is, they give up their lives, their sense of independent power, saying, "Everything is from the Holy One," for it is He who gives us power to do anything, He gives us understanding and wisdom to serve Him. That is the meaning of "a person dies in a tent"—a person who does not act with a sense of independent power but knows that everything is from the Holy One, this person dwells in God's tent. "All that is in the tent (with the corpse) shall be impure for seven days" (Numbers 19:14). Alternatively, a person who sees himself as a tzadik, who serves as if he were indeed fully devoted to God, as if he were sure that he was already in God's tent, shall surely defile the seven days, which are the seven divine aspects and qualities (*middot*) of God. And, he will need to work to repair them.
>
> (Avodat Yisrael, Parah,
> s.v. zot hatorah adam ki yamut ba'ohel)

I am heartened and challenged by this teaching. Death is not only the end of our physical existence, our annihilation. We can also be dead in the midst of life. When we are mired in self-centered concerns, regretting every loss, begrudging every payment we have to make, resisting every challenge to change, and blind to the needs and distresses of others, we are dead to the world and to God. When we devote the personal drama of our lives and our expectations to God's service with joy and love, we gain life. When all of our efforts are toward realizing God's presence in our lives and in the world, we come fully alive. We can live in God's tent, but we have to be willing to let go of our habits of thought and our expectations of "how things ought to be," in order to live fully in the face of the truth of life.

I was called to the home of a ninety-year-old man who had died. I went to visit with his wife, to prepare for his funeral. We sat in her kitchen, talking about him, about their life together. They had no children. They had lived simply. They had been married for over sixty-five years.

After a pause, she sighed and asked, "Why couldn't we have had a little more time?"

There are many ways to understand her question, and the least charitable would be to say that she was greedy. But, she spoke a truth that many of us feel even more acutely if we are younger, or if we lost a spouse at an early age, or when we worry about our children, family, and friends. We want more life. We want more connection with loved ones. We don't want to lose anything.

Why can't we have more?

A young widow reflects on her husband's death at the hands of terrorists. "He was my life. We had so many plans, so much we had hoped to do. It's so tragic. Now he's gone." What are we to do with loss? What happens to our plans when they are left undone, when our hopes die without hope of fulfillment? What happens to us?

I sat with the parents of a girl who had celebrated her bat mitzvah in my congregation and now was dead, at just twenty-six years old. In the midst of the shock, in the emptiness of loss, the questions came: "Why not me? She was so young and had so much to look forward to. Now, who will I have lunch with? Who will make me laugh? How can I go on?"

How is it that we actually survive loss, tragedy, suffering, pain? What are we to do when our world crumbles as one of its pillars is removed? Why is it that even though our world crumbles, not all of it falls? Why is there a world at all when our hearts are broken?

The question stands from the beginning of time. We read the story of Cain and Abel, about the first death and its aftermath. Cain, of his own accord and seemingly without any precedent, brings an offering of grain to God. His brother follows suit, bringing of the choicest of the firstlings of his flock. God "paid heed" to Abel's offering but not to Cain's:

> Cain was much distressed and his face fell. And Adonai said to Cain, "Why are you distressed, and why has your face fallen? Surely, if you do well, there is uplift. But if you do not do well, sin crouches at the door; its urge is toward you, yet you can be its master."
>
> (GENESIS 4:5–7)

Cain then has some conversation with his brother Abel, and then, in the field, he rises up and kills him. God then comes to Cain and asks, "Where is your brother Abel?," to which Cain responds dismissively, "I do not know. Am I my brother's keeper?"

This is all that we know of Abel, and it is very little. In the whole of this short narrative, God's speech is directed solely toward Cain, never to Abel (even when God "pays heed" to his sacrifice). Moreover, from verse one to nine, from Cain's birth until Abel's death, Cain is mentioned nine times and Abel merely seven, and then Abel appears only once more: "Adam knew his wife again, and she bore a son and named him Seth, meaning, 'God has provided me with another offspring in place of Abel,' for Cain had killed him" (verse 25). Abel appears in the Bible again only because he is being "replaced"—and then he is really gone. Nothing more is heard from him or about him in the rest of the Bible.

Unless, of course, we consider the words of Ecclesiastes to be a long meditation on Abel's life and on the futility of human existence. The name Abel is *hevel* in Hebrew, which means "vapor" or "breath." The King James Bible translates the second verse of Ecclesiastes as "Vanity of vanities; all is vanity *(hevel)*," while the New Jewish Publication Society translation offers, "Utter futility! all is futile." Over and over, Ecclesiastes observes the world around him, human endeavors, strivings and failures, and all he sees is Abel—all is *hevel*. "Men are mere breath *(hevel)*; mortals, illusion; placed on a scale all together, they weigh even less than a breath *(hevel)*" (Psalm 62:10). If we were to place all of humankind on one side of the scale, they and their accomplishments would come to no more than a breath, all of Abel's accomplishments. There is no permanence in success, no salvation in wealth, no hope in wisdom. Whatever we may do—thinking that we will put off death, prevent loss, establish a lasting name in this world—is futile and vain. In the end, it is *hevel,* and we are all Abel. "*Adam lahevel damah;* Man is like a breath (like Abel)" (Psalm 144:4). We appear, we work, we find some success, and it is taken away from us—we die.

For all this, the Bible does not dwell on the futility of human life, or on the lost figure of Abel. Rather, the disappearance of Abel reflects the biblical author's preference for the concrete, the sense that what counts is what exists. That which is present before us is susceptible to our control and open to change. Motivation and antecedent are not as important as consequence. In the same way that Cain evades God's question, the narrative ignores all discussion of motive and extenuating circumstances. It is not "why" that interests the Torah, but "what now." The story of Cain and Abel teaches us that, in the end, we can only deal with what is left over, with the survivors, with outcomes. We cannot change the past; we can only deal with the present, with what is at hand.

And so, after Abel's death, the Torah focuses on Cain. He is the survivor. He can be called to account. He can experience the consequence of his acts, and in his response he can make a difference. Just as God spoke to Cain before the murder, God speaks to him again after the murder—because only Cain is left. The Torah is interested in what happens to Cain; the story of his punishment is a necessary counterbalance to Abel's murder. Abel lived and died and, having no successors, his memory fades from the earth. Cain is called to account for his actions, for his brother's death. "Therefore, you shall be more cursed than the ground, which opened its mouth to receive your brother's blood from your hand. If you till the soil, it shall no longer yield its strength to you. You shall become a ceaseless wanderer on earth" (4:11–12). This is pretty harsh stuff. For a farmer such as Cain, this must have been unbearable. His whole life is turned upside down: cut off from the land, forced to wander like his brother the shepherd, nowhere at home. Cain is certainly punished—but is justice done? Is it fair that we pay so much attention to Cain, in the end? Does it make sense that Cain should have a life, any sort of life, while Abel lies dead on the ground?

But Cain does live on. The Torah reports it all, and his life almost seems "normal." That is, he marries and he has a family. Surprisingly, he even settles down, building a city that he names after his son. Further, Cain's lineage extends even to the sixth generation. Among Cain's last descendants are those who are the ancestors of all who dwell in tents and amidst animals (Jabal, 4:20), those who play the lyre and the pipe (Jubal, 4:21), and those who forge all implements of copper and iron (Tubal-Cain, 4:22). The father of these generative men was Lemech. With these last two generations Cain's story then ends. The final word on Cain's line, the lament of Lemech, suggests a kind of symmetry. Violent death is again reported: "I have slain a man for wounding me, and a lad for bruising me. If Cain is avenged sevenfold, then Lemech seventy-sevenfold" (4:23–34). Cain's fame, which should have been as the "first child" and the head of the generations of man, is instead as the first murderer. His legacy to his descendants is death. While there may have been moments of glory, they are still fleeting, and his lineage ends as it began, with death. We hear no more of Cain. His line comes to an end.

In this one chapter, in twenty-four verses, the Torah established a truth that would characterize the world from that point on: narrative, history, and moral interest rests in what can be done *now.* The Torah will from now on teach about consequences, not motivations. We may mourn the dead, but we cannot bring them back to life, and their story can only live on in that of the living. But, the dead have no voice; only the living tell the story, because the ongoing story is only about them. Because the Torah focuses on consequences, it deals with justice. Although Cain lives on after Abel's death (something that will not be tolerated so easily later, when human judicial systems evolve), he does not go unpunished. He is uprooted from his work in the soil and exiled from his land. He struggles to make a living and has no rest; he is an outcast among men. He may have had accomplishments (such as building a city), but they are ultimately washed away (along with his descendants) in the Flood. The Torah tells us, indirectly, that the consequence of his act continued to work its way out in his life and in the lives of his descendants. The ultimate payment for his crime may not be stated explicitly, and it may not seem at all connected to the original act. But, justice is finally done. Even Cain cannot escape the end of all flesh: to become Abel himself, a fleeting breath, a mortal consumed by death.

Is this something that we know in our own lives, experience in our bodies and souls? When we pay close attention to the unfolding of our lives, we realize that what is true and accessible is only this moment. We realize that what has happened in the past cannot be undone, and we do not know what the next moment will bring. All that exists is the awareness of this moment and how it shapes the intention of our hearts. When we act poorly, when we sin against another, we are still responsible for making amends, for seeking reconciliation. But what shall we do when we realize that the one we have harmed is no longer here, is no longer alive? We cannot change the effect that we had on that person. We cannot change the harm that we did. We are still alive, and we live out the story of those consequences in our own lives. How we live next, what we do to change our behavior to avoid harming others, is our charge. We fulfill that charge in our lives, with each next breath, each next step, each next day. So long as we are alive, we experience ourselves as Cain over and over again.

However, it often takes us time to realize our failures and own up to our mistakes. How much longer may it then take for the full effect of those mistakes and the consequences of our realizations to finally appear? Do we not know that if justice has not been done in this moment that it may yet be done in the next? The absence of justice in this moment can propel us to seek reconciliation, perhaps even inspire us to do justice always. But that is a dedication that must be renewed each moment, and whose outcome will only be known over the course of time, if at all.

So much of the story of our lives has to do with what we experience in any given moment, how we understand that event, and how we respond to that moment. The end of the biblical story was not foreshadowed at its beginning. Cain, the firstborn—the first child in all of Creation—responds to the spontaneous and natural movement of his heart and brings an offering to God. He models devotion and piety for his younger brother, who, in turn, brings an offering. This was not a competition. Both acted with purity of heart. But Cain's "face fell" when he sensed that God had "paid heed" to Abel's sacrifice, and Cain acted on his feelings. In that moment, he created a crisis. He allowed jealousy, anger, or fear to cloud his heart. He interpreted God's action personally, and, on that basis, rewrote the narrative of the offerings. He turned the offerings into a competition, he made up the rules, and he defined the apparent meaning of the outcome.

Then God speaks: pay careful attention, Cain. Look at your heart. What is true? Have I suggested to you that I do not care for your offering? That I pay heed to Abel's is merely that: now, at this moment, I pay heed to Abel. Do you know what I want from you? Can you determine how I will respond to your next offering? And what difference would that make, anyway? You brought Me an offering out of the goodness of your heart, the deep sentiment of your spirit. Do you need Me to tell you that you did well, that your action was good in and of itself? "If you do well," if you pay attention to the truth—you are angry, you are jealous, you are afraid—you have not failed. But you can also do well, you can survive this moment—"there will be uplift"—if you can wake up in your life to know that you are blessed whether I "pay heed" or not. In that manner your offering will be true because your intention was true. "But, if you do not do well," if you allow your feelings in this moment to cloud your vision and constrain your heart, "sin crouches at the door." The story that you are making up will lead you to sin, to acts that are unkind or worse. You will not act out of generosity of spirit or compassion of the heart; you will act selfishly, to soothe your ego. Ego will blind you to the truth. You will lose sight of the full humanity of your brother. Ego's (or sin's) "urge is toward you, but you can be its master."

Cain, like all of us, experienced a moment of crisis: he created a story that blinded him to the truth. God told him that he had the capacity to see clearly, to do well. So, too, do all of us. Each time we stop in the midst of our inner turmoil to listen carefully to the workings of our egos, we experience a moment of choice. Sin crouches at the door in the possibility that we may act to soothe our vain spirit and thereby bring suffering to another (and to ourselves). But we can master it. We can stop, take a breath, reflect in a mindful manner, and ask the questions: What is true? What is it that I feel? Where does that feeling come from? Does it flow from an accurate assessment of the situation? What will happen if I act on the basis of this feeling? Do I know the true intentions and motivations of the "Abel" who stands before me and with whom I am in contention? Do I know all of the extenuating circumstances or exigencies that have led "Abel" to act in this manner? Do I know all of the conditions and exigencies that have led me to act in this manner? Has "Abel" actually done anything against me, or am I just responding to my own feelings of uncertainty and fear? What will be most just for both of us? What would be a compassionate response—both for me and for "Abel"? Asking these questions before we act gives us the opportunity to relax, reconsider, and return—even if only for a moment—to a balanced, open heart. In this manner we can experience uplift, and perhaps master sin, overcoming the forces of our egos. We can choose to respond out of compassion and mindful clarity.

Cain did not do this, however. He failed to understand God's words, and he acted out of pique, anger, frustration, jealousy, fear—all to protect his ego. Sin crouched, he opened the door, and it pounced. Instead of the spiritual uplift, the joy that he could have experienced in celebrating his brother's honor, he rose up and killed him. The rabbis recognized this. They highlighted it through irony: in their story Cain recognizes that the situation calls for compassion, but he perverts its purpose. Instead, Abel extends his spirit in openheartedness and suffers in the end.

> Rabbi Yoḥanan taught: Abel was indeed stronger than Cain. When the Torah says, "He rose up," it means to tell us that Cain had fallen under Abel. Cain then said, "There are only the two of us in the world. If you kill me, what will you go and tell our father?" At these words, Abel was filled with compassion for him. Cain immediately got up and killed his brother. From this came the proverb: "Do not do good to an evil man, and evil will not befall you."
>
> (GENESIS RABBAH 22:8)

Cain recognized that the moment was open to compassion. He may not have felt it for his brother, but he understood that other people would be affected by his actions. Yet, he closed his eyes and his heart to the fullness of that knowledge, and remained stuck in his anger. Moreover, he used it to manipulate Abel, to throw him off balance, and so gain advantage. In the guise of compassion, Cain instead did injustice.

We are thus led to the conclusion of this text. Is this the lesson of this story? Are we prepared to divide the world so clearly into "good" and "evil" people, to only do good to some and not to others? Being thoughtlessly permissive may lead us to unwise actions. Too much pity can lead to injustice when we explain away the actions of another, finding extenuating circumstances to explain their violence or cruelty or insensitivity—and thus permit crimes to go unpunished and cruel acts to pass without resistance. When we allow this to happen, we ignore one of the tenets of mindfulness: knowledge of the truth of the moment permits us to respond with wisdom. Wisdom includes awareness of the need for justice, the appropriateness of firm, but dispassionate, resistance to malevolence. Not to respond would be to sustain the evil that is being done, to permit its persistence. What we want is to respond in such a manner that we do not open the door to sin, that we not enter into a contentious wrestling match that will blind us to our own potential for malicious acts. We can maintain a compassionate heart even when we say "No" to injustice. "If you do well, there is uplift. But if you do not do well, sin crouches at the door; its urge is toward you, yet you can be its master."

Let us return, though, to the issue of Abel's disappearance from the Bible. It seems wrong that the criminal remains the focus of attention, and the innocent victim is ignored. Part of the reason that it seems so unfair is because we see ourselves as Abel. We do not want to be forgotten; we anticipate that we, too, will disappear. We fear death. We know that when we die we will no longer have consciousness of our own existence, and we worry that no one else will remember us, just like Abel was not remembered. The psalmist shared these feelings:

> The bonds of death encompassed me; the torments of Sheol overtook me. I came upon trouble and sorrow and I invoked the name of Adonai, "O Adonai, save my life!" Adonai is gracious and beneficent; our God is compassionate. Adonai protects the simple; I was brought low and He saved me. Be at rest, once again, O my soul, for Adonai has been good to you. You have delivered me from death, my eyes from tears, my feet from stumbling. I shall walk before Adonai in the lands of the living. I had believed it when I said, "I am suffering terribly," when I said in my haste, "All men are false."

> (PSALM 116:3–11)

In the face of suffering and death, for a moment, the psalmist had feared annihilation. Now, restored, he reconsiders what had happened. He can see that he drew a false conclusion about people, and about God. When it appeared that death was at hand, when he believed that he was really suffering, he lost all trust in people. "All men are false": they do not care about me now, and they will not remember me when I am gone. When the psalmist says that he called upon the name of Adonai, it means that he took stock of his situation. He asked, "Is my assessment of my situation correct? Even when I am brought low, am I completely lost?" The answer that the psalmist finds is one of reassurance: "When I look around, I realize that there are other people in the world, not just me. There are others who suffer, those who are simple, and God cares for them, too. I am not alone in my suffering, and I am not forgotten. How do I know that I am not forgotten? 'I was brought low, and He saved me.' I am still here! I can regain my composure, some sense of balance."

In this moment, the psalmist invites us to realize that when we suffer we are not dead. When we stumble, we are not obliterated. To allow our hearts to close, our eyes to be clouded by tears, is to lose sight of the myriad ways that we are still connected to all that is. Fear of disappearance cuts us off even from the people who do, indeed, love us and care for us. It leads us to a sense of being separate and alone—what it means to experience "death" even in the land of the living. But that need not be the only conclusion that we can draw. Suffering need not be the only end; rather: "I will walk before the Lord in the lands of the living." We can regain our composure by opening our hearts, even in the midst of our fear.

This is wisdom, manifesting as hope. This awareness of the presence of God is the antidote to fear. Rather than submit to anxiety over disappearing after death, or worrying about the great injustice that our own death seems to us, the psalmist suggests that we would do better to use each moment to be fully alive now. What comes afterward cannot be accounted. "The heavens belong to Adonai, but the earth He gave over to man. The dead cannot praise Adonai, nor any who go down into silence. But we will bless Adonai now and forever, Hallelujah" (Psalm 115:16–18). There is no other moment than now. Worry about the future, about what will happen after we die, is misplaced, a distraction from the present moment. The dead cannot praise God—that is, they cannot live in this moment. They are dead. There is nothing more that they can do. Only we, the living, have the capacity to awaken to the possibilities of this very moment. Only we can remain alive. "I shall not die but live and proclaim the works of Adonai. Adonai has punished me severely, but did not hand me over to death. . . . This is Adonai's doing; it is marvelous in our sight. This is the day that Adonai has made—let us exult and rejoice in it" (Psalm 118:17–18, 23–24).

Our sympathy for Abel, our sense of injustice at his disappearance, is largely our own fear of disappearing. Over and over in the course of our lives we feel threatened. We experience physical suffering. We go through periods of depression. We fear loss, loneliness, abandonment, rejection. We face death. Over and over we sense that we could become another Abel. And yet, in that moment we actually respond more like Cain. When we sense a crisis, we feel the need to act to preserve ourselves, to protect our egos, to negate "unfairness." We can allow the bonds of death to encompass us, giving in to fear. We can allow pain to become suffering, and lose faith with other people, and ourselves. At such times we are at risk of flailing about in blind anger and frustration, of becoming Cain—yet we cannot deny the unresolved fear that we are actually Abel. If, in that moment, we perceive our fear and recognize our confusion and irrational response, we learn that we can choose otherwise. We can rise to the awareness that there is no other moment than this—the only moment in which we can experience anything, even suffering. This makes it possible for us to master the urges that threaten to overwhelm us, acknowledging their presence while denying their power. We can choose to remain in the land of the living, acknowledging the full truth of the moment (that we may yet become Abel), or we can give in to our fears, and to death (and, so, become Cain).

As hard as it is to acknowledge that human existence carries the risk that we will be Abel, it is also painful to see ourselves as Cain. The Cain perspective reminds us that in this moment we are alive, and we remain alive even when other people die. Sometimes we even forget them when they are gone. Moreover, at moments it creeps into our consciousness that we go about our lives ignorant of all of the other Abels in the world, the thousands upon thousands of people who die short of fulfillment, who go to the grave unknown, unmarked, unremembered. And so, we live in fear that we will be the next Abel, and we rise up against the Abel in us, transforming ourselves into Cain. Thus, we are at once both the manipulative, selfish, fearful Cain, and also the innocent Abel. We are potentially both wicked and righteous. In each moment, however, we are given the chance to choose life, to resist the pull of sin whose urge is toward us, to master our blindnesses. We can recognize when, in our haste, in our fear, in our shortsightedness and closedheartedness, we blame other people for our suffering. God offers us a moment of choice: "If you do well, there will be uplift." In choosing against our anger, against giving in to our fears, we enter fully into the land of the living.

The rabbis knew this as well. They had a sense that one could be dead even in the midst of life, just as one could be alive even in death.

> "[For he who is reckoned among the living has something to look forward to—even a live dog is better than a dead lion—] since the living know they will die. But the dead know nothing; [they have no more recompense, for even the memory of them has died.]"
>
> (ECCLESIASTES 9:4–5)

Rabbi Hiyya Rabbah and Rabbi Yonatan were walking in front of the bier of Rabbi Shimon ben Yose ben Lekunia. Rabbi Yonatan's garment dragged on his coffin. Rabbi Hiyya Rabbah said to him, "Son, lift up your cloak so that they (the dead) will not say, 'They are coming to us tomorrow, and yet they insult us!'" He replied, "Rabbi, doesn't the Bible say, 'but the dead know nothing'?" He said, "Son, you may know Scripture, but you do not know Midrash. 'The living know' refers to the righteous, who even when they are dead are referred to as being alive, and 'the dead know nothing' refers to the wicked, who even in life are considered dead."

(ECCLESIASTES RABBAH 9:4)

"I will walk before Adonai in the land of the living." So long as we are conscious, we have the capacity to be fully alive. But at the same time, we can choose death. Who are the righteous here? They are those whose intention is to master their egos, to overcome the urges of the moment and see the truth; they are thus fully alive. The choice to respond in haste and see everyone, all life, as false, is wickedness: this is to be dead. In every moment we can become alive. The choice at any given moment for life does not guarantee future life. It only redeems this moment. The ways of righteousness demand constant vigilance. There is no moment that is not threatened by clouded vision or selfishness. Over and over we must choose life if we wish to live among the living. Or we can choose death, even while we are alive, and be among those who "even in life are considered dead."

I am reminded of the movie "Remember the Titans." There, in the newly integrated South, the white quarterback opens his heart to his black teammates. His initial motivation is to keep his position as quarterback, and to win one more season before graduation. In the end, his commitment to them expands so that he sees them as full human beings, and he keeps these friendships even at the expense of his standing among the white students. Before the championship playoff he is injured in a car accident, paralyzed from the waist down. He celebrates his team's victory vicariously, and with their support and others', he ultimately makes a life for himself, including victories in the Para-Olympics. And then he dies, killed by a drunk driver.

At each step in this story, the quarterback could have chosen blindness over clear-sightedness, yet he did not. That is what makes him a hero, and it is also what makes his death seem tragic. What is significant, however, is that until the last scene in the movie, we do not know that he has died. We are living out his story, his heroism, his openheartedness. We are caught up in the moment. The heroism of his life, his goodness and his openheartedness, are no less true when finally we find out that he is dead, except that we know that he will not be able to extend those qualities into the future. We mourn his death, and we grieve the loss of his influence and his goodness into the future. But the good that he did, the force of his inner growth, translated into communal good, still stands. Even in death he is still alive.

A more painful instance. A young man had planned to spend his junior year of college studying abroad, specifically in Israel. As the summer before his departure passed, the political situation in Israel deteriorated. It seemed that no one in Israel was safe from terror, and the cycle of violence was grinding more and more deeply into war. His parents asked that he not go, that he stay in America where he would be safe. He got a job for the fall, working in New York City, in the World Trade Towers. He died on September 11, 2001.

Were his parents wrong to ask him not to go to Israel? Could they have foreseen that he would die in a terrorist attack in his own country? Would they have sent him to Israel if they had known that the World Trade Center would be attacked, yet also knowing that the likelihood of a terrorist act was greater in Israel? They were not wrong (given the evidence at that time), and they could not have known what would happen on September 11. They made the best decision they could and he made the best choice he could, in that context, to do something meaningful and productive with his time. At each step, they acted according to the truth that they could see, wholeheartedly, with faith in their decision. It is tragic that the boy died, even painfully ironic. But looking backward in time, there are no grounds to second-guess what happened. They all chose life; they looked for the opportunity to expand goodness, to be fully alive in the midst of life. Despite his death, that is no less true.

That these people are young makes their stories that much more painful. We hear in our hearts, "They had so much to look forward to, so much good yet to do. Family, work, community service, travel, philanthropy, love, old age. What a loss. What a waste." We realize this at a distance, reflected in these "other" lives, but we know, as well, that this is our deepest fear. We live with the unsettling awareness that we may not see our children's children, that we may not finish our current project, that we may never have the chance to say "I love you" one last time. How can we live with that threat hanging over our heads? How can we accept that we or our loved ones may be the next Abel? The author of the *Sefat Emet* addresses this challenge below.

> We are told that "whoever participates in the pain of the community will get to see the community's consolation" (cf. Ta'anit 11a). Thus it is written about mourning for the destruction: "Rejoice in gladness with her, all you who did mourn for her" (Isaiah 66:10). How shall we understand this teaching? If the rebuilding of Jerusalem happens in our day, won't everyone alive then see it, and

not just those who mourn it, even now, in its destruction? Alternatively, if we live to the time of Jerusalem's rebuilding, won't there still have been others who joined us in mourning its destruction, other righteous people, who may have died before that time? The way to understand this lesson is that we are being invited to develop the capacity to see the consolation of the people even in the midst of their suffering, since the exile (and its suffering) is only a matter of hiding. Whoever is able to remove this quality of hiding, through the clarity and transparency of their heart, will also be able to see the consolation of the people, just as it says, "Rejoice . . . with her." That is, rejoice with the community of Israel (also, the Shekhinah); even though she may be in exile, nevertheless joy is still hidden with her. She knows that in the end she will be raised up to be the crown on her king's head. Thus, anyone who joins with her in her suffering will merit to see this joy, too.

(SEFAT EMET II 11, SHEMOT 5643)

I feel that our text sets out the problem very clearly here: those who are promised that they will see the outcome for which they so longed, for which they worked with devotion, may not actually live to see it, while those who were not so dedicated may enjoy that benefit. All Abels die without posterity, without uttering a word, innocent—is that really all that we can hope for? Even the Cains of the world have hopes and dreams for their families, for themselves. Is it right that they get to take pleasure in these joys while Abel lies dead on the ground? Is it possible to commit wholeheartedly to any endeavor knowing that we may not see it through to the end? Do we have the will to open our hearts in love even if the objects of our love may be lost, to strive even if we may fail?

This text suggests that it is possible to "remove this quality of hiding" through the clarity and transparency of our hearts. The "quality of hiding" is our willful turning away from hope and commitment. It is the denial of the ultimate good of life, the promise of consolation, even in the midst of our personal suffering. We can make our hearts pure when our devotion to doing the good is ultimately for the sake of the good. Our hearts can become clear when our love is finally for the sake of others. Alternatively, any plans that we project into the future may turn into the "hiding." That is, any thought of what is "due" us, what is "right" or "just" or "fair," only clouds our hearts. When we are so fixed on what we anticipate, on what we hope for, we may become blind to the immediacy of the blessing of the moment. Even in the deepest exile, in the shadow of destruction, we have the capacity to raise the joy in life's possibilities, in the blessing of the moment over the pain of loss or the fear of unfulfilled expectations. The challenge is to make our hearts pure, to clarify them of all false expectations.

It is only this moment that we possess, not the future. This text calls us to commit ourselves so fully to this very moment in all of its richness that it will also include all future moments. When our hearts are open, when no one is excluded from our prayers for good and redemption, we step closer to experiencing that good and redemption in our own lives. If our intention is to see the greatest good for the greatest number, without self-serving evasions of responsibility, without blaming others for our current failures, we may actually experience that good in our own lives. That is how we can experience the promise that "whoever participates in the pain of the community will get to see the community's consolation." That I do not yet have in my hand all that I wish for does not mean that I have failed, nor does it mean that it will not yet come about. I do not have it yet, but I still hope for it. I enjoy fully that ultimate possibility without fear, grounded in the present moment.

My father was sixty years old when he died. His younger daughter had died thirteen years before that. He had lived to see four grandchildren born to his two older children, yet he would never know the four now born to his younger two children. He had projected his life out into the future: how he hoped to retire, to travel with my mother, to volunteer his expertise to help emerging economies and struggling people. He did not live to do that. I'm sure that when he first heard the diagnosis of his brain tumor he could not imagine that he would not still enjoy his future. He lived as if it would yet come. But that is how he had always lived. He enjoyed each moment for what it was. He certainly had hopes and plans. But he knew that he had been only seventeen when his own father had died. All of his own accomplishments in life came in the darkness of his father's absence. Yet he enjoyed them in the spirit that his father would have enjoyed them. He lived them completely, with openness of heart and a full belly-laugh. Whatever hopes he may have had remained alive despite personal loss and pain. Whatever expectations he may have had of life and for his future were fulfilled at the end of a family meal, topped off with some good cognac and a fine cigar. "Who would have thought that the son of immigrants, a kid from the Lower East Side, would have traveled the world, would have done all I've done? Who would have thought that I would have all this? Hah!"

"I shall not die, but live." That is a vain expression, a boast that will not stand, unless it is attached to the end of the verse: "and I will proclaim the works of Adonai." The wonders of Adonai are nothing more than this moment. There is no greater blessing than this moment, no hope for more life than this. Every breath is a blessing, each moment a gift. Our every attainment is more than Abel ever enjoyed. The possibility of enjoying our lives in the present will be undermined if we allow our hearts to shrink in fear of "what might happen," or the dim awareness that "we may not live so long." To the extent that we experience blessing in this moment, we will be prepared for the arrival of any future blessings—hopeful, without anxiety, and always aware that whatever comes will be the wondrous work of Adonai. "This is the day that Adonai has made" is every day, for in every day will be found all future days, in all of their possibilities. Therefore, "let us exult and rejoice in it." This will strengthen us, keeping us connected to and engaged in the world despite its pain, despite its suffering. The more fully we remain open and present in each moment, seeing it clearly and responding with compassion, the more likely we will merit "rejoicing in the consolation of the community." Even in our death we will be considered among the living. Rabbi Shelomo Hakohen Rabinowich of Radomsk, in his work *Tiferet Shelomo* (early nineteenth century, Poland) challenges us in the text below to become fully present in this very moment, to be fully alive.

"This is the instruction regarding a person who dies in a tent" (Numbers 19:14). The sages taught that the Torah is sustained only by those who give up their own lives over it (cf. Berakhot 63b). This seemingly contradicts the verse, "You shall live by them" (Leviticus 18:5). But consider: we should be diligent in engaging in Torah while we are still alive, experiencing this world, and "not say, 'When I have time I will study,' lest [we] not find time" (Avot 2:4). Therefore, we must cherish this day and this hour that we are in this world, for it is in our power to repair everything through devoted study. For after we die, even if we were to offer everything in the world for just one day to return to this world to fix that which we had spoiled, it would not be given us. . . .

"This is the law" (Numbers 19:2): that we should devote our lives to repentance, self-transformation, and yearning to serve God fully. Just imagine: if "a person dies in a tent" and then looks for a way that his soul might return to this world even for one day—he would work, devoted to Torah, *mitzvot,* and good deeds on the one day that was given to him as if it were his whole life. That is the meaning of the teaching, "Repent one day before you die" (Avot

2:10). Imagine that this day is the one that was granted to you to return from heaven to this world to perfect your ways before you die. How precious would this day be, since you will never have it again.

This is the import of the teaching that Torah is only sustained by those who give up their lives over it. That is, it is as if they die each day, and consider, in turn, the death to come the next day (Heaven forbid). Thus, if they are still alive the next day, they sense it as a gift from Heaven, one more day in which to perfect themselves before the death that awaits at the end of the next day. In this manner, all of their vital force, their life and livelihood, is solely for the sake of Torah each and every day.

(TIFERET SHELOMO, ḤUKKAT,
S.V. ZOT HATORAH ADAM KI YAMUT BA'OHEL)

When I read this text I am reminded: this day, this very moment, I am alive. That fact, despite all else, offers the opportunity to live in God's presence. When I acknowledge the truth of the moment, without turning away from its pain and without grasping its joys, I let go of my selfish interests and self-imposed limitations. I realize that there is no other time than now, no other opportunity to appreciate, accept, and embrace life than this moment. I am then able to cherish it, seeking to fill it with meaning, to do my best in every way. And, even if I cannot do everything that needs to be done in that moment, on that day, I will at least have acknowledged it all. I will have accepted my responsibility.

This is to participate in the pain of the community—my pain, the pain of my neighbor, the pain of existence. When I fully place myself in it, I transform it. I taste its conversion from agony to joy, from mourning to celebration. I am complete in the moment, so I am complete in my life. I have died to everything but this moment, and so I live in eternity.

Chapter Four

Mindfulness and Connecting with Others

*T*he practice of mindfulness requires that we develop the skill of paying attention—both to the totality of the events that surround us and sweep us up as well as to the minute and precise ways in which we respond to those events. Just as there is a difference between a newspaper story that reports events and an article that analyzes the meaning of those events, so too there is a difference between what happens to us and our response to what happens to us. To see more clearly what exactly is happening, we must find a way to step back from our responses, to cut through the layers of our reactions and biases (the interpretations we overlay on events), to gain some perspective and to put some space between our reactions and the event itself. The capacity to see clearly in the moment what is true, to avoid vision clouded by habitual responses, helps us to respond with wisdom and generates a heart of compassion for ourselves, and for others. This is the goal of mindfulness practice.

The most popular technique to develop this capacity is meditation. But both in popular perception and in the very nature of its practice, there seems to be a conflict between means and ends. That is, meditation is a private practice, taking place within the practitioner. It often is accompanied by closed eyes, suggesting a withdrawal from the world. And, it tends to focus attention on the practitioner—his or her inner life, feelings, and experiences. Compounding this sense that meditation removes us from the world, there are forms of practice that teach that we are to prevent all thoughts of the phenomenal world, even denying its reality.

The Torah makes clear that human existence is meant to be in relationship: "It is not good for man to be alone; I will make a fitting helper for him" (Genesis 2:18). The rabbis understood the phrase "He did not create it (the earth) a waste, but formed it for habitation" (Isaiah 45:18) to suggest the imperative of procreation (Gittin 41b), but it might as easily imply a human obligation to make the earth habitable. Together, men and women are to engage in the work of life: providing sustenance and shelter for themselves and others, transforming the earth for the well-being of all. Once engaged in this endeavor, they have additional responsibilities toward one another—and even toward strangers. No one is to be left destitute, without sustenance or support (Deuteronomy 15:7–11). No one is to be forced to work in such a manner as to deny him or her human dignity (Deuteronomy 5:12–15). Along with our work in the world that brings us into relationship with other people, we are also to give of our time and effort to serving God, and to studying God's Torah.

"And God saw all that He had made, and found it very good" (Genesis 1:31). Rabbi Levi in the name of Rabbi Ḥama bar Ḥanina opened his lesson: "It is the glory of God to conceal a matter, but the glory of kings is to investigate a matter" (Proverbs 25:2). From the beginning of the Book [of Genesis] up to this point, "It is the glory of God to conceal a matter"; but from this point onward, "The glory of kings is to investigate a matter": it is the glory of the words of the Torah, which are likened to kings, as it is said, "Through me kings reign" (Proverbs 8:15), to be investigated.

(GENESIS RABBAH 9:1)

To investigate and understand the workings of the world are glorious endeavors. That is our charge. We can come to a deeper comprehension of the world and our place in it, as well, through the study of Torah. Torah-study and scientific investigation demand neither withdrawal from the world nor denial of its existence, but engagement in it. Ultimately, as the Zohar teaches, the world was created so that God might become known (Zohar II 42b). Through the world we come to know God.

Thus, if the goal or outcome of mindfulness practice were to remove us from engagement with the world, it would be a betrayal of Jewish life and tradition. But it is not. Mindfulness practice does require that we pay close attention to the workings of our minds and hearts; it does have that internal focus. The purpose of that investigation, however, is so that we will be better able to sustain an open heart while living fully *in the world*. That is, each of life's accidents—in the sense of every event that touches us, affects us, happens to us or around us—triggers a reaction. This response is spontaneous, encoded in our genes and formed over time through family interactions, friendships, habits, etc. It happens on its own, simply "in response." Mindfulness practice helps us to see the nature of our minds, the patterns of our reactive selves. Seeing this, we recognize how often our responses are inappropriate to the circumstances, flowing from an inaccurate assessment of the situation. When we are able to see this, we can begin to choose to control our responses, to change our reactions to external (and internal) stimuli. The goal of this process is not only to experience our lives with less anxiety, stress, or contention (so that we will suffer less). It is also so that we will be less likely to hurt other people, or to induce negative responses in them, so that they too will suffer less.

In mindfulness practice we ask over and over, "What is the truth of this moment?" The answer varies, of course, but when we recognize what is truly happening, we find that our responses change. That is, when I sit to meditate and there is noise around me, the answer to the question may be, "I am sitting here; there is noise; there is anger." In the moment that I recognize that, beyond the simple facts of sitting and noticing sound, I also identify that sound as an annoying noise and connect that sound to an emotional response—anger—I have the opportunity to determine why I feel angry. What would cause me to be angry? I can then pay attention to my mind as it spins out: "I have only a little time to meditate, and I can't when there is so much noise! Why can't those people take their conversation elsewhere? Why can't they fix the heating system so that it makes less noise? It's just like it always is—no matter what I want to do, someone is always interrupting . . ."

This stream of thought has led me astray from my intention to meditate, to pay attention to my life. I am now telling myself a story about my circumstances, rather than about the bare facts of the situation, trapping me in my self-centered concerns, leaving me angry, frustrated, and defeated. But if I am truly attentive, watching the workings of my mind, I will begin to notice that I am creating a story about the noise. I will see that I have written a whole play about the inconsiderate people who are talking, about the maintenance crew, or about others. I have projected out all of my anxiety and anger, and displaced my discomfort onto other people. In my clouded vision, I thought I was unhappy because of these other people, but in actuality I have made myself unhappy. The truth simply is: "There is sound." Everything else is a story, a reaction that flows from "It's just like it always is . . ."—that is, my habitual response pattern. Learning to see clearly what is true, I have the possibility of responding in a number of ways. I might simply treat the sound as another phenomenon on which I can rest my attention, like my breath. That is, simply notice "loud noise; voices; noise; noise; noise; noise," and eventually the noise itself will no longer be "noise" that is distracting and invasive sound, but just "sound." Impersonal, amoral, unintentional sound. And, I will then be able to let go of my reactions, undoing the story, and passing through the interruption.

Another response would be to investigate more fully the train of thought that flows from "It's just like it always is . . ." That is, what do I mean by that? How is it always? When did I first feel that it is "always" thus? What image, voice, or inner feeling accompanies my awareness of "it is always this way"? My capacity to follow this line of thought dispassionately, without telling more of the story than "annoying sound; interruption; no privacy; loss of intimacy; crying; baby sister" may help me to recognize a deep pattern of response. My capacity over time to pay close attention to this sort of phenomenon and the reaction it produces may allow me to see how I overlay this history, this part of my life experience, onto every other experience in my life. When I see this, I realize how I create my own additional pain every time I am interrupted. That is, interruption is difficult enough—distracting, impeding, impolite— but I make it worse with the story I tell. When I realize this, I can then offer myself some compassionate care for this suffering. I may then be able to release myself from having to be angry whenever I am interrupted, liberating myself from responding out of my conditioned habit to "noise" or "interruption." The product of that sort of freedom will be less inner strife, and also the potential to respond to others with less anger and more compassion: less anger because I will no longer express my habitual response; more compassion because I will have experienced compassion for myself over my self-inflicted pain, and because I now understand how much pain other people may also suffer. I will not want to suffer any more myself, nor cause anyone else pain.

This is the process of mindfulness practice, and it is difficult. It requires practice, returning over and over again to the question, "What is the truth of this moment?" Over and over we must seek to distinguish between our habitual reaction and the stories it generates and the most truthful description of the moment. It is hard to let go of our habits. We have had most of them for a long time. They serve us well, orienting us in our world, defining us with or against others, reassuring us of who we are, how we are "right." Until we can see the habits of our mind we are trapped, bound to react without control, harming ourselves and others, digging ourselves deeper and deeper into those patterns of thought and feeling. The psalmist expresses this in the starkest of terms: "I am imprisoned and I cannot go out, I will not go out, I shall not go out *(kalu velo eitzei)*" (Psalm 88:9).

The speaker in this psalm feels abandoned by God, cut off from the living, shunned by companions. So far as he can see, there is no way out. What is so striking is that if this were true, the whole enterprise of the psalm would make no sense. That is, what is the good of calling out to God if there is no hope? The opening, middle, and end of the psalm belie the poet's claim. "Incline Your ear, O Adonai, answer me, for I am needy and poor" (verse 3). "Is Your faithful care recounted in the grave, Your constancy in the place of perdition?" (verse 12). "As for me, I cry out to You, Adonai; each morning my prayer greets You" (verse 14). If the poet were so completely cut off, if there were no hope, it would make no sense to call out and pray to God: there would be no purpose in cajoling God to pay attention. The capacity to pray, the realization that the psalmist is still alive and not really among the dead (despite his claim "I am numbered with those who go down to the Pit; I am a helpless man abandoned among the dead, like bodies lying in the grave" [verses 5–6]) ought to open up a door to him, an escape from his suffering. But, it does not. Instead, he is caught in his habitual response to trouble and suffering: "Imprisoned, bound, I cannot move."[1]

Seeing the truth is the means to liberation, release from the prisons—emotional, psychological, spiritual—in which we feel bound. The Baal Shem Tov and the hasidic teachers who followed him also wanted people to learn to see the truth. For them, the truth is drawn from the verse, "It has been clearly demonstrated to you that Adonai alone is God; there is none beside Him" (Deuteronomy 4:35). Their interpretation is: Adonai is God (even the aspect of strict judgment and constriction, "God," is an expression of love and compassion, "Adonai"); there is nothing else. That is, there is nothing but God. Even the physical world, in all its diversity and concreteness, is nothing other than a manifestation of God's Oneness. This idea is expressed pointedly in this quotation from *Or Torah,* a collection of teachings attributed to the Maggid of Mezritch, collected by Rabbi Yeshayahu of Donovitch.

> The seal of the Holy One is Truth *(EMeT).* The letters that make up this word constitute the first, middle, and last letters of the alphabet, hinting that the Holy One surrounds all worlds, fills all worlds, and contains all worlds, and therefore there is no place devoid of God at all.
>
> (Or Torah, al aggadot ḥazal,
> s.v. ḥotamo shel HKB"H EM"T)

---

[1] Norman Fischer, *Opening to You: Zen-Inspired Translations of the Psalms* (New York: Viking Compass, 2002), p. 109.

In this text we are reminded that to learn to see the truth is to learn to see nothing but God in all things: to see that all things are God. God is present in all of Creation, and God surrounds and sustains all of Creation. Nothing moves except as God moves it—even when we wiggle our little fingers, in the end it is God who is moving. Nothing occurs that is outside of God's being.

When we act, our endeavors can contribute either to revealing the Divine in all things or to obscuring it. The Baal Shem Tov's instructions encourage us to strive toward the former, to seize the opportunity in every moment to uncover divine sparks. The problem is that these sparks of divine presence are hidden. Not only are they obscured by the material nature of Creation, but they are buried in it, held fast in "husks." These husks (sometimes characterized as negative forces, distracting ideations, our inclination to evil) enwrap and conceal the sparks, at times even actively resisting attempts to remove the divine light from them. Seeing the Divine in the wonders of Creation is one means of revealing these sparks, and that is often spontaneous and easy. Yet, we are also challenged to find the divine spark even in the least likely of places: the ugly, the polluted, the violent, the debased. Our capacity to locate the divine spark in all things, in all places, at all times, will enable us to find the path of compassion and lovingkindness as well, as we learn in this text by Rabbi Gedaliah ben Yitzhak of Lunietz, *Teshuot Hen.*

> The quality of Truth is the vital force sustaining all Creation. The sages exemplified this in the story told about the city known as *Kushta* (literally, "Truth"). (Cf. Sanhedrin 97a: In this city everyone told the truth and no one died before his time.) Truth is contained even in the husks *(kelipot),* and its force sustains them as well. This is the mystery of the verse, "You keep them all alive" (Nehemiah 9:6), and the teaching of the sages, "Any falsehood that does not also have some truth in it will not in the end be sustained" (cf.

Sotah 35a). . . . Thus, Truth is the common denominator of all of God's qualities. It is the attribute that stands in the middle of God's thirteen attributes of mercy (cf. Exodus 34:6–7, "Adonai, Adonai, a God compassionate and gracious, slow to anger, abounding in kindness *and truth (ve'emet)*, extending kindness to the thousandth generation, forgiving iniquity, transgression, and sin, and remitting punishment"), in the mystery of "and truth," *vav—emet*. This signifies that *emet* (truth) contains the six (*vav* has the numerical value of six) attributes that preceded it as well as the six that follow it. Truth is thus the vital force that vivifies the other twelve, for any quality that is not true in its fullest expression is not an attribute.

(Teshuot Ḥen, Re'eh,

s.v. o yomar dehinei hadavar yadua)

When I read this passage, I am forced to stop and reconsider my habitual sense of order: good is good and bad is bad and they never mix. But, as our text reminds us, even in the *kelipot* we will find the divine spark, the Truth. And, when we find it, it will lead us toward compassion and forgiveness.

My younger son went off to college and set out on the next stage of his life. I was happy for him, and happier still that my new home would be closer to his school, making visits easier and more likely. Indeed, he came home for Thanksgiving as well as part of his winter break. I visited him at school once during the fall semester. As the winter moved toward spring, I began to look forward to Passover and his presence at our seder, a pleasure I had not had with his older brother.

Our conversation about his attending the seder got off to a bad start: we disagreed about co-ed sleeping arrangements in the house. I took my stand as the "father," laying out my position, my concerns, my expectations in terms of my professional role and the values I felt I needed to uphold. He kept pointing to the reality of his life at school, to his values, to the unimportance of my "role" in our relationship as father and son. Into this already roiling mix I added my concern—my exasperation—that he would not set aside his needs for even two nights to attend the seder! What would he do instead? His response, that the seder was not so important to him, after all, threw me completely for a loop (even though I already knew he no longer involved himself in Jewish activities). I ranted and raved, argued from every angle I could come up with— and got nowhere. I kept trying to convince him that I was right, and I kept looking for holes in his argument to show him that he was wrong. I refused to accept that he could see the world so differently from me. What broke the conversation open, what revealed the light in this darkness, was the moment he said, "Dad, if you keep thinking of me in terms of your life, your values, your Jewish commitments—if you only see what you see, what you want to see, what you think there is to be seen—then you're not really seeing me." I stopped short. What could I say in response, other than, "I want to see you—as you are."

In the end, he did not come, and despite my disappointment I was also grateful. As much as I had witnessed the ways he had been changing, even before he left for school, I had not adjusted to his growing maturity. I was stuck in my role as "father," that is, the one who knows best, the one who sets the agenda, the one to whom the children come for family celebrations. I wanted him to be like me, to value what I value, to think what I think. I had allowed a husk to grow around my heart and a membrane to cloud my eyes. But in one moment he broke them open and the light of the truth penetrated my core. I let go of my views, my desires, my expectations, to listen to the person who was actually speaking to me, to hear again what he had to tell me. It was not easy to do, and it was a little painful. But that discomfort was much less than the suffering of anger, resentment, disappointment, recrimination, and alienation that would have filled my heart if I had not opened up. My love for him is not and cannot be dependent on his living as I would like him to live. It was only truth—his truth, my truth, the truth of our relationship—that transformed a moment of conflict into one of compassion and love.

It is difficult to see the truth, particularly the truth of our own self-imprisonment; that we are the cause of our own suffering. Often, the harder we try to see clearly, the more forcefully our habits of mind and heart will cling to the stories that have shaped us, the stories by which we recognize ourselves and our world. I hear this echoed in the teaching of Rabbi Moshe Shoham ben Dan of Dolina, a student of the Baal Shem Tov.

> The essence of our existence is to find, raise up, and reveal the divine sparks hidden in the world. . . . This is our mission. But, for this endeavor we need a great deal of help from God. Haven't we experienced how difficult it is to pull the holiness out from the husks, as if the husk fights against us? Indeed, the holy spark within provides the life-force for the husk, and if it should be withdrawn then the husk would lie lifeless and without power. Therefore, the husk fights against us, trying to get us to sin so that we will not have the power to release the divine sparks. Indeed, in this struggle, the husks seek even to gain power from our very endeavor.
>
> (Divrei Moshe, Lekh Lekha,
> s.v. veyuvan vazeh ma'amaram z"l)

The message in this text seems to be: the harder I try to see clearly, the stronger the resistance. While here the divine sparks are depicted as being outside of us, inside something else from which we seek to extract them, these same sparks also exist inside us. They are present in our experiences, in every interaction and thought. The divine spark—that is, the truth of the moment—is difficult to find, and the habits of our minds and hearts work hard to prevent us from doing so.

How is this truth similar to the truth that we may identify when we pay close attention to our lives? To clear away all of the stories that arise when we are surprised, hurt, angered, and so on, we must slowly and painfully disengage from all of the ways that we allow our egos to define who we are. That is, the stories that we tell ourselves about what is happening largely begin with "I": "I am angry," "I am jealous," "I am annoyed," "I am afraid," "I am ashamed." All of those feelings translate into a sense that our person—our ego—has been assaulted, insulted. As we look carefully at what is really true, we find that all of these feelings and thoughts are transitory. They pass away as quickly as they arise (much of the time). They are not really attached to us, since they are but transient reactions and responses that flow from the habits of our egos. As angry or as scared as we may be, we can quickly come to see that we do not explode from anger nor disappear from fear. When we feel these emotions in our bodies, we have the impression that these feelings are as substantial and as permanent as our physical selves. But they are not substantial; they pass through us, they are not us. There is something else that exists: the particular manifestation of God in our physical existence through which these feelings pass. That is real, but the feelings are not.

What is permanent? What lies behind our fleeting reactions and our constantly changing, aging, corruptible physical bodies? "There is nothing but God"; only God, only the truth of the universal, eternal unfolding of God's Being. All thought processes, all emotional reactions to stimuli that obscure our awareness of God's presence in us and around us, have no substance or reality in the face of

God's universal and unitary being. We do not, we cannot stand outside of God: there is no place that is devoid of God's presence, not even our hearts or minds. But, our egos stand in the way of our perceiving this. Our egos and all of their products, manifested in our habitual reactions, are the *kelipot* (or "husks") that prevent us from seeing the truth. The rabbis understood how potent the ego is as a source of distraction, how attached we can become to our own feelings and thoughts—even to the exclusion of God. "Rav Ḥisda taught, and there are those who say that it was Mar Ukba: Of the one who has a haughty spirit the Holy One says, 'He and I cannot dwell in the same world'" (Sotah 5a). Ego squeezes God out of our hearts and minds, just as ego hides the truth from us. As we clear away the products of our egos in action—the habitual reactions of our minds and hearts—we are able to perceive the truth more clearly, to sense God's presence in all things, in every moment. Then we can truly say, "There is nothing but God."

In the same manner that we seek to see the truth of the moment, we also seek to perceive the truth of God's presence in all things. The ego will not relinquish its place of pride without struggle. Learning to see the truth requires action; it does not happen on its own. That, then, is the value of practice—whether through meditation or some other intentional inner process. Hasidic sources do not rely solely on meditation, instead offering intellectual exercises that are practice techniques designed to help us see ourselves clearly, and so be prompted to change. In this manner, studying these texts helps to create another sort of discipline: conscious awareness of the signs of ego in action, allowing us to stop and consider, "What is true?" Rabbi Yaakov Yosef of Polonnoye, one of the primary students of the Baal Shem Tov, offers just such an exercise.

> It appears to me from what I have received from my teachers and colleagues that this is how to behave with compassion toward all

others. Even when you see something ugly or unbecoming in another person, you should turn your heart to thinking that the Holy One dwells there too, since there is no place devoid of Him. It is therefore for your good that you have seen this, since you have some aspect of this same ugliness in you as well, and this will move your heart to *teshuvah*. Even if you should be distracted from your study of Torah or prayer by someone's conversation, you should take note of being distracted and consider that this is for your good, either because you were not praying or studying properly, or so that you will bring a different intention to your sacred service. Through this process you will come to accept this situation as good, and ultimately that it truly is for your good.

(TOLDOT YAAKOV YOSEF, ḤAYYEI SARAH,

SECTION 2, END)

As I read this text, I understand that the spiritual practice that will help us to see the truth is to "turn your heart to thinking that the Holy One dwells there too." The prompt to do so is when we are irked by something that we see or that happens to us. Whenever we sense a negative feeling arising in us—jealousy, aversion, anger, fear, lust—our response should be to ask, "Where is the divine spark here? How can I see God in that which causes me discomfort or stimulates habitual responses?" When we see God's presence in that which rankles us, our habitual responses soften. Rather than reacting angrily or with resistance, we will be drawn to look lovingly, respectfully, reverently at this receptacle of God's divine spark. Looking for the divine in the other leads us to compassion, even if our ultimate response is to challenge the "offending" actor or event. Further, we are challenged to discern how that which has distracted us is also part of our own make-up. How is the very thing that bothers or interrupts us present in us, as well? Knowing that it does exist in us, admitting that we are just as "guilty" of "ugly" and "unbecoming" behavior, will lead us to have some compassion for ourselves as well.

Part of what makes this practice helpful is that it immediately short-circuits the habitual process in which we begin to tell stories about others. That is, just as we are about to complain that so-and-so is doing something that irks us, distracts us, angers us, offends us, we are told to look first at ourselves: "Rabbi Yoḥanan said in the name of Rabbi Shimon bar Yoḥai: From the forest itself comes the handle for the axe" (Sanhedrin 39b). Without discounting that what we observe may indeed be offensive, we are directed to consider what it is in us that causes us to respond so negatively, or so strongly. The answer, we are told, is that we actually share something of the offending or exciting behavior. We may be blind to it, at the moment. But if we pay attention to our responses, if we observe how they arise, what they feel like, where they sit in our bodies, and what other associations they generate, we will often come to see that we are angry or ashamed or otherwise concerned for our own egos.

When I engage in this practice, I find that I am constantly refining, fine-tuning my attributes. That is, over and over when I am challenged by someone else's behavior I first ask, "How am I like that person?" I look at my habitual responses, and seek that which stimulates my reaction, some way in which I am like that which offends me. I can then see how my reaction is an attempt to hide from my own flaw by attacking it in another. It is not easy, but when I recognize that in me, rather than cringing in shame, I try to open my heart to accept it, with compassion. In that manner, I can begin the process of change, to repair the flaw. I feel that I become softer in the process. I lash out in self-protection less often, and I am less likely to blame my discomfort on someone else. In addition, in this process I also come to view other people differently. I more quickly come to recognize the divine spark in them, and, in turn, I find that I have more compassion for them. After all, they are just like me—

burdened with flaws, with habitual responses. Just as I experience compassion for myself as I face my ego, I ultimately also come to feel compassion for others. This sentiment was given expression in a classical form by Rabbi Uri Feivel ben Aharon of Dubenka in Poland in the late eighteenth century in his book *Or Haḥokhmah*.

"As face answers to face in water, so does one man's heart to another" (Proverbs 27:19). The Baal Shem Tov interpreted [the verse] this way: When we look in the water, we see our full reflection there, and we look big. As we stoop down, our reflection gets smaller. The more we crouch down next to the water, the smaller our reflection becomes until we actually have our face in the water. At that moment, our reflection comes to meet us. So, too, with "our hearts toward others." When we think of ourselves as great, then our fellow is also great. And when we make ourselves smaller before our fellow (deflating our ego), so, too, does our fellow become small (and more accessible to us). Even if we go so far that we cannot become any smaller, even then our fellow will become that small, too. In this manner, we find a balance *(shivui)*, and we become equal *(shavim)*. . . .

That is what David the Psalmist meant when he wrote, "I place *(shiviti)* Adonai before me always" (Psalm 16:8), I want to get to the point of being equal *(shaveh)* (with God). [The word *shiviti* here is a play on words, with *shaveh* and *shavim* meaning "equal."] That is, when I place Adonai before me I can then understand how much the Holy One contracts Himself (as it were) and does good for me. This leads me to make myself smaller, more humble, and more present before God, and in this manner I come to the quality of equanimity [*hishtavut*, another pun].

(Or Haḥokhmah, Vayak'hel,
s.v. od yesh lomar re'u kara Y"Y beshem betzalel)

This text reminds me that the goal of our mindfulness practice is both to gain perspective on and then control over our habitual responses, freeing us to live in the truth of the moment, and to increase our capacity to hold other people in our hearts with compassion. The text above illustrates both of those experiences. We are able to respond to others with compassion when we see them fully as our equals. That is easier said than done. Our egos, fed by our desire to preserve our self-esteem, largely get in the way. We define ourselves in comparison with others—better or worse than, larger or smaller than, but rarely equal to. When we pay close attention to the habitual responses of our hearts and minds, we find that we are quite critical of others. We may not outwardly express our criticism of them, but it still arises in us, and it shapes our response. This is a source of great unhappiness—for us and for others. Alternatively, when we learn to discern this critical voice, to identify how we insert a story generated by our egos into our interactions with others, we might more readily see others in their fullness. We would understand that we are indeed equal.

The step that comes first, the practice that aids us on the path toward compassion for others, is to see the truth; that is, to look fully and attentively into God's face. However great we may consider ourselves to be, when we see God's face (as it were) before us, we are forced to take stock: "I am not as great as God! How is it, then, that we are face to face? God must have 'come down' to meet me. What humility! And look at me and my ego! Let me meet God truly, honestly. Let me see myself clearly and see others, as well, in a balanced, loving manner. Let me open my heart to God's presence."

When we place God fully before us, perceiving that there is nothing else but God, we realize how much we are blessed in every minute. Indeed, moving beyond this thought, we realize that even to think of "nothing else" maintains some sense of separateness, as if there were an "else" from which to observe God. Our sense of "I" or "me" dissolves when there is nothing but God. When there is nothing but God, blessing is manifest in me and all that occurs through me.

It is very difficult to remain in a state of ego-less contemplation, and we return to our normal sense of duality: the world and God. But even then, we sense how our very self is a gift each moment from God. God is present in every part of our being, in every thought and action, in our waking and in our sleeping. God's blessing sustains us with each breath, with each meal, with each step. When we see God before us always, we realize that no matter how obnoxiously we may have behaved, how ego-centric we may have been, God has nevertheless provided these gifts to us. That God has been our partner while we have been both big and small is startling, but also reassuring. We come to realize that no matter what we have, much or little, it is a blessing. With this awareness, we are able to receive with equal joy and gratitude whatever comes to us. God's constancy helps us to learn equanimity. That we wish no more than we have and are grateful for what we've been given releases us from our habitual reactions and allows us to respond to all others with compassion and love.

Maintaining a sense of equanimity is difficult. Over and over things pass before us—thoughts, images, people, material possessions—and habitual thoughts and feelings arise in us. Our hearts and minds reach out toward them, to grasp them or push them away, desiring them or despising them. And so, over and over we are challenged to notice how we respond, what impulse seeks expression, and then determine if it is correct to act on that inclination. We strive to substitute intention for inclination, for when we are driven by inclination, by our habitual reactions, we regularly make mistakes, even those that would be considered a sin. "Resh Lakish taught: No one would commit a sin without being invaded by the spirit of mindless distraction" (Sotah 3a). The word that the Talmud uses for "mindless distraction" is *shtut*, which is otherwise translated as "folly." This image is made more concrete by Rabbi Avraham Yehoshua Heschel of Apt:

> In truth, it is difficult to conceive—how can a person, created in the divine image, embraced and surrounded by supernal lights, actually commit a transgression? It comes about when, in a moment of mindless distraction, a spirit of folly enters our limbs, and the divine image then flees. Therefore, we must be very careful to prevent this spirit of folly from entering our minds or hearts, our eyes, ears, or speech. In this manner will the spirit of God remain hovering over us always.

> (OHEV YISRAEL, LIKKUTIM ḤADASHIM, BERESHIT,
> S.V. BEMIDRASH RABBAH)

I hear in these words the suggestion that our natural response to the world and its phenomena (that is, God who embraces, surrounds, and fills us and all things) is one of gratitude and equanimity, ease and compassion. What disturbs our sense of being in God's presence, what removes the divine image from us, is folly that arises in mindless distraction. That spirit enters our body—it creates visceral reactions—and it takes over our reason. To prevent this invasion of folly, we must pay attention always—using our minds and hearts, watching carefully over all the means by which we perceive the world—what we think, feel, see, hear, and say.

I was supposed to leave work before five o'clock so that I could meet my family for a special outing. But, just as the last hour of my shift as a volunteer chaplain rolled around, a person with whom I had spent some time earlier in the day called to see me. (In our earlier conversation she had taken interest in the fact that I was a rabbi without a congregation—and she was a member of a small, newly founded congregation without a rabbi.) She was unhappy with how she had been treated by others, having been refused the help that she had requested from a social service agency. She was caught up in her anger, accusing people of selfishness, of insensitivity, of misplaced values, of duplicity. It was difficult to see her in such pain, and I thought that, perhaps, I might be able to help her see things a little differently, to shift her sense of powerlessness (a victim at the hands of bureaucrats) to one of empowerment (could she write a letter?). But, she was quite agitated, and it was slow going. And, the clock was ticking.

I should have recognized that I would not be able to accomplish what I had hoped. Moreover, I should have remembered that this was not really my job as a chaplain. This was something that deserved more long-term attention and the skills of a mental health professional or social worker. Yet there I was, and her need caught me—and my ego held on too. I kept hoping that the next thing I would say might make a difference. But it wouldn't. And so I tried another tack, a different approach, thinking that I would yet find success. In that moment, I was seduced by my own ego needs to help her, to be the person who would not disappoint her. I was in over my head, and instead of taking a breath and looking for a way to shore, I kept flailing about. Seized by mindless distraction, I was trapped by my ego.

Moreover, I forgot (or ignored) the previous obligation I had to my family to be on time, to be where I had planned to meet them so that they would not worry. I allowed our conversation to continue until I was close to half an hour late. Instead of having the wisdom to extricate myself from an intractable situation and fulfill my duties to my family, I allowed a "spirit of folly" to take over, and consequently I failed myself, my family, and this woman.

The context of Resh Lakish's teaching above is in the tractate Sotah, which is concerned with matters related to the "suspected wife" of Numbers 5. Verse 12 in the Torah reads, "If any man's wife has gone astray *(ish ish ki tisteh ishto)."* Resh Lakish reads it as if it said, "Any man who is foolish *(ish ish ki tishteh)."* He puns on the word *tisteh,* converting it to mean something related to *shtut,* folly. His comment precedes the following discussion: "The School of Rabbi Yishmael taught: A man does not become jealous of his wife unless a spirit enters into him, as it is said: 'but a spirit of jealousy comes over him and he is jealous of his wife.'" At this moment the man does not know if his wife has gone astray, having had relations with another man, or not. Yet, a feeling arises in him, a "spirit" possesses him, and he sets out on a course that will publicly embarrass him and his wife. Would anyone do so if a moment of mindless inattention had not permitted jealousy, fear, anger, possessiveness, pain to take over mind and heart, if "folly" had not entered his body?

"Rabbi Eleazar HaKappar taught: Jealousy, desire, and honor remove one from the world" (Avot 4:23). These are three of the habitual responses that "invade" us, that take over our minds and hearts, generating our reactions to the events of our lives and our interactions with others. "Rabbi Yehoshua taught: Stinginess, ill will, and the disdain of others remove one from the world" (Avot 2:11). These are three others. When we let them take over our lives, when they are the mode in which we react to the occurrences of our lives, they make us unhappy, and they distance us from other people. This is the meaning of "remove one from the world." Maimonides, in his commentary on these texts, treats this phrase naturalistically. That is, regarding Rabbi Yehoshua's lesson, he suggests that stinginess and ill will are antisocial traits. Further, Maimonides interprets the term "disdain of others" to mean the disaffection toward others that results from our stinginess and ill will. The more one approaches the world through those qualities, the less one will desire the company of others. Regarding Rabbi Eleazar HaKappar's teaching, Maimonides suggests that these behaviors will undermine faith in the ways of the Torah, impeding the acquisition of intellectual, spiritual, and ethical qualities; without them, one's life is no life.

We would likely agree. How do "jealousy, desire, and honor" remove one from the world? That is, how do they undermine healthy, honest, and compassionate connections with others? Consider three stories from Scripture: Elijah (1 Kings 18–19), the People of Israel following the episode of the scouts (Numbers 14), and Jonah. Elijah was a prophet, a servant of God, who fought against the apostasy of the royal house of the Northern Kingdom and its people. In a dramatic confrontation, Elijah presents the people with proof of the vacuity of the pagan gods they had begun to worship and the supreme power of the God of Israel. Having been embarrassed by Elijah's "defeat" of her servants, the evil queen Jezebel sought his death. Despite his faithfulness, his life was still not secure and so Elijah ran to the wilderness where, alone and tired, he sat under a broom bush and prayed that he might die. "'Enough!' he cried. 'Now, O Adonai, take my life, for I am no better than my fathers'" (1 Kings 19:4). God intervenes, sending an angel to provide him with sustenance by which he makes a forty-day journey to the mountain of God at Horeb.

> Then the word of Adonai came to him. He said to him, "Why are you here, Elijah?" He replied, "I am jealous for Adonai, the God of Hosts, for the Israelites have forsaken Your covenant, torn down Your altars, and put Your prophets to the sword. I alone am left, and they are out to take my life." "Come out," He called, "and stand on the mountain before Adonai." And lo, Adonai passed

by. . . . Then a voice addressed him: "Why are you here, Elijah?" He answered, "I am jealous for Adonai, the God of Hosts; for the Israelites have forsaken Your covenant, torn down Your altars, and put Your prophets to the sword. I alone am left, and they are out to take my life" (verses 9–14).

Receiving this response, God informs Elijah that his term as prophet has ended.

Elijah was, indeed, a faithful servant of Adonai, zealous and jealous for God's honor. He stood up against great danger and terrible odds to demonstrate God's power, and he remained faithful when it seemed hopeless. Yet his zeal—his jealous hold on his commitment to God's honor—also removed him from the world. He loses his job and disappears into the heavens, leaving his work incomplete as a result. Why does this happen? It is due to Elijah's mindless inattention, his inability to see beyond his habitual response.

In response to God's first query, Elijah tells his habitual story: I have been Your faithful servant and still they want to kill me. We are thus presented with the ground from which he works, the perspective from which he views the world. But God offers him the opportunity to see the world differently. Led to Horeb, where Moses met God face-to-face, "Adonai passed by" Elijah, just as with Moses (Exodus 34:6). Elijah could have woken up to a larger truth in that moment, but he didn't. He could have understood that although he has played a role for God, he is not God; that his life has purpose even when he feels like a failure; that his ego has clouded his vision and limited his perspective to himself alone, and not to God's will. Over and over he is presented with phenomena of power, like those he used in his battle with idolatry—rock-shattering wind, earthquake, and fire—and senses that God is not in those forces. Then he hears "a still, small voice," which he could have recognized as indicating the presence of God, yet he responds by hiding himself: "he wrapped his mantle about his face" (verse 13). His resistance to learning something new—about God, about God's power, about himself and his role as a prophet, about God's enduring care and concern for him, and about the inevitability of God's victory over paganism—is made clear in his verbatim response to God's second query. Nothing has changed for him. He is still the same Elijah he was before God passed before him. Rather than break out of his habitual self-conception, he remains trapped. His deep emotional, psychological, and spiritual investment in being "jealous for God" ultimately removes him from the world. His mission among the Israelites as prophet and comforter ends.

Two years after the Exodus, God is ready for the People of Israel to move on from Sinai to the Promised Land. He has Moses send scouts into the Land to determine its fortifications, the nature of the inhabitants, and the quality of the land. The scouts return after forty days and, while they confirm the bounty of the land, ten of them offer a negative report on the strategic situation: "However, the people who inhabit the country are powerful, and the cities are fortified and very large; moreover, we saw Anakites there" (Numbers 13:28). In horror at the fearful reaction of the people to this report, "Caleb hushed the people before Moses and said, 'Let us by all means go up, and we shall gain possession of it, for we shall surely overcome it'" (verse 30). But the other scouts continued to spread calumnies about the land, saying, "The country that we traversed and scouted is one that devours its settlers. All the people that we saw in it were of great size . . . and we looked like grasshoppers to ourselves, and so we must have looked to them" (verses 32–33). At that, the people railed against Moses and Aaron, refusing to take up the march, even suggesting, "Let us head back for Egypt" (verse 14:4).

God's response is quick and harsh. He determines to destroy the people then and there and to start over again with Moses. Ever the royal opposition, seeking the good of the people while still serving God, Moses intervenes, and God relents. "I pardon, as you have asked. Nevertheless, as I live and as Adonai's presence fills the whole world, none of the men who have seen My presence and the signs that I have performed in Egypt and in the wilderness, and who have tried Me these many times and have disobeyed Me, shall see the Land that I promised on oath to their fathers" (Numbers 14:20–23). To bring that about, God decrees that the people will remain in the desert for forty years, a year for each day of the scouting operation, during which the older generation would die off. When Moses repeats these words to all the Israelites, the people are overcome by grief. Early the next morning they set out toward the crest of the hill-country, saying, "We are prepared to go up to the place that Adonai has spoken of, for we were wrong" (verse 40). But Moses says, "Why do you transgress Adonai's command? This will not succeed. Do not go up, lest you be routed by your enemies, for Adonai is not in your midst. For the Amalekites and the Canaanites will be there to face you, and you will fall by the sword, inasmuch as you have turned from following Adonai and Adonai will not be with you" (verses 41–43). Yet they defiantly march toward the crest of the hill-country, though neither Adonai's Ark of the Covenant nor Moses has stirred from the camp. And the Amalekites and the Canaanites who dwell in that hill country come down and deal them a shattering blow at Hormah (verses 44–45).

Here we have the people who have been redeemed from Egyptian bondage with signs and wonders, who have been sustained with supernatural manna and divinely provided water in the wilderness, and who, for all that, have no faith in God's providence.

Their habitual response to adversity is to doubt, to fear, to retreat, and to complain. Despite the suffering they experienced in Egypt, they recall it with favor over and over, seeking to return there as if to paradise. The desire for safety and security, to be free of struggle or adversity, is deeply rooted in their hearts and minds. Even when presented with the bounty of the land, and the hope for an easy life in its midst, they fall into their old habits: they complain, they reject Moses (and God), and they remain stuck in place.

Moreover, when the consequences of their actions are presented to them, when God's judgment is announced, they resist its truth, just as they had rejected the faithful truth of God's sustaining help in the past. Rather than look carefully at their previous actions, rather than examine their habitual reactions to learn about their inner lives, to realize how they are trapped in a self-destructive pattern of behavior, the people react out of fear. They run from the truth, again. Unable to accept God's blessings and providence, they are also unable to accept responsibility for their own actions. The unsuccessful foray into the land, intended to show faith in God, can only result in tragedy, since it is a blind response. Over and over the people run from the truth, seeking only to fill their desire to be free from responsibility. Desire, covetousness, lust, and craving are all are based on irrational expectations: I want what I do not have and I want to have it without taking responsibility or having to work. They are all distractions from the truth, and they all remove us from the world, as they did with the People of Israel in the wilderness.

The story of Jonah is, among other things, a story of the costs of seeking honor. Called by God to go to Nineveh to proclaim its destruction (for its wickedness), Jonah flees in the opposite direction. Caught by God and returned to his mission, Jonah makes his way to the great city of Assyria to broadcast God's word: "Forty days more, and Nineveh will be overthrown!" (Jonah 3:4). The people of the city take Jonah's words to heart, and seek to supplicate God through fasting and mourning. When word reaches the king of the situation, he follows suit and proclaims a public fast (of both man and beast), adding, "Let everyone turn back from his evil ways and from the injustice of which he is guilty. Who knows but that God may turn and relent? He may turn from His wrath, so that we do not perish" (verses 8–10).

The king and his people hear Jonah's proclamation and see the truth. They have been evil, they have been wicked, and they are being called to account. In response, they confess their sins, fast in contrition, and pray for forgiveness. The king understands that these acts are not guaranteed to prevent punishment; he couches his announcement in the conditional voice. Rather than respond out of habit, rejecting God's power and denying their wickedness or culpability, the people seek to change their ways. Indeed, they intend the change to be universal, including their children (who are not responsible for their wicked deeds) and their animals (who cannot be evil, since they have no independent will) in the rituals of repentence. "God saw what they did, how they were turning back from their evil ways. And God renounced the punishment He had planned to bring upon them, and did not carry it out" (verse 10).

Jonah, however, could not see the truth. His response was to remain stuck in his original frame of mind, with his concern only for his person and his ego. "He prayed to Adonai, saying, 'O Adonai! Isn't this what I said when I was still in my own country? That is why I fled beforehand to Tarshish. For I know that You are a compassionate and gracious God, slow to anger, abounding in kindness, renouncing punishment. Please, Adonai, take my life, for I would rather die than live'" (4:2–3). Jonah fled from his appointment as prophet not because he was afraid that he might fail (and no one would listen to him), and not because he feared for his life. Rather, he sought to avoid his task because he feared that he would be seen as a fool, announcing destruction to come, but being proved false. For this embarrassment, apparently, he would rather die than live.

God then opens a door for Jonah to reconsider his first reaction, to look again at the truth and respond differently. "Adonai replied, 'Are you that deeply grieved?'" (verse 4). God further provides Jonah with an experience through which he might review and reevaluate his habitual concern for his own honor. While Jonah sits overlooking the city to see what will happen, God causes a plant to grow over him, its leaves providing him with shade from the sun. The next day, God provides a worm that attacks the plant so that it withers. "And when the sun rose, God provided a sultry east wind; the sun beat down on Jonah's head, and he became faint. He begged for death, saying, 'I would rather die than live.' Then God said to Jonah, 'Are you so deeply grieved about the plant?' 'Yes,' he replied, 'so deeply that I want to die'" (verses 8–9). Again, Jonah's habitual response was, "Things are not going the way I want them to. I am unhappy. I am uncomfortable. This is not the way I should be treated. I wish I were dead." Even when prodded by God's rhetorical question—"Are you that deeply grieved?"—Jonah cannot remove himself from his prison of egocentricity. This point is then driven home in the last words of the book.

> Then Adonai said, "You cared about the plant, which you did not work for and which you did not grow, which appeared overnight and perished overnight. And should I not care about Nineveh, that great city, in which there are more than a hundred and twenty thousand persons who do not yet know their right hand from their left, and many beasts as well?" (4:10–11).

Jonah is concerned only with his own ego comforts. He cannot see the larger truth of the infinitely complex and interconnected nature of all Creation. He cannot place himself in anyone else's shoes, either to consider their needs or to acknowledge their claim on him. And, apparently at all costs, he refuses to consider the truth of God's constant sustaining power in the world, expressing itself through both justice and mercy. Jonah's last words are, "I want to die." His egocentrism, his quest for honor, removes him from the world.

In each instance—jealousy, desire, and honor; Elijah, the People of Israel, and Jonah—the underlying concern that prevents us from seeing the truth is ego. "I must do," "I must have," "I must be seen as" are all expressions of defense against what we perceive to be attacks on our persons, on who we think we are. Our egos are projections of our inner states, ways in which we make our habitual sensations and reactions concrete in the world. We hold onto them, we reinforce them, we fight to protect them. We fear that if our ego-projections were to fall away, we would disappear. In the end, we fear our own annihilation and death. This theme runs through each of the narratives brought above. Elijah feared for his life at the hands of Jezebel; yet, even more he feared that his work, all the energies he expended to create his ego-projection, would come to naught. The People of Israel feared death at the hands of the Amalekites and the Canaanites, yet they also feared death at God's hand. More than that, they feared the end of their self-contained life, the irresponsibility of both slave and dependent. Jonah was clearest about his ego-concern. His expression "I want to die" revealed his personal sense of loss of face, of dishonor. Unable to consider God's needs, or any needs beyond his own, Jonah feared only for his own loss, his own emotional death.

For me, the most important line of the mishnah follows Rabbi Eleazar HaKappar's teaching about jealousy, desire, and honor: "All who are born are to die" (Avot 4:22). This fundamental truth, when I bring it to mind, wakes me from the dream of my story. When I remember mortality, then jealousy, desire, and honor, stinginess, ill will, and the disdain of others disappear. No matter what we do, no matter how hard we try to create a sense of permanence through our investment in our egos, we will ultimately die. There is no permanence. There is no protection from death. All of our attempts to avoid that realization, denying the truth, protecting our egos, will come to naught. All that exists is God, and God alone. There is nothing else. Not our person. Not our accomplishments. Not our stories. Not our egos. As the mishnah continues: And do not think that you can hide in blindness to the truth. For against your will were you conceived, and against your will were you born; against your will you live and against your will you will die. And ultimately, against your will you will have to face the truth and be held accountable for the ways in which you allowed your habitual responses to cloud your vision, leading you farther and farther away from God, out of this world. You were dead, even as you struggled to avoid death, and you did not know it. So, wake up, pay attention, and live.

The cost of our attachment to our egos is that it removes us from the world. As Maimonides put it, it disconnects us from other people. Caught up in ourselves, in our own stories and habitual responses, we are unable to truly see others. In that blindness, we are doomed to constantly bump into them, step on their toes, shout over them, ignore them, leave them hungry and wanting. When we follow the lead of our egos, we play into the hands of the husks, the dark coverings that hide divine sparks of light from us and keep our own inner light from us. The husks will suck out our energy, and we will be less able to look below the surface of all that we see— particularly the people with whom we live and work—to see God's presence. God's image will depart from us, and we will be blind to it in others. In that darkness, not only will we suffer, but we will be useless to others, unable to help them. The divine flow of love and compassion will be cut off both from us and from others. In the moment, the opportunity to wake up, to see clearly is always before us. It is our choice—"if you do well, there will be uplift"—to reject becoming Cain and to transcend our fears of becoming Abel. We can do well, and with that bring compassion, love, and wholeness to ourselves and to others.

Section Three

Avodah

Chapter Five

Mindfulness and True Awareness (*Kavanah*)

*F*or several years I have attended mindfulness meditation retreats on a regular basis. The routine of each day is stripped to the minimum: sitting meditation practice, walking meditation practice, meals, and sleep (and time for personal prayer). The instructions for the walking meditation are essentially the same as for sitting meditation: pay attention. The difference is where we turn our attention. When walking we can attend closely to the concrete physical experience of each step: raising, moving, and lowering each foot; the sense of pressure and no-pressure; shifts in weight from side to side and from back to front; etc. Each step offers us a renewed awareness of where we are, of exactly what is happening in the moment.

In addition, since walking is a willed activity (as opposed to breathing), we can also give our attention to the very activity of connecting will to action. Over the course of several retreats I have tried very hard to see the internal movement from the thought "take a step" to the actual initiation of action in my leg. This is not so simple as it may sound. Of course, I can think, "I want to walk" and then just set off to do it. What I am looking for, however, is to sense the actual connection between my intention and my actions. So, I find that I stand in place, sensing my weight on my feet, feeling my feet on the ground, aware of my place on the road, and then articulate to myself the instruction, "Take a step." Because I want to be aware of the movement from my intention to my action, I wait until I feel that I am paying full attention to this process. I wait until my mind clears of other thoughts, until the breeze on my skin or the sound of the crows or the sun on my back no longer draws my attention. I wait until I sense that I am not watching myself watching myself take a step. I try to feel inside myself the direct connection between thought and action, between my head and my leg, between my intention and my behavior.

Often I find myself standing still for a long time without taking a step. Sometimes I can actually take the first step fully aware of my intention and my response to it, but that awareness rarely continues beyond the second or third step. Sometimes I am aware of having the initiating thought, of waiting and watching to make the connection, and then, in the briefest moment of distraction, I take a step. It is as if I allow myself to be distracted so that I can set out on my walk, so that I can move on. Perhaps I really was more interested in walking than in experiencing the connection between intention and thought. Perhaps I truly was aware of my intention and the feeling of linking it to my step, but I got too caught up in thinking about it. Perhaps, in fact, I had focused too hard, had generated too much tension in my attention, and could not move at all. This reminds me of the saying of the rabbis, "Three things come when we are not paying attention: the Messiah, a found object, and a scorpion" (Sanhedrin 97a). If we look too hard, if all we do is look for something that may or may not be present in the moment, our attention may become too focused, too intense, and we will not be able to see what is really in front of us.

Is the answer then not to pay attention, not to give thought to what I am doing, not to feel myself in my body as I go about my life? The Baal Shem Tov warns us against being too careless with our attention: "It is a teaching of the Baal Shem Tov that wherever our thoughts may be, that is where we really are" (*Keter Shem Tov,* No. 56). We may think that we are present in our lives, that we are in control of our daily affairs, that we connect with the people in our lives—but if our minds are wandering, if our thoughts are elsewhere, then we are not truly present. The challenge is to develop the capacity to be fully aware of the workings of our minds and hearts, to be able to sense when our actions fully express our intentions, without closing off the fullness of our awareness.

This challenge is one that I also face daily when I pray. I want to be able to express each word of prayer with my full intention. I want to mean what I say; I want to know what I mean; and I want to say what I mean. And I want to be able to pray this way while using the words of the traditional prayerbook—so I want to bring my attention fully to those texts, to know what they mean, and to mean what they say, and to have them say what I mean. And I want to pray without being distracted, without my mind wandering elsewhere. At the same time I also want to be aware of what it is that distracts me, so that I can learn the content of my own heart and mind. If I can do this in prayer, then perhaps I will be able to do it in the fullness of my life as well—and, so, live mindfully aware of the truth of my life.

The Bible takes prayer for granted as a natural and spontaneous response of human beings to the truth of their existence. Cain and his brother Abel bring offerings from the work of their hands in gratitude to God. Noah offers a sacrifice immediately upon his debarkation from the Ark. The Patriarchs build altars for thanks, supplication, and prayer throughout their lives. Moses prays on behalf of his people as passionately as he prays for the cure of his sister Miriam's leprosy. Hannah prays wordlessly for a son, and Jonah prays from the belly of the great fish. King Hezekiah prays at length that his city be saved from the Assyrians, and he offers a brief prayer when faced with his own death. There seems to be nothing more natural than prayer.

At the same time, God also commands a form of service, of worship.

> "Now, if you dutifully obey my commandments which I command you this day, to love Adonai your God, and to serve Him with all your heart and all your soul" (Deuteronomy 11:13). Now, is there some sort of divine service that takes place in the heart, as our verse suggests? Indeed, it is prayer.
>
> (SIFRE DEUTERONOMY, EKEV, 5)

As much as we may be inspired to pray on our own, we are also commanded to do so. This imperative came to be expressed, over time, in the form of fixed prayer services to be recited at particular times of day, each day. While historically there may have been some latitude in the actual wording of the prayers to be recited, over time they have become quite fixed. In rehearsing these particular words in the proper form and order, in the proper time and in a community, one can fulfill one's obligation to pray.

Yet, even in antiquity, the rabbis were sensitive to the danger that reciting fixed prayers in a rote manner would undermine the powerful imperative at the root of mandatory worship, which is to serve God with our hearts. "Rabbi Shimon taught: Be mindful in reciting the *Shema* and the *Amidah* (the primary texts of the prayer service). And when you pray, do not make your words rote. Rather, let them be prayers of compassion and supplications before the Holy Blessed Place *(Hamakom)*" (Avot 2:13). How can we keep our hearts open and souls attentive when we engage in regular, daily prayer? How can we wake up in our lives, to see the truth clearly and to know how to respond with compassion? How can we make certain that we remain present in our minds, in our words, in our prayers?

Every moment brings its own challenges and wonders, and in each instance we are called to see the truth and to open ourselves to God's presence. When we allow habit or regulation, insecurity or fear, ignorance or familiarity to limit our vision and close off our hearts, we are unable to bring our full attention and open hearts to prayer. We need to find a way to make every moment and every action one of devotion, one of divine service. We need to prepare so that we can wake up in our lives. We can learn how from Moses in Egypt, as he argues with Pharaoh. He demands that Pharaoh allow the People of Israel to leave Egypt to go and worship God in the wilderness, yet Pharaoh refuses. Following the ninth plague,

> Pharaoh then summoned Moses and said, "Go, worship Adonai! Only your flocks and your herds shall be left behind; even your children may go with you." But Moses said, "You yourself must provide us with sacrifices and burnt offerings to offer up to Adonai our God. Our own livestock, too, shall go along with us— not a hoof shall remain behind—for we must select from it for the worship of Adonai our God. And we shall not know with what we are to worship Adonai until we arrive there."
>
> (Exodus 10:24–26)

This is a mindfulness prayer instruction. When we approach the worship of God—that is, when we set out to meet God in our lives, whether in formal prayer and ritual or in any other experience—we cannot limit ourselves. Pharaoh would have the Israelites (and us!) hold back, leaving some of their possessions— and themselves—behind. Moses responds that not only are we to bring our own belongings, but we must be open to and include everything around us in our awareness so that we will be prepared for whatever comes. "We shall not know with what we are to worship Adonai until we arrive there." Only in the moment, in openhearted attention to the fullness of our lives, will we be able to meet God fully, and serve God with devotion.

Every moment is a potential meeting with God. If we are to be prepared, we will need to be mindful, to be awake and alert and engaged, to bring our whole being to every moment. Nothing can be excluded from our awareness. When we are present to every truth as it arises, and nothing is allowed to overtake our awareness, we will be more able to choose how we will respond. We will be more aware of how predispositions and habits of mind threaten to cloud our attentiveness. When we bring our full attention to the fullness of each moment, when we are fully present, we will then become aware of how we are to respond. In moments of clear vision, we see the truth of God's presence in everything that comes before us and we can discern how to respond—how we are to worship Adonai.

Over and over, we realize that we are not paying attention. We set out toward God's mountain, toward clear-sighted attention to our lives, and then we lose track of what we are doing. We set out to pray, to offer our thanks and devotion to God, to acknowledge our needs before the Merciful One, and we are distracted. How can we allow ourselves that inattention? "Rabbi Yoḥanan said: 'Would that a man would go on praying the whole day!'" (Berakhot 21a). If only we could pay attention all the time, attentive to the needs of the moment, able to choose the proper response to what arises before us and in us!

Is there anything more significant for us to do than pray? Indeed, if we were to experience deeply what it means to live in God's world, to benefit from all of Creation and the fullness of life— and that there is no way that we can compensate God for this gift—

what could we do, other than offer our thanks in every moment? Aside from the need to find sustenance and to procreate, what other need is greater than waking up to the truth of our lives and acknowledging that truth in prayer? As it says in the psalm, "How can I repay Adonai for all His bounties to me? I raise up the cup of deliverance and invoke the name of Adonai. I will pay my vows to Adonai in the presence of all His people" (Psalm 116:12–14).

The hasidic tradition dissolved this tension by elevating the idea of *avodah,* divine service, removing it from the realm of the Temple service and formal prayer and generalizing it. Rather than an activity set apart in time and space from the ongoing activities of life, *avodah* became the paramount and all-embracing spiritual practice toward which all people could strive. It is true that prayer and Torah-study are the prime examples of this practice. But the hasidic masters highlighted the possibility that one might engage in *avodah* in every instance, in every activity. Simply remaining awake and aware in each moment is to serve God. This is the teaching of the Baal Shem Tov, as reported by his grandson, Rabbi Moshe Ḥayim Efraim of Sudylkow:

> "Do not turn to idols" (Leviticus 19:4). Our sages interpreted this to mean, "Do not turn to that which you conceive in your own minds" (Shabbat 149a). We can understand this according to the teaching of my grandfather (the Baal Shem Tov) regarding the verse, "that you turn away and worship other gods" (Deuteronomy 11:16). He interpreted thus: "'that you turn away'—as soon as you turn your attention away from cleaving to the Holy One—'you will worship other gods'—it is as if you have become an idolater." Although his teaching is very deep, my feeble explanation is this: Anyone who serves God in all his ways, seeking to fulfill the injunction "know Him in all your ways" (Proverbs 3:6), will do everything mindfully. Eating, drinking, sleeping, engaging in con-

versation in order to bring others closer to God, or to help dispel their sadness, or to help them in their business to sustain them so that they may devote more time to serving God—if even these (worldly) activities are done mindfully, then they also constitute divine service, *avodah.*

(DEGEL MAḤANEH EFRAIM, KEDOSHIM,
S.V. AL TIFNU EL HA'ELILIM)

From this teaching we learn that there is no activity that is not, or cannot be *avodah.* We can, in a sense, pray all the time. All of our intention, our motivation, and our focus can be toward serving God. When we are distracted, when we turn away from paying attention, we stop serving God. According to the Baal Shem Tov, any activity that is not devoted to God, that does not bring us and others closer to God, is idolatry. The invitation in this text is to learn how to hold our attention steady, to remain awake and attentive to our lives, to become mindful. Mindfulness is not limited to meditation, or to certain specific times or activities. Our goal is to be mindful all the time—to our inner experience, and to the world around us. Similarly, prayer and *avodah* are not limited to synagogue services or particular days or seasons. Our goal is to pray all the time. The attainment of this goal is called *deveikut,* which means cleaving to, becoming attached to, being devoted to God. *Deveikut* is the goal of *avodah,* the result of making all activity an expression of divine service. This is the message, for example, of Rabbi Menaḥem Naḥum of Chernobyl.

> "Know Him in all of your ways" (Proverbs 3:6). Everything you do should be for the sake of Heaven, even those activities that are most mundane and worldly. For, of everything that exists, "Adonai made everything for a purpose" (16:4), and "Everything that the Holy

One created, He created for His glory" (Yoma 38a). Therefore, God's glory abides in every thing. Now, regarding a king of flesh and blood, he and his glory are not coexistent—whereas the Holy One and His glory comprise a complete unity. (Let the wise discern this.) Thus, in every thing the glory of the Blessed Creator abides—indeed, "the whole earth is full of His glory" (Isaiah 6:3), for there is no place devoid of Him. Everything mundane and worldly that we do—whether regarding food or drink, or regarding business dealings—it all expresses the glory of the Blessed Creator. . . . Therefore, we must remember that the King is always present before us, as it says, "I have placed Adonai before me always" (Psalm 16:8). Even when we are doing business for our own needs, to our own ends, the Holy One, the King, King of Kings, is hidden, garbed in all we do.

(ME'OR EINAYIM, LIKKUTIM,
S.V. KETIV BEKHOL DERAKHEKHA DA'EHU)

What this passage directs us to see is that no matter what we are doing, we could and should be serving God. No matter where we turn our gaze, we could and should perceive God. *Avodah*—in prayer, study, and all our worldly engagements—is to be our constant practice, directed toward the end of *deveikut,* experiencing the totality of God's Being.

This connection between *avodah,* serving God every moment, and *deveikut,* cleaving to God in every moment, requires constant attention. It requires us to set our intention clearly, to know what it is that we wish to do in our lives, how we would like to live. We cannot pay attention in our lives without first determining that this is what we wish to accomplish. In Hebrew, the term that embodies this step is *kavanah.* This is the intention to make every moment and every action one of devotion, of divine service. This is the shift from a defined, determined experience to be achieved in prayer, to an experience to be anticipated in every moment. As Moses said, "We shall not know with what we are to worship Adonai until we arrive there." *Kavanah* is the intention to remain awake and prepared for every moment, for every experience to become the means by which we know "we are there"—where we are—and what we are to do. Thus, it is through *kavanah* that actions become *avodah*. It is in this manner that the hasidic tradition, for example, in the teachings of Rabbi Yaakov Yosef of Polonnoye, takes up Rabbi Yoḥanan's plea, insisting that one should actually engage in *avodah*, in prayer and service, all day long.

> Initially [Rabbi Shimon bar Yoḥai and his son were] convinced that the only practices that constituted *avodah* were Torah-study, prayer, fasting, weeping, and the like. Therefore, when they (came out of their cave and) saw that people were not engaged in these practices they were enraged and said, "They leave off dealing with eternal life to engage in the life of the moment." Their intolerance increased anger in the world, until a divine voice told them to return to their cave, and they then understood that this was to teach them a new way of being in the world, a way of compassion (cf. Shabbat 33b). This path is serving God through every aspect of every act, giving heed to the fact that the Holy One is there, too. This is manifest in the way that the great masters are able to accomplish great unifications (a form of *avodah*) even while telling stories with a friend . . . and to remove sadness by engaging in some business. Even when seeing something unseemly in another person, or when another person distracts us from study or prayer, we should recognize that even this is from God, to accomplish some divine end through us. . . . This is clearly the meaning of the verse, "Know Him in all your ways" (Proverbs 3:6). Moreover, "I place Adonai before me (*l'negdi*, also opposite, over against me) always," even when I expe-

rience opposition or hindrances, nevertheless "He is at my right hand, I will never be shaken." Therefore, "my heart rejoices" in arousing compassion, mercy, and joy in the world, and so "my body rests secure" (Psalm 16:8–9).

(TOLDOT YAAKOV YOSEF, VAYEITZEI, SECT. 5,
S.V. VEHA'INYAN SHEKATAVTI L'EIL)

I know that at times I am distracted by other people, and I close my heart to them, shutting myself off from God as well. When we learn that it is possible to serve God in every moment, in every activity and interaction, we realize how much of our lives we pass through asleep. There is no "time out" from *avodah;* when *deveikut* is our goal, our intention to wake up becomes more pressing. We need to develop our capacity for *kavanah,* for mindful attention. *Kavanah* helps us to wake up again and again to the truth of the moment. As we work past the hindrances and obstacles that cloud our minds—like Rabbi Yochanan and his son, who could only see people engaged in their daily lives and missed their inner devotion to God—we realize how a closed heart clouds our vision, how compassion opens our eyes and hearts. We are better able to sense that there is no other moment than this one, regardless of how it feels or seems. In this moment, we sense the awesomeness of existence, the wonder of Creation in its manifold forms and unfolding nature. In the wonder of the moment our hearts fill with gratitude, our response becomes *avodah.* When we sustain that awareness from moment to moment, we experience more and more deeply the oneness of all existence, that there is nothing other than the One. In joy we will experience *deveikut.*

Mindfulness meditation, the contemplative form of practicing awakened, present attention, is a way to develop *kavanah.* Initially, however, holding our attention steady, without distraction, is difficult. We often find that our minds wander. Distracting thoughts arise, and we find that our minds trail off into various discursive trains of thought. Often, we are troubled by inner conflicts, emotional responses to the practice of meditation that inhibit an open and free perception of each moment in its fullness. Mindfulness practice can help us to learn neither to respond with harshness to banish those thoughts from our mind, nor to blame ourselves for not being able to hold our thoughts constant. When we learn to recognize these disturbances and inner conflicts, we employ skillful tools to counter them. Often, when we are able to respond with compassion, we can acknowledge that this is the nature of an active mind, and the product of living a life. We depend on our minds to be inquisitive, analytical, and capable of memory, so it would be silly to reject these capacities when we sit down to meditate. In the course of any endeavor there are moments of doubt, frustration, slothfulness, etc. Recognizing this, we may be better able to remember that in this instant, these thoughts are merely distractions, perhaps hiding deeper truths from us, perhaps entertaining us while we are trying to learn to appreciate the stillness of just "being." Without contention we can more easily put these thoughts aside so that we can sense our body and spirit, in just this moment, right here. We can transform distraction into renewed intention.

While *avodah*, service of God, demands our full attention in all instances, its primary expression is in prayer (along with study and fulfilling *mitzvot*). Even if we intend to bring our full attention to our every act, at the very least we should try to develop our capacity for *kavanah* in prayer. This is as difficult to accomplish in prayer as it is in meditation. One of the innovations of the Baal Shem Tov, the founder of Hasidism, was to offer a method for dealing with distractions in prayer. He called these thoughts *maḥshavot ra'ot,* wicked thoughts, and *maḥshavot zarot,* strange thoughts. The negative connotation is twofold. As we have seen already, anything that distracts us from contemplating God with reverence and awe in a sense leads us to idolatry. In that sense it is "wicked." The other is a general denigration of all things physical—passion, desire, food, sex—common in mystical and spiritual traditions. In that sense, thoughts that keep us focused on the concrete and physical are distracting or "strange." Related to both of these types of thoughts are those that flow from the ego, anything that is in the least bit self-inflating, self-congratulatory, self-concerned, or even self-referential. These thoughts may arise in the course of prayer, just as they do in meditation.

There were those who viewed these thoughts as impure and defiling, and who urged us to battle with them, to banish them. The Baal Shem Tov offered a different path. He argued that since there is nothing that does not contain God's glory, and there is no place devoid of God, then even the strange thoughts that come to us must have a divine source. If this is true, then these thoughts cannot be wicked; they must in some manner be part of God. Realizing this, we are enabled to raise up these thoughts to the divine plane in two ways. The first is tied to the mystical tradition related to the power of speech. Thoughts (which we experience and think about in the form of speech) are made up of words, which are, in turn, made up of letters. These same letters are the means by which God created the world: God thought of Creation, then spoke words that brought it into being. The words of Creation were made up of letters, and these letters, then, participate in the divine realm. When we identify the holiness in the letters of our speech we can return them there with our positive intention, as we learn from the Maggid of Mezritch.

> *Maḥshavot ra'ot* are also known as *tamar* (palm tree), since (initially) it is bitter *(mar)*, but in the end it is harmless *(tam)*. This is like the verse, "I have seen slaves on horseback" (Ecclesiastes 10:7). The letters that make up the prayers are the horses, and when a

strange thought rides on them we are struck with wonder *(tamah,* a pun on *tamar)* to see a slave riding on the King's horse. But, then we consider: are not these strange thoughts also made up of the holy letters, only they are not combined in a good way. Therefore, when we bring these letters to our thoughts (that is, when they enter our thoughts and we pay attention to the phenomenon without also being caught up in them), we can raise them up to the world of transformation *(temurah,* another pun on *tamar),* and thus make of these (defective) combinations (of letters) other words: words of Torah out of words of foolishness.

(MAGGID DEVARAV LEYAAKOV,
LIKKUTEI AMARIM, NO. 95)

This teaching reflects the mystical idea of the downward chaining of letters in Creation. The combinations of letters in divine speech brought about the initial acts of Creation. The ongoing chain of interaction and recombination into lower and more coarse realms brings into being all that is—including strange thoughts. The letters themselves are still connected to the original divine speech, and are therefore holy. We might be deceived into thinking that impure thoughts and actions are impure by nature and therefore outside of the divine realm. But these letters have simply been combined in defective ways. When we recognize that fact, we can redeem them and raise them up again to God, experiencing again that there is nothing outside of the Divine.

When we pay attention to the workings of our minds, we find that they swirl with images and thoughts, with ideas and plans. If we were to approach these phenomena with a judging mind, determined to rid ourselves of these thoughts or ideas, we would enter into competition with them for space in our minds. We would be fighting them always, and potentially find that as we engage with them they become more prominent, more persistent, more difficult to remove from our consciousness. What the Baal Shem Tov suggests is that we undermine the power of these strange thoughts by seeing through their disturbing qualities and understand them for what they are: manifestations of an aspect of the Divine. In that manner we can defuse the irritating quality of "strange thoughts" and make them simply "thoughts" that might lead us again to God.

This is the same technique we might use in mindfulness meditation. We see thoughts arise and simply identify them as "thoughts." We do not enter into a contentious relationship with them; we do not judge them. We note them, giving them their due, and then return to our point of focus. Rather than getting angry at being distracted, we accept the presence of "strange thoughts" without assessment, acknowledging that the mind produces these thoughts, and then we put them aside. Rather than being distracted (and perhaps then pursue a path of foolishness and unhappiness), we transform our own strange thoughts into moments of grace. If we can hold them in our minds, without contention, we experience a moment of liberation, of freedom from anger, frustration, self-judgment, fear, or shame, and the thoughts pass easily, of their own accord. We return to the truth of the moment—the activity at hand, the intention of our hearts and minds—and experience equanimity and peace.

The second method that the Baal Shem Tov suggested we might use to raise up "strange thoughts" and so to be freed from their distracting and engaging quality is to see them as fallen manifestations of divine qualities. In the following passage, the Baal Shem Tov gives a strikingly new interpretation to a problematic verse in the Torah to illustrate this point.

The Baal Shem Tov (may his soul rest in supernal treasuries) taught regarding the verse, "If a man marries his sister . . . it is a disgrace *(ḥesed)*" (Leviticus 20:17): the love that arises when we are attracted to illicit sexual relations is actually *ḥesed,* that is, it derives from the realm of *ḥesed,* the realm of the love of God. It is up to us to select (the good love) out of the bad and connect it to its divine source, and not to be drawn after the wickedness that is in it. And this is true regarding all of the other divine qualities. The essence of our service *(avodah)* is to rise to such a level that we can separate out the divine sparks in all things, selecting the good out of the bad in which it is clothed.

(Me'or Einayim, Shelaḥ,
s.v. kemo she'amar haBeSHT)

I want to compare this teaching to the one that preceded it. Whereas in the first example the divine quality was found in the letters that make up the strange thought, here it is in the actual quality of the thought or feeling that we find the Divine. That is, even a love so perverse as the sexual attraction of a brother toward his sister has the potential to point to the highest love, that of God for us and us for God. Thus, should a sexual or other "strange thought" arise—whether in prayer, in study, or in any other circumstance—we might find ourselves distracted, ashamed, disgusted, or angry. If we react with judgment and force, trying to remove the thought from our minds, to blot it out in anger or shame, we will not succeed. What the Baal Shem Tov suggests is rather that we should observe what the feeling or thought actually is, asking: What are its qualities? To what is it related? How can this feeling or thought lead me to God? In this manner we might come to discern the positive element of this phenomenon—that is, the part of it that is connected to a divine quality. We then can turn our hearts to serving God through this quality. At the same time, we can more easily let go of our attachment to the actual content of the "strange thought"; we need not be subject to its compulsions or urges. In this manner, the strange thought can be transformed, raised up, to become a means to proper service of God.

This, too, is similar to what we might do when practicing mindfulness meditation. Thoughts or feelings arise in the course of meditating. Often, when they arise, they produce a response—anger, fear, shame, passion, or desire. At first, we may be tempted to extinguish the feeling, to run from it, to deny it, to remove it. Doing so, however, we enter into a contentious relationship with the strange thought, and are distracted from the truth of the moment: thoughts and feelings do arise. If, for a moment, we were to examine our responses to the thoughts or feelings, we might better understand their source. We might come to understand "why this thought at this time," or better understand the nature of our minds, the ways in which we deny the truth of each moment. We might see how we close ourselves off from painful or embarrassing events or aspects of our personality. In the moment that we learn to hold the thoughts or feelings, without judgment and without contention, we find that they are no longer frightening or disgusting. In accepting that part of our past or personality as the truth, as who we were or how we are at the moment, we will be better able to choose how to respond when such thoughts or feelings again arise in our daily affairs. We will not be blindsided by them, but will allow them to be present without being overcome by them. In this manner, we are choosing good out of evil, seeing the truth in the midst of turmoil, and so we find a moment of peace and equanimity. It is as if we are raising up the strange thoughts to the divine level.

Disengagement from contentious responses to strange thoughts flows from the awareness that there is nothing but the Holy One. As we read above, the goal of all *avodah* is to perceive fully that everything is God. This, in turn, demands that we reconsider our normal, fundamental sense that "things" have independent reality. It is certainly true that a chair is a chair, and has a "thingness" to it, such that

I can sit on it. And to the extent that I can learn to see God when I see it, the chair will not lose its substantiality such that I would fall on the floor if I sought to sit on it. But, I have to be careful not to confuse the "thingness" of the chair with separateness from God. The chair only exists by virtue of the vital force that sustains it, a force that flows from God (through the letters that make up the word or idea "chair," or the spark of divine vitality that is found in all things). The challenge to see clearly, as posed here by the Maggid of Mezritch, is always before us.

> It is a great accomplishment for a person to reflect and to consider in his heart always that he is next to the Holy One, and that He surrounds him on all sides. In this manner he will cleave to Him so intensely that he will not have to convince himself regularly that the Holy One is next to him. Let him only perceive the Holy One with his mind's eye, that the Holy One is "the place of the world"—that is, He was before He created the world so that Creation abides in the Blessed Creator. One should strive to cleave to God so completely that all he will perceive is the Holy Creator, and not that by seeing the world he thereby sees the Creator. Rather, let the focus of his vision be only the Blessed Creator.
>
> (LIKKUTIM YEKARIM, No. 54)

I find this a great challenge: to see God all around me, and not to see the physical embodiment of God in Creation first. And if it is difficult to see beyond the physicality of the chair, which is external to me, how much more will it be true for thoughts and feelings, which are hidden inside me! One of the greatest (if not the greatest) impediments to clear vision and the perception of God in all things is our sense of self. That we see ourselves as substantial, as permanent, as powerful, creates a wall that separates us from a clear perception of the truth: there is nothing but God. We sense our consciousness in our bodies; we hear our voices talking even when we are silent. We sense the flow of our thoughts. We consider, we reason, we plan, we act. Our actions make changes in the world around us. We believe, on this basis, that our intentions are substantial, that our wills and determination make things happen. Because it is true that we are instruments of action—the chair only comes out from under the table because I pull it out—we might confuse what we do with the actual creation of existence, its persistence, or its ultimate disposition. But, at most we manipulate things, and in the end we are participants in a larger dance that includes all of existence. We are a part of God, and our actions are merely expressions of the ongoing playing out of the divine will.

When we practice mindfulness we also come to realize the insubstantiality of things. As we return over and over the truth of each moment, we realize that the fears and angers and other experiences that come to mind or fill our hearts are, in the end, passing phenomena. Indeed, all things are passing phenomena. Breath arises and passes away. Pains and discomforts rise and fall in intensity. What occupies our minds one minute can be swept away by some other event—a sound, a sensation, a scent, a scene, a memory. From moment to moment what we take to be continuously existent, we realize actually dissolves and is recreated.

I remember an episode of the renewed version of "The Twilight Zone" from the 1980s. In it, a man absentmindedly turns a corner into an alleyway and suddenly finds himself in what seems like the backstage of his town. That is, stage managers and directors are giving instructions to little blue stage workers (blue, suggesting that they would not be visible against the "blue screen" of "reality's" video stage production). The workers are rebuilding the set—that is, the town in which he lives, and so, we suspect, all of reality, from moment to moment. The point of this episode was to suggest that what we take to be permanent, substantial, and continuous is actually recreated anew in every moment. We impose continuity on it. If we saw clearly, we would recognize the miracle of existence from moment to moment.

That we hold onto past events, nursing them and cherishing them as proof of our long-suffering nature or justification for our righteous indignation, is a reflection of our insistence on making the impermanent permanent. We hold onto our egos and their concerns with such intensity that we gloss over the renewal of each moment. When we acknowledge this truth, our grasp on these events—and on our sense of self and all that attaches to it—loosens. The insults and injuries that we suffer in our lives—from skinned knees to bruised egos—we come to see as unique events. When we slow down our thoughts and responses, when we break the pattern of spontaneous and habitual reactions, we come to see the world from "backstage." We learn that each moment is the only moment. What we are experiencing in this instant is all that we have. We can let go of the past, relinquish our expectations of the future, and rejoice in the truth of this very moment. The author of *Me'or Einayim* invites us to attain to a sense of immediacy in each moment.

> "For Adonai is a devouring fire" (Deuteronomy 4:24). That is, God is the fire that consumes all fires. What does this mean? Whatever it is that we become accustomed to ceases to make an impression on us. [So how can we wake up?] Consider this illustration: One who is regularly in the king's presence does not feel fear and reverence for the king as one who does not see the king often. Therefore the Torah warns, "Let the words of Torah be new to you as if they were given today" (cf. Rashi on Exodus 19:1 and Deuteronomy 26:16), that is, don't let your experience of each moment grow old, depriving you of the impression it should make.

Now, we have many different spiritual capacities, and we become enthused by one or the other, yet, over time, we become accustomed to this experience; it feels natural, customary. As a consequence, the fire of our enthusiasm lessens and is extinguished. This is so, also, when we listen to Torah teachers and preachers. When we do not hear their words as new, our hearts do not respond passionately. But, when we listen, attaching our attention to God at the same time—the God who enlivens all life and is the boundless life—we find that these words are always new, and we are inspired with renewed vitality.

In this manner, we do not remain the same from moment to moment, for at every moment we are renewed. This is the meaning of "fire that consumes all fires": before the outpouring of the fire and enthusiasm of the Creator all other passions are quenched, leaving nothing but the flames of enthusiasm that the Creator renews each day and instant. In this manner, we are continually filled with passion for our lives, since each moment is new—which would not be true otherwise.

(ME'OR EINAYIM, LIKKUTIM,
S.V. TA'AM SHE'AMRU KI H' EISH OKHLAH HU)

I am inspired by this sort of teaching. Negating physical existence and natural phenomena before God does not mean that there is nothing to the substantial world. Rather, it means that we recognize that whatever exists, exists because of God's sustaining vital forces, which are renewed each day, each moment. We can go on eating and drinking, procreating and creating, interacting, praying, and studying, since the world itself will continue to exist through God's ongoing renewing vitality. That is what it means to be alive—to receive God's revivifying blessing, and to respond by engaging in the full range of human activity. Yet beyond this, there is a further challenge: to be *aware* of the fact that we are renewed, from moment to moment; to sense in our lives that we receive renewed vital force from the Blessed Creator each day. That is, in any given moment, we must both engage in whatever activity is before us while at the same time recognizing that in itself the undertaking has no ultimate value. It is merely the occupation of the moment, and its only real meaning and value is as an expression of the constantly renewed divine force sustaining the world. And what is true of our activities is true for us as well. Our existence is "real" only as we experience it and express it as testimony to God's ever-renewed sustaining power. It is this awareness that can transform all of our actions, in turn, into *avodah*.

Balancing between the immediate experience or activity and awareness of the ultimate moment-by-moment dependence of all things on God's sustaining power is difficult. That is, there is much to enjoy in this world—physical pleasures, aesthetic pleasures, relationships. And that which brings us pleasure and enjoyment may also bring us pain, unhappiness, and disappointment. To be fully engaged in our lives—and not just passing through without making contact with anyone or anything, as a hermit cut off from the world—we need to be open to experiencing both the pleasure and the pain. What this suggests, however, is that we need a point of perspective from which to view the immediate experience. We can step back from being too caught up in it, too attached to it. We can change the way in which these experiences seem to fill our consciousness and hearts to the exclusion of all other concerns. The height of this sort of self-absorption is expressed in the words of Lamentations: "Look about and see: Is there any agony like mine?" (1:12). Just as we often experience our suffering so acutely that we lose sight of all others who suffer, so, in our joy, we often have no room for the needs or limits of others. The practice of mindful presence offers us a way to look beyond, around, or through our own suffering or pleasure to see the whole, to experience a larger awareness.

This larger awareness can be achieved through self-negation, as suggested above. It can also be attained through self-transcendence. This latter is accomplished by shifting all concern from oneself, or one's immediate circumstances, to another point of focus. Opening up our perspective in this manner allows us to see our own situation, and that of others, from a different, often broader, point of view. The classical expression of this move in Jewish mystical and hasidic teaching (here expressed by the Maggid of Mezritch) is to move our attention from the mundane toward the divine realm, to the suffering of the *Shekhinah*.

> You should always consider yourself as nothing (*ayin*, like the nothingness of God's infinite, indefinable nature), forgetting your selfness completely, so that whatever you may request in your prayers you request for the sake of the *Shekhinah*. In this manner you can transcend even time, reaching the World of Thought (*mahshavah*) where everything has equal valence—life and death, sea and land. This is what the Zohar suggests when it refers to the verse, "Why do you cry out to Me?" (Exodus 14:15) (Zohar II Beshallah 52b). What this means is that the Israelites were to have renounced themselves and forgotten all of their troubles so that they could arrive at the World of Thought, where everything has equal valence (and then they would have been able to walk on the water), which they could not achieve when cleaving to the physical world (and their particular situation). This world is one of dichotomy, of the separation of good and bad that characterize the seven days of Creation (and are found in the balancing of the seven lower *sefirot*). So how would it be possible for them to tran-

scend time, to the place where all is one complete Unity? Thus, when you think about yourself as something (distinct) and request that your needs be fulfilled, the Holy One is not able to clothe Himself in your prayer, for He is *Ein Sof* (Infinite) and no vessel can hold Him. But this is not the case when you think of yourself as *ayin* (nothing).

(MAGGID DEVARAV LEYAAKOV, LIKKUTEI AMARIM, No. 159)

I hear the Maggid saying: When all we are able to see is our own suffering or need, we actually leave no room for the Holy One to enter and to help us. Raising our consciousness to see that our suffering is like that of others—and particularly, to understand that God is in need as well, to be united with the *Shekhinah* and for all of Creation to be made whole—we open ourselves to God's help. Negating ourselves and our needs before God—becoming *ayin*—makes room for God (*Ein Sof*) to join with us in our suffering.

When we practice mindfulness as a meditation we often become aware of our own suffering first. In meditation we may become frustrated that we cannot keep our minds from wandering, or we may experience tension or pain while sitting still. If we allow these experiences to fill our awareness, we find that our suffering increases. Alternatively, we can offer ourselves a moment of compassion, recognizing that all that has happened is that our minds have wandered or that we are experiencing pain. We can name the pain as such, not expanding it into unbounded or interminable suffering, and then choose to return our attention to our breath. In that moment, we find that the distraction or the pain is easier to bear. In the movement from a constricted mind—closed off by anger, frustration, or pain—to a more open and freer mind, we can see the fleeting nature of life. We move from the center to the periphery, from something to nothing. Further, we can look more compassionately at our suffering, recognizing the ways that we made ourselves feel worse. We can understand how all other people, whether meditating or actively engaged in their lives, experience moments of frustration, pain, and anxiety. In this realization, we learn to have compassion for them. In all, we come to take a more compassionate approach to all other people and our own burdens become easier to bear. The Maggid of Mezritch expresses it this way:

"[Hillel used to say:] If I am not for myself *(im ein ani li)*, etc." (Avot 1:14)—when you pray, you must strip yourself of physicality so that you have no sense of your separate presence in the world, and therefore can say, "I am nothing *(ayin*—like *ein*, nothing)." That is, when I am stripped of my awareness of my physical existence and separate consciousness, where I do not know of or sense the world at all, then certainly I need not have any fear of strange thoughts. For, what strange thoughts can actually come close to me when I am stripped of my worldly experience? That is what "who is for me *(mi li)*?" (the concluding phrase of Hillel's teaching) means: what strange thought can come to me (if there is not me)?

But (Hillel continued), "when I am for myself"—that is, when I think of myself as something real, with separate existence, a permanent part of the physical world, then I actually count for nothing. That is the meaning of (the concluding phrase) "what am I *(mah ani;* I am a what, a something)?" That is, it is as if I want to highlight the ways that am I important, and how my *avodah* is important before the Holy One. But, when I think that I am something *(mah)*, then strange thoughts will indeed trouble me, and my endeavors will have no purpose, since the essential reason for human existence is to serve God, and I cannot because I am distracted by strange thoughts. (Then, indeed, "what [good] am I?")

(LIKKUTIM YEKARIM, No. 41)

To the extent that I can lift up my awareness beyond my personal concerns to see those of others, then I will be more likely to sense some relief of my own suffering. I will not deny my experience. Rather, I will come to see it differently, to experience it in a new way. When I can make myself nothing/*ayin,* when I diminish my ego concerns *(mi li),* I will experience fewer distracting thoughts, fewer troubling feelings. I will be less caught up in the passing phenomena of life, and more able to see the truth of each moment. My pain will only be pain, not suffering; my frustration will be a passing moment, not real. In that, I will also have the capacity to express more compassion and concern for other people. This is the goal of *avodah,* divine service in all of its forms (from Torah-study and prayer to mundane interactions). It is also the goal of mindfulness practice.

Over the course of two years I participated in a training program, a series of five-day meditation retreats at a Jewish retreat center in upstate New York. During those retreats, always with the same people, I established a certain rhythm of personal practice. I knew what kind of chair I preferred and where I liked to sit, what I preferred to eat at each meal during the course of the week, when I would go running, and so on. I came to know the facility fairly well and I was looking forward to returning for another retreat two years later. When I got there, I found that the meditation sessions had been moved from the building lobby to a smaller downstairs room. This was not a bad decision since this new "meditation hall" was quieter, more intimate. But I was thrown off a little. I would no longer be able to sit in my accustomed place. Still, I made a point of bringing the sort of chair I preferred into the hall, so that comforted me. After the second meditation session, it became clear to me that I was very uncomfortable. Whatever had been "right" with this chair before was now clearly "wrong." I had a stiff back and a sore neck, and I found it very difficult to maintain focus during my meditation.

I saw all of this happening, and I tried to work with it. I found a new spot in the hall and made it "mine." I reminded myself not to get too bound up in the pain in my back and neck. I thought that I was doing all the right things to see the truth clearly, trying not to make up a larger story, remembering to appreciate "what is." At the end of the second day I met with one of the instructors for a private conference. Although my first response was to say that I was doing just fine, I did go on to talk about my discomfort. The instructor responded, expressing compassion for my suffering and offering me encouragement to acknowledge it, know it, feel my reaction to it in my body, and so also see through it. I bristled a little, since I didn't think I was suffering. That is, I didn't think that I was making more of the story than it was; I wasn't making the pain anything other than pain.

As the conversation unfolded, however, I was suddenly struck, in a very new way, with how I was, indeed, suffering. The instructor had reflected back to me the way I was talking about my experiences: "my chair," "my place," "my back," "my pain." I had made out of all of this "my story," and I was stuck in it. I was not able to see through the events because I was at the center of them. I was suffering because I felt out of place; my expectations had not been met. Things weren't as I had anticipated, and I wanted to force them back into place rather than have to fully adapt. Barring that, I wanted to be able to control my responses, to "move beyond them." Following the instructor's directions, I opened myself up to fully feeling the pains and sensations of loss, to accepting them fully in the moment. In that way, as soon as I was able to have a little compassion for myself and for my constricted mind, I found that my heart opened up. I relaxed, my back eased up, and I was less critical. What I found at the retreat was what was—nothing more or less. I was the one who was "out of place." Letting go made me, and it, right.

What I then found was that my whole perspective changed. I sensed that my inner perception of the other participants softened—which is to say, I discovered that under my breath and hidden from my heart I had been judging them. I now saw them differently, more aware of the fact that several people had to lie on the floor rather than sit, due to back problems. So I wondered how many other people were dealing with sore legs or backs or necks. I realized that there were people on the retreat who had never meditated, who were probably struggling with the whole enterprise, wondering what they were doing sitting in silence while the world outside (and particularly Israel) was up in flames. And my heart opened more—both for them and their labors, and for all the other people in the world who simply wished to live in peace yet lived in terror and deprivation. I ended the retreat in a very different place—in my heart and in my head—than the one in which I had started.

This is what it means to say, *"mi li,"* to remove oneself from the focus of the picture and to see the larger whole. I had made myself a *mah,* a something, a someone—the center of my attention and concern. When I was able to let go of "my story," my personal struggle and suffering, I realized *"mi li?"*—who am I and my pain? I created it, I sustain it, I suffer it. But it will pass, since it is only the product of my resistance to change and my disappointed expectations. And, indeed, the strange, troubling thoughts passed. Similarly, I found that as I loosened my grip on my own suffering, my focus of concern shifted: first to the other people on the retreat, then to the people in Israel and Palestine, and finally to all people who suffer. Isn't this like the shift of attention from my own personal needs and concerns to those of the *Shekhinah* in exile, bereft of her God and Lover, suffering loneliness, loss, and pain?

My teacher Sylvia Boorstein once encapsulated mindfulness practice with these three instructions: "Pay attention. Tell the truth. Don't duck." I did pay attention. I saw my disappointment. I saw that I was physically in pain. I thought that I was telling the truth when I spoke about it—that is, I thought that I was able to distinguish between my experience and the thing itself. But I wasn't. I ducked. The larger truth was the one I learned when I didn't turn away, when I didn't duck. When I finally acknowledged that I was holding onto my pain and experience as my story, my experience, rather than as just a passing phenomenon, I was finally liberated from that suffering.

Mindfulness practice, then, like prayer, is ultimately about telling the truth. *Kavanah* is a means to move toward speaking the truth. The Maggid of Mezritch connects prayer and mindfulness in the following passage.

> The primary field of battle with the *yetzer hara* is in the service of the heart, which is prayer. We can't engage in this fight all day long, since we don't have the right weapons. But, when we engage in prayer, we wrap ourselves in our *tallit*, crowned also with the *tefillin*—and these are our armor against Satan. With these we gird ourselves to overcome our (passionate) inclinations, to direct our soul, preparing it with pure thoughts toward the Creator by means of a double-edged sword. That is, first we employ the holy words of the sacrifices and *Pesukei Dezimra*. Then, we take a spear (*romah*) in our hands—that is, the 248 words (the numerical value of *romah*) of the recitation of the *Shema*—defeating a great army with them. In this manner we are able to direct (*lekhavven*) our soul with proper thoughts in the silent prayer (the *Amidah*), such that our thoughts and our words are as one.
>
> (Likkutim Yekarim, Second Essay, No. 33)

I learn from this that the result of *kavanah*, when it is practiced properly and prepared for carefully, is that we are able to say what is true—"our thoughts and words are as one." Getting to that state is not easy. The author of this text presents it as if it were a battle. The opponents are depicted as the *yetzer hara,* our passionate inclinations, and Satan, the Accuser, who seduces and tricks us into failing our highest ambitions and not living up to our highest ideals. We might understand our opponents as our inclination to make ourselves a "something," to hold onto our egos and our personal needs, or the sorts of "strange thoughts" that arise in our minds. To resist these opponents we are encouraged to first prepare physically, putting on the uniform of battle (the *tallit,* or prayer shawl) and our protective garments (the *tefillin*). Strengthened in this manner, we will be able to enter into battle. There are two preliminary stages to the battle: recitation of the passages of sacrifices in the early part of the service, followed by the recitation of psalms and other sections of praise. These prepare us to then employ the power of God's unity (and God's Name) to bring our attention fully into the battle. Only then will we be ready to fall into silent devotion, with full attention. Only then will we be able to discern what is true among all the disparate thoughts that fly through our minds. Only then will we be able to speak the truth, connecting our thoughts and our words.

Our goal is to become awake and aware in the midst of our lives. We want, as much as possible, to be mindful of our whole being, and all that we are sensing, thinking, and experiencing. But it is difficult to do this in the midst of all that constitutes an active life. Therefore, we often set aside time to practice paying attention, in meditation or in another exercise. We pay attention to physical aspects of our practice—such as our posture when sitting—to support us in our endeavors. We sense that our breath can serve as a constant point of focus, helping us to quiet the mind. Letting our posture and our breath support us, we are prepared to begin paying attention to what our minds present—and then slowly, compassionately, to let go of the distractions and diversions to see more clearly what is actually happening, what is true. Eventually we may be able to tell the truth, and not duck. We may be able to admit to ourselves, in thought and words, what is true: how we generate, sustain, and sometimes invite our own suffering over and above that which occurs to us. We also become more able to see how we have made other people into the villain when we have avoided taking responsibility for our own actions. And we ultimately realize that just as we are suffering in our own confusion, so, too, is everyone else in theirs. Our hearts then open in compassion and love for them, too. This is how the Maggid of Mezritch expresses this awareness.

> Even if at that moment we are not able to pray with full reverence and love of God, our words of prayer can still rise up to the degree that we have fully connected ourselves to others saying, "I now take on myself to fulfill the positive commandment of 'Love your neighbor as yourself.'" In that moment, we must bind ourselves with bonds of love to the souls of all the righteous of our generation, particularly if we can imagine their faces, which will increase our capacity to make our thoughts and words one.
>
> In truth, I learned this from Rabbi Yeḥiel Mikhel of Zlotchov, who said, "Before I pray I connect myself with all Jews, both great and small. The reason that I connect with those greater than I is so, in that manner, they can raise me up. And, I connect with those lesser than I so that I can raise them up."
>
> (LIKKUTIM YEKARIM, SECOND ESSAY, NO. 33)

I love this teaching. We learned earlier that the battle with the *yetzer hara* often requires intense preparations, utilizing the full panoply of uniforms and weapons available in prayer to quiet the mind and help support *kavanah,* the unity of thought and word. Yet not everyone is able to employ those tools, so there must be another method to rise up toward God, to experience wholeness in God's presence. That other path is loving all other people, though this, too, requires a degree of self-awareness. To recognize whether someone else is "greater" or "smaller" than oneself first requires a clear assessment of one's own inner life, one's faults and one's strengths. This path may not be so direct, and therefore the struggle may not be as pitched, but in either case the work must be done if one wishes to stand before God, to come close to God, to cleave to God. *Kavanah,* the unity of thought and word, leads to openness and compassion for other people, which leads to *deveikut,* cleaving to God. The *avodah* of taking on the *mitzvah* of love for other people leads to unity of thought and word, which leads to *deveikut.*

Avodah is not only Torah-study or prayer, but it includes anything that we do with *kavanah,* with the intention of achieving *deveikut.* Still and all, the texts that we have presented, and the overall system of Judaism, assume that there are, indeed, fixed, specific practices that constitute *avodah.* We are still not free of the tension between spontaneous, personally directed prayer and that which "must be done," which may not express our inner experience. At the same time, our spontaneous urge to pray stems from deep need and heartfelt necessity. How can that prayer lead to *deveikut?* Will not our self-concern interfere with our desire to get out of the way, to remove ourselves from the center of attention? How can we keep our personal concerns from leading us only to focus on selfish ends?

Ultimately, all is in the hands of God. There is nothing but God, and still our comprehension of the Divine is extremely limited. What is it, then, that we think we accomplish when we cry out "give me this," "provide me with that"? Is our particular wish so important that its fulfillment should take precedence over all the other needs and concerns of all the other beings in the world? Is it possible, on the other hand, to place ourselves before God, acknowledging our dependence on God's mercy, announcing our need, without treating God as merely the dispenser of good? The Maggid of Mezritch addresses this question.

> "Rabbi Shimon taught: Be mindful in reciting the *Shema* and the *Amidah* (the primary texts of the prayer service). And when you pray, do not make your words rote, but rather let them be prayers of compassion and supplications before the Holy Blessed Place *(Hamakom)*" (Avot 2:13).
>
> That is, don't pray only for your own needs; rather, pray always for the *Shekhinah* to be redeemed from exile. That is the import of the phrase "let it be a (plea for) compassion and supplications before the Holy Blessed One"—that is, pray always before the Holy Blessed One, that is, for the sake of the *Shekhinah*, who is known as "the Place *(Hamakom)*."
>
> This is why the Zohar calls those who pray only for themselves and not on behalf of the *Shekhinah* "shameless dogs who cry out incessantly 'give, give' *(hav hav*, a pun: the sound dogs make and the Aramaic word for 'give')."
>
> (MAGGID DEVARAV LEYAAKOV, LIKKUTEI AMARIM, No. 13)

Here, again, we are told to pray for the sake of the *Shekhinah*. Were we to remain fixed on our own needs, we would be nothing more than "shameless dogs," mindlessly yapping about this and that for which our instinctual and habitual minds hunger. But in this case, we are taken farther than in the previous texts. Now, not only are our eyes lifted from our personal concerns to see that others, even the *Shekhinah*, are in need of help. We are told that no prayer is real prayer—pleas for compassion and supplications—if it is not directed for the sake of the *Shekhinah*. That means, in a sense, that whatever our prayer, it is ultimately a prayer for God's sake. Our concern must finally be God's concern. That is the goal of prayer as Rabbi Menaḥem Naḥum of Chernobyl expresses it here:

> Therefore, you should not have any other intention in your study or prayer, no other goal, than to pray for God's sake. Even when the fixed (petitionary) prayer (of the *Amidah*) seeks some extra good or end for people, this is only an outer garment. In the end, we can only connect with inner spiritual matters by means of external garments . . .
>
> Ultimately, God's will is to do good for His creatures, and His glory fills all Creation. Therefore, we should pray with this intention: that His glory and goodness should fill all Creation, which is His will.
>
> This is the meaning of the verse, "As for me, may my prayer come to You *(lekha)*, O Adonai—not just "to You" but "for You, for Your sake *(lekha)*"—"at a favorable time" (Psalm 69:14)—that this moment should be like the moment of God's will at the time of Creation. [The phrase *eit ratzon* can mean both "a favorable time" and "a time of desire or intention."]
>
> (Me'or Einayim, Likkutim,
> s.v. vekhol zeh k'sheyiftaḥ teḥilah sha'ar hayirah)

I learn from this that God's concern is for all of Creation. As the hasidic teachers frequently say, "it is in the nature of the Good to do good," and at the time of Creation God's intention *(ratzon)* was to do good to all. "Adonai is good to all, and His mercy is on all His works" (Psalm 145:9). God's goodness and mercy are universal, reflecting the manifest presence of God's glory in all things. What it means to pray for God's sake, then, is to pray for the sake of all Creation, that God's goodness should be manifest everywhere, always, that every moment be an *eit ratzon*. Even when we pray for particular needs to be filled, even when the mandated prayers put these words in our mouths, our intention should be that our prayer be for the sake of God, for the wholeness of the *Shekhinah*.

This shift in focus, from personal needs to those of the *Shekhinah*, from mundane concerns to divine concerns, reflects a fundamental component of Jewish prayer. The Hebrew verb for prayer is *lehitpallel*, a reflexive verb that ultimately points us to "self-judgment." When we pray as Jews, we are challenged to see ourselves clearly, to scrutinize our lives, to inspect carefully our behavior. To even begin to address our needs to God we must first be certain what they are. How do we know if what we sense to be a "need" is not simply a whim, a hunger, a jealousy, a passing passion? Our primary prayer is to see clearly who we are, how we live, how we engage with others and with the world, so that we might discern what it is, in fact, that we might truly need. Our self-awareness, our mindful self-assessment, is the outcome of *tefillah*, our self-judgment in prayer.

Nevertheless, we are sometimes trapped in the language we use. English is, for most of us, our primary, native language. Our understanding of the word "prayer" is not only derived from the culture that surrounds us, but from the etymology of the word itself. "Prayer" is ultimately derived from the Latin *precari*, "to beg or petition for." We are left, then, with the sense that praying means asking God for things. Our attitude toward God follows: God is the divine dispenser of all goods and benefits. We are instructed, in these hasidic texts, to change that view. That is, even when we have personal needs, we are called to set them in the context of the whole of Creation. As one text above suggested, we are to step out of time and space, to consider our needs from the point of view of all needs and concerns. Further, the needs and concerns of all are actually manifestations of the Divine, for God fills all things. There is nothing but God. If we sense a lack, it suggests a flaw in the overall garment behind which, or through which, we perceive God. To pray for a lack to be filled, a concern to be addressed, is to realize our desire for God to be whole, and that we might be whole with God *(deveikut)*. In mystical terms, that is to bring the *Shekhinah* out of exile, to reunite her with her God and Lover.

When we shift our attention from the personal to the universal, we are not left behind. Our needs may still be met. But, our sense of what it might mean for them to be met—in what manner, through what mechanism—will change. And, quite possibly, we will come to see others' needs being met through us as well. This is the meaning of the following teaching of the Maggid of Mezritch.

> If you need to ask something of the Holy Creator, imagine that your soul is a limb of the *Shekhinah*, as it were, a drop of water in the whole of the sea. Then, ask on behalf of the *Shekhinah*, since what you need is also lacking in Her. Believe fully that your concerns are solely for the *Shekhinah*. And, if you cleave to the *Shekhinah* in this way, then the outflow of blessing for Her will flow over to you as well. This is like when a person is happy and she claps her hands even without intending to, but her joy spreads throughout her body and produces this effect. So it is if you consider yourself a limb of the *Shekhinah*, as it were, that the flow moving through Her will affect you, as well.
>
> Further, you should see yourself as merely a vessel, and your thoughts and words are extensions of the supernal worlds. The World of Speech, which is the *Shekhinah*, makes its requests of

the World of Thought by means of your words. When the light of the Holy Creator fills your thoughts and words, your request should be that the divine outflow spread from the World of Thought to the World of Speech, and that it should come by means of the matter that you need filled, and God will thereby also fulfill your request.

This is the meaning of the phrase (in the Sephardic *Seliḥot* poem), "Be present for us in our requests." That is, may the Holy One be present for us in the very things that we request. Thus, as the sages say (Zohar, *Vayishlaḥ,* 1 178a), "Just as the power of the worm is in its mouth to produce silk thread for cloth, so, too, the power of Israel is in its mouth to produce silk to clothe the *Shekhinah.*"

(MAGGID DEVARAV LEYAAKOV, LIKKUTEI AMARIM, NO. 66)

Our needs are not effaced altogether. Healing, sustenance, peace are not meaningless concerns. They are not unique concerns, either. In this process our hearts and eyes are lifted out of our own particular set of circumstances and tied to the cosmic drama of God and the *Shekhinah,* of exile and reconciliation. Just as when we place our needs in the moment of Creation, realizing how truly the Creator desires our good, and we therefore pray for the good of all, so, too, here, when we place our concern in the resolution of the brokenness of the universe our prayers will be answered in the larger process. What we truly want, in our heart of hearts, is for God and the *Shekhinah* to be united, for all conflict and opposition to be resolved. Our particular need, our lack, is the result of the cosmic imbalance, and a reflection of it. We come to understand that for our need truly to be filled the larger problem must also be resolved.

Prayer, then, is ultimately a mindfulness practice. Although we may start out with a particular concern in mind, a need that we wish to be filled, through *kavanah* we come to see it, and ourselves, differently. We are led to realize that our needs are not the only ones in the world. Not only do other people hunger, not only are others sick and in need of healing; indeed the *Shekhinah* Herself is in exile, suffering all that we suffer. She is dependent on us to help reunite Her with the Holy One. Moreover, the structure of the traditional prayer service leads us to an awareness of God's Oneness, and our place and participation in God's infinite Being. As we try to experience a sense of unity with God and God's purpose, our perception of what constitutes "the good" changes. We begin to see the world beyond time and space, from the perspective of the Creator at Creation. Our personal needs and concerns shift to become God's needs and concerns. What we want and need comes into line with God's desire and will.

When we pay attention to our lives, from moment to moment we become aware of "needs." Whether we sense aversion or attraction, resistance or attachment, the object of our attention becomes the need of the moment. When we notice that reaction, we become able to relinquish our habitual modes of response. That is a moment of liberation. We are no longer trapped in servitude to instinct or tendency. When we ask ourselves, "What is true?" and can respond, "This is aversion" or "This is attraction," we are released again. We see how in this moment we are caught up by a passing emotion or habit, and can then choose to let go of it. We can treat ourselves with compassion—for having first been caught up in our habitual response and also for the loss of "shelter" that habit provided. Our sense of ourselves changes. We see ourselves larger, no longer constrained by our past. We see beyond our immediate concerns, the needs of the moment, and recognize the needs of others. We understand better how other people struggle with their own bondage, how they also have needs and concerns. Our hearts open to them in compassion as well.

As over and over again we come to recognize the truth of the moment, we come to see how our perceived "needs" are the product of the moment. We recognize how often what we yearn for, what we "pray" for, is merely a habitual response to the challenge of the moment. Seeing this does not mean that we may not ultimately find that it is, indeed, imperative that we fill that "need." But we will come to that conclusion in a different manner, with a different sense of purpose, and with a different relationship to the people around us. As we pay attention to what starts out as "prayer," we see it slowly transformed into confession. What we "need"—in the sense of yearning, compulsion, or aversion—becomes "what is": "This is my habitual response. This is my fear. This is my hunger." In the moment of awakened awareness we attain a sense of acceptance: "This is true. I don't have to fight it; I don't have to like it. I simply must accept it in this moment." We sense that our experience coheres: it could not be other than what it is at this moment. We see our lives from a different perspective, from the standpoint of the whole of Creation. Everything that has happened up to this moment, to us, to those around us, to those we know and those we will never know, has brought about this very moment. It could not be different. It is the truth of this moment.

In the end, prayer is confession. It is telling ourselves the truth, and acknowledging the truth before God. In the moment of confession, in recognizing the truth, we experience the relief of liberation and the obligation of compassion. We see our lives more clearly, and we see all others with an open heart. If we are to learn to pray, if we are to learn to be fully awake in our lives, then we must be prepared for every moment to be one of meeting, of service, of truth-telling. We cannot prepare for this, except by striving over and over to lift our eyes and hearts, by training our minds and spirits. We must learn to bring our whole selves, carrying with us every part of our past and the awareness of our connection to all others. This requires that we be truly present in each moment, that our minds and intentions be united because "We shall not know with what we are to worship Adonai until we arrive there." We shall not arrive without acknowledging the truth, without *kavanah.*

Chapter Six

Mindfulness and the Experience of Prayer

*P*rayer is one of the primary forms of *avodah*, of divine service. It is the mechanism through which *kavanah*, mindful, balanced attention to the truth of the moment, leads to *deveikut*. "Rabbi Yoḥanan said: 'Would that a man would go on praying the whole day!'" (Berakhot 21a). The hasidic teachers embraced this intention, and sought to make all activity a form of *avodah*, but as we read earlier:

> The primary field of battle with the *yetzer hara* is in the service of the heart, which is prayer. We can't engage in this fight all day long, since we don't have the right weapons.
>
> (LIKKUTEI YEKARIM, SECOND ESSAY, NO. 33)

It may not be possible to pray all day, but perhaps when we pray we create the possibility that the rest of our endeavors will reach the level of *avodah*.

For the most part, when we speak of prayer in a Jewish context, we mean participation in formal, mandatory prayer services. For this, we turn to the siddur, the book containing the prayers in their "order," which is what *siddur* means. In the morning service (the standard form of daily prayer) there are four main sections: the Preliminary service, comprised of blessings greeting the day (and, in Orthodox prayerbooks, biblical and rabbinic selections describing the sacrificial service); *Pesukei Dezimra,* selections of biblical passages, largely taken from the Book of Psalms; the recitation of the *Shema* (Deuteronomy 6:4–9, 11:13–20; Numbers 15:37–41) and the three prayers surrounding it; and the *Amidah,* the standard standing devotion composed by the rabbis (which, on weekdays, includes a series of petitionary prayers). How can following the prayers as set out, as "ordered," be useful as a tool in spiritual development? How can we use the siddur as a mindfulness guide? In this chapter we will examine a number of the prayers from each section of the morning service as a means of answering these questions. As an introduction we will present an extended passage from a hasidic text, suggesting how the order of the service itself, along with the specific content of the prayers, helps us to generate a sense of *deveikut,* to experience participation in formal prayer as a spiritually moving mindfulness practice.

To find our way into the experience of prayer as a mindfulness practice, let us examine this selection from *Or Hame'ir* by Rabbi Ze'ev Wolf of Zhitomer, a disciple of the Maggid of Mezritch.

The Men of the Great Assembly established the twelve intermediate petitions of the *Amidah*—for health, sustenance, the fall of our oppressors, and so on, among the many things that we need. Yet, can there be any change in the divine will (Heaven forbid!)? Let it never be suggested that there is any change in the will of the Creator of all, as it says, "I am Adonai—I have not changed" (Malachi 3:6). Rather, the process really has to do with those who are the recipients (of God's blessings).

(OR HAME'IR, ROSH HASHANAH II, S.V. VERZ"L NITORERU)

I want to pause here to note: What a refreshing and candid declaration! Our prayer is not to change God in any way. Rather, it is to change us. This is what we found at the end of the previous chapter: petitionary prayer is ultimately confession. When we list that which we truly need, we declare the truth of our lives—where we stand today, how we perceive our lives, our fortunes, the unfolding of our relationships. When we confess the truth, we acknowledge that which may be missing; our desire for it to be fulfilled is not a wish for a magical intervention but a reflection of our deepest intentions to live openly, honestly, and lovingly. At best, we express our desire for the capacity to change ourselves, to resist our baser instincts, to have patience.

My earliest recollection of personal, spontaneous petitionary prayer is set in elementary school. I may have been in fourth or fifth grade. My interest had been piqued by a television commercial, and I had latched onto the "need" for an electric train set. I remember standing at the edge of the playground during recess. I was alone, turned away from my classmates, looking off into the distance. I remember praying, "Dear God, I really would like an electric train set. Please, please, would You help me to get it?" As soon as the thoughts had arisen in my mind, I felt awkward. I realized something was not quite right. I think that then, given my family background and sensibilities, I felt conflicted about asking for something for myself, and in particular, something frivolous, something superfluous, something material. I wanted something—a *thing*—and felt guilty about my desire. Further, I knew that even though I wanted the train set, praying for it made no sense. God did not deliver train sets, and would not change my parents to make them do it. I had to deal with my desire, with my guilt, with my pain, with my sense of need. In time, I learned that seeing my life clearly, feeling everything fully, and confessing that truth is worthy of expression to God in prayer. That is what mindful Jewish prayer is about. That is what we learn as we continue with our text.

So observe: first we recite *Pesukei Dezimra* (passages of praise). Our sages taught, "Why are they called *'pesukei dezimra'*? Because we trim off *(mezamerim)* the husks . . . from our hearts and inner beings." So, for instance, when we recite "Great is Adonai and highly praised" (Psalm 145:3), we find that we start to turn toward the Holy One, thinking, "'Do I believe what I am saying' (Psalm 116:10)? Adonai is great and the whole earth is full of His glory—so, why have I behaved in this (unseemly) manner, doing this and that?" And, indeed, each one of us knows our inner flaws and the sorts of thoughts that preoccupy us. When we stop to think, we begin to regret our actions and to look with incredulity at what we've done. Then, when we read, "Adonai is good to all and His mercy is over all His works" (Psalm 145:9), we find that we take these words to heart, and ask, "If this is so, then why am I deficient (in experiencing goodness)? Am I not also one of God's works?" We realize that if we do not sense the good in our lives, then the lack is in us, that we have not prepared ourselves to be a proper receptacle to receive that good. We then determine to ornament ourselves with good qualities, casting off all alien contacts, so that God will dwell in our every limb and sensation.

In this manner we continue with all of the psalms, trimming off the husks, the negative qualities that we sense in ourselves.

I see in this section that our first steps in prayer require us to consider who we are, where we stand, how we perceive ourselves, our lives, our place in the world. The words of the psalms can be tools in this process, waking us up to the truth of our lives. As we move through this section of the prayer service, our eyes and hearts are opened, our vision clears, and we are prepared to see more clearly what it is that we truly wish to pray for. Only after this preliminary process:

are we truly able to pray, that is, to connect our innermost thoughts with the exaltedness of the Holy One, attaining a complete unity when we recite the *Shema* . . . becoming completely united with the Holy One, such that we gain the capacity to nullify evil decrees, compelling God to do good for all, as the sages taught, "The Holy One makes decrees and the righteous person nullifies them" (Mo'ed Katan 15b). Thus, when we arrive at the word "one" (at the end of the *Shema*) and unite ourselves with the Holy One completely, our purpose will be so great that we can nod in all six directions, the six paths through which the world was created, directing them according to our will, and, standing outside of time, we can change the times and switch the seasons from the depths of complete unity with God. . . .

When we then come to recite the *Shemoneh Esrei (Amidah)*, adorned from head to heel (with good qualities) and prepared to serve as a proper receptacle for the divine blessing—having trimmed the husks away in *Pesukei Dezimra*, and having attained a complete unity in reciting the *Shema*—then of itself the divine flow will pour out blessing from above, since nothing is lacking in the King's palace. Therefore, there is no change in (God's) will; rather (after having trimmed away the husks and having become a vessel prepared to receive) the change is in us. In a sense, we become like a vessel that was ready to receive from the start, and we then sense how much we, like God, only desire the good of all creatures.

This is the intention of the sages in their teaching, "A person should first rehearse his praises of the Holy One, and then pray" (Berakhot 32a). That is, by means of the praises that we experience internally, we come to realize our imperfections, the flaws that limit us. And, anyone who has a blemish cannot approach the altar (Leviticus 21:18), that is, anyone who is flawed cannot bring himself close to God, who is complete in the most absolute sense of completeness. Still, after we order our praises in *Pesukei Dezimra*, trimming off the husks from within us, and we are incredulous over our earlier actions, we become whole, and can approach the Holy One. That is why we must first order our praises before we can pray. This process allows us to connect ourselves to the Holy One, as noted above.

The process, then, is that when we trim off the husks with *Pesukei Dezimra*, we are fit to pray and request the fulfillment of our needs, since certainly we will not direct our attention to filling our bellies, but turn to higher concerns, praying for higher needs. Even when we recite the twelve intermediate blessings in which we ask for healing, sustenance, the fall of our oppressors, etc., our appeal is to ease the suffering of the *Shekhinah.*

I want to make clear, of course, that this extended passage is not the only or the last word regarding the significance or the meaning of the traditional prayer service. It is suggestive, however, of a number of concerns that we have seen before and of matters that we may wish to attend to as we review the specifics of the morning service. In this passage we see again the transformation of our personal prayers into appeals to ease the suffering of the *Shekhinah*. We are, thereby, lifted up out of the mundane realm of time and space to share in the divine perspective. Thus we see as well, in a more developed manner and with greater force, the sense that when we truly unite with God we are transformed. At those times when I have started to pray, filled with personal concerns and needs, and realized that my will has become God's will, I have felt changed, and inspired that we and not God are changed. I feel my intention to be God's intention. My heart is no longer focused only on my good; I am not in competition with the rest of the world to fill my needs. Moreover, as I see that my needs and concerns are those of the whole world, I sense that it is possible to desire good for all beings. My prayers, particularly my petitions, are lifted out of the realm of personal interest and mundane needs, and I feel relieved, realizing, with pleasure, that I desire only the good for all beings. Through prayer we come to desire only the good of all beings, just as God desires that same good.

In addition, this passage invites us to consider the steps required to reach this exalted state. The author assumes that one cannot arrive at a deep unity with God automatically or sponta-neously. Rather, it takes work and is attained in stages. And while this is not directly stated in the text, it also takes time and practice. The purpose of reciting passages from the Psalms and other selec-tions from the Bible is to hold up a mirror to us, to challenge us to look carefully at who we are, how we behave, what we think and feel. We are told that each psalm *(mizmor)* can be a pruning knife by which we can remove *(mezamerim)* a *kelipah,* a husk that sepa-rates our heart from God. That is, the recitation of and reflection on the psalms are means by which we come to see ourselves with clear eyes, removing self-interest and haughtiness, egotism and self-concern. Only in this manner can we hope to let go of our sense of "self," and open ourselves to truly uniting with God.

This is the work of mindfulness. As we are increasingly able to bring a calm, balanced attention to each moment of our experience, increasingly able to recognize the confusion caused by our fears and passions, we see the ways in which we create and sustain our own self-deception, cutting us off from other people, from ourselves, and from God. The more we see clearly, the more we are able to let go of our ego preoccupations, our self-righteousness, or our self-depreca-tion, and accept the truth of the moment. Without the false bound-aries that we create to maintain our separateness from others, to protect our hearts and minds from the challenges of truly seeing the other and relinquishing our inner sense of mastery and selfhood, we open ourselves to all of Creation and to all others. We are increasingly able to experience ourselves as part of the larger whole, to realize our innate unity with all beings, and with God.

Here are a few of the early passages in the siddur and in *Pesukei Dezimra* that are especially moving to me personally. My experience is that they regularly bring me up short, make me catch my breath, challenge me to pay attention and consider who I am and what I am doing, and to tell the truth. They may thus serve as examples of how the texts of *Pesukei Dezimra* might help us to prepare for the recitation of the *Shema* and the *Amidah.*

The Preliminary Service

Modeh Ani

"I thankfully acknowledge You, living and enduring Sovereign. You have returned my soul within me with loving compassion. Your faithfulness is abundant."

These are the words the siddur offers to recite upon awakening in the morning, words that overwhelm me each time I say them. The first word is one of thanks, a conscious orientation of all thought and activity for the day to follow. I like that the first thing I say is "thank you." When I wake up, I recognize my mortality before God's immortality: my need for sleep, and its intimations of death, before the One who is eternal. I feel that to have awakened again to life is to experience God's love and faithfulness.

The last phrase, "Your faithfulness is great," is taken from the Book of Lamentations, the scriptural dirge mourning the destruction of the First Temple. There it appears in this context: "Adonai's love has not ended; His mercies are not spent. They are renewed every morning—Your faithfulness is great! 'Adonai is my portion,' says my soul; therefore I will hope in Him" (Lamentations 3:22–24).

Our personal experience of sleep and awakening is related to that of our people's suffering—of destruction and the hope for renewal and redemption. That we have awakened this morning heartens us that in every aspect of our lives we will be able to witness hope overcoming despair, trust sustaining faith in the face of travail. This is the import of the following instruction in spiritual practice offered by a hasidic teacher of early nineteenth-century Poland.

> At the moment that you wake from your sleep—whether to rise for prayer and study at midnight or at daybreak—don't lie about lazily, for of the *Shekhinah* it is written, "She never eats the bread of idleness" (Proverbs 31:27). Rather, stir yourself to get up to do the will of your Creator, who has returned your soul and spirit and life to bring Him pleasure. (Happy are we and how pleasant our lot that God has taken us to be His servants!) Then, turn your thoughts to *teshuvah,* to making yourself whole, with all of your capacities, and then recite *Modeh Ani.* After that say, "The power of the Creator is in the created," to arouse in you the sense that God's power is in you. Should the outpouring of blessings or the vital force that God gives us depart from us for a moment, we would be as nothing. Let this arouse in you great reverence and awe of the Holy Creator.
>
> (HANHAGOT TZADIKIM,
> RABBI TZVI ELIMELEKH OF DINOV, NO. 1)

I hear in this that from moment to moment we can wake up again to our life. From breath to breath we are renewed, and our capacity for hope, faith, and love is strengthened. In every moment we open to the infinite, relinquish our attachment to the temporal, and rejoice in our lives, even when faced with adversity. Since our lot is the Eternal, we are part of the unfolding of all Creation, and what is happening at any moment is true. To acknowledge this is to find grace and hope.

L'olam yehei adam yerei shamayim baseter uvagaluy

"At all times a person should be God-fearing in private and in public, acknowledging the truth and speaking the truth in his heart."

This sentence stands as the introduction to the prayer-passage that follows it, but it also carries its own profound message. To be one who fears God is to acknowledge that there is no real "private domain." There is no place to hide. Even the deepest recesses of our hearts are not hidden from the One. Our concern is to bring to light all that we can, to learn the most that we can about our hearts, our heads, our spirits, so that we can tell the truth—even if it is only to acknowledge that truth to ourselves. Again, hasidic teachings, this time of Rabbi Moshe Teitlebaum, the nineteenth-century Polish author of *Yismah Moshe*, focus on the central importance of truth to any spiritual endeavor.

> The whole of the Torah is contained in the quality of truth. If we desire to grasp the quality of truth fully, without any deception at all, then we will find that all of our interactions with other people and all of the Torah are bound up in truth, and we will then experience fear of God in private and in public. In turn, we will answer truthfully to those who delegate our tasks to us—ultimately that is God, who has sent us out into the world.
>
> (Yismah Moshe, introduction, s.v. venakdim od)

I understand this as the ongoing work of mindfulness: "Pay attention. Tell the truth. Don't duck." We learn, when we pay attention, that nothing is finished and done with. Whatever we may think we know about ourselves, it is always subject to change, to evolution or development. What we think we have resolved may come undone; what we fear may never be at ease may suddenly loosen and come to rest. "At all times" we have to pay attention—to our hearts, our minds, and our spirits. When we do that to the fullest extent we can, then we will be more likely to tell the truth—to ourselves, to others, and to God. Fear of God is not dread of punishment. It is awesome reverence for the demands of truthfulness, and dedication to living truthfully.

Lo al tzidkoteinu anaḥnu mapilim taḥanuneinu lefanekha

"Arise and say: Ruler of the Universe, it is not on the basis of our righteousness that we cast our supplications before You, but due to Your great mercies. For, what are we, what is our life, what is our kindness, what is our righteousness, what is our capacity to save, what is our strength, what is our might? What can we say before You, Adonai, our God and God of our ancestors? Are not all the mighty as nothing before You, the famous as if they had never been, the wise as if devoid of knowledge, and the discerning as if devoid of intelligence? For most of their deeds are nothing, and the days of their lives insubstantial (vanity, *hevel*) before You. The pre-eminence of man over beast is nothing, for all is vanity *(hevel)*."

When we bring our full attention to our lives we discover this truth: our lives and all that we do are ultimately insubstantial. Everything passes away. Nothing is eternal but God and God's eternity. There is no more profound truth. When we understand this, when we accept that our accomplishments have no more meaning than those of the animals in their myriad species manifest and hidden, we may at first feel lost, unbalanced, bereft of a resting place or a point of reference. When we stay with that awareness, when we stay focused on that truth, we slowly come to feel instead as if we are being freed of our skins, the husks in which we have secured our egos and protected our self-images. As we loosen our grasp on our particular story, as we relinquish our claim on primacy and priority, we actually open to a new awareness of our place in Creation. We learn to see ourselves differently.

"Nevertheless, we are Your people." The prayer continues, offering a new platform from which to see ourselves and all others. We belong to God, and not the other way around. We are the heirs of a tradition that has constantly led its practitioners to awareness of this truth, and to celebrate its implications. Abraham, Isaac, and Jacob, each in his own way, demonstrated his devotion to the service of God. Each set aside his personal needs and desires, the story that he wished to have fulfilled for himself and his family, to acknowledge the truth of each moment. They each experienced in dramatic fashion the dead-end of self-service, they were freed of their ego-identities, and they emerged as new personalities devoted to God.

We can follow in their footsteps. We, too, can look beyond the "normal" story of a life, the expectations that lead us into traps of selfishness and fear, of jealousy and anger. We can also relinquish the self-satisfaction that accompanies success and ease, prosperity and comfort. Everything can and does change. Nothing is eternal but God. It is not for our sake that we have been created, but for the good of all beings, for the service of the Holy One.

"Therefore, we are obliged to thank You, to praise You, to glorify You, to bless and sanctify and give praise and thanks to Your Name. Happy are we, how good is our portion, how pleasant our lot, how beautiful our heritage. Happy are we that we can rise early in the morning and tarry in the evening, twice daily reciting '*Shema Yisrael*—Hear O Israel, Adonai is our God, Adonai alone.'"

When we allow ourselves to see the truth, we do not come to despair. That all is vanity, that our works and accomplishments are insubstantial, is not cause for depression or nihilism. Rather, it is a call to engagement. Not for gain, not to attain immortality or permanence, but to live with joy and devotion. When we learn to see that what is true at this moment cannot be anything other than what it is *at this moment,* we can rejoice in it. Knowing our limits, and knowing also our real powers and capacities, allows us to work to improve the lives of those around us, to live with greater compassion, to bring more justice. To recite the *Shema* is to endeavor to let go of our narrow, personal perspectives, to see the truth that there is nothing but God, and to open our hearts and minds to making our behavior a manifestation of that truth.

This prayer was composed by Rabbi Yoḥanan for use in the Yom Kippur confessional service (cf. Yoma 87b). To recite this passage every morning reminds us that the work of telling the truth and making amends for mistakes is not a once-a-year endeavor, but a daily practice. Each day, in a sense, shares something of Yom Kippur. Each day can be a time of transformation, of cleansing our hearts, and of being reborn into the truth of this moment. And when we remind ourselves each morning that this is true, we recommit to making each waking moment one in which we will strive to be as whole as we are at the end of Yom Kippur.

Mizmor Shir Ḥanukat Habayit (Psalm 30)

The theme of this psalm is one of thanksgiving for recovery from illness, which the psalmist then generalizes to the movement from anguish and despair to redemption and joy. For the psalmist, the experience of illness and recovery is only one manifestation of all of the various ways that we experience the regular cycle of suffering and release. Having witnessed this process, the psalmist declares: "For He is angry but a moment, and when He is pleased there is life. One may lie down weeping at nightfall, but at dawn there are shouts of joy" (verse 6). God's anger, the psalmist suggests, is what we experience when we are sick, when "enemies rejoice over" us, when we are terrified, or when we believe that our life is coming to an end. Recovery from illness, justification before one's enemies, the return of security and ease are all moments when we sense that we have been brought back to life through God's favor.

If this theology is meant to suggest that our job is to appease God, always in fear of God's anger, it is unsatisfying. But that is not the sense that comes from the end of the verse: "One may lie down weeping at nightfall, but at dawn there are shouts of joy." That is, the alternation of weeping and joy is recurrent, the expression of the downs and ups of life. If we pay attention, we learn to expect— or at least accept—these swings. It is not that God is angry, but rather that in our anguish or pain we feel cut off from God, and interpret our alienation as God's anger.

The flow of the psalm helps us to learn this truth. "When I was untroubled I thought, 'I shall never be shaken' . . . You made [me] a firm mountain, but then when You hid Your face, I was terri-fied" (verses 7–8). The self-assurance in verse 7 voices a sense of security that was to be proven false. We think of mountains as per-manent, stable, eternal, but they can shake and shudder; they crumble over the course of time. To think that any achievement, or any state of heart or mind, is permanent is to be self-deceiving. Out of that state, we tend to blame our disappointments and failures on others, or we feel guilty ourselves. God hiding His face, then, may actually be rhetorical and reflexive in meaning: "(I thought) You hid Your face," the psalmist says, but then realizes, "No, it was I, terri-fied and confused!" God did not hide His face as punishment, as a sign of disfavor or a signal of disinterest. Rather, the psalmist says, I allowed complacency to cloud my vision, permitted habit to shape my sense of the moment, and so I was shaken. The psalmist, as "king of the mountain," lost sight of how things change. He took his eyes off of God, and allowed his ego to fill his heart. As a consequence, eventually he came to sense that God was not with him.

The Talmud teaches:

> Rabbi Ḥisda said, and according to another version it was Mar Ukba: "Of every man in whom there is haughtiness of spirit, the Holy One declares, 'I and he cannot both dwell in the world.'"

> (Sotah 5a)

When we fill up our hearts with our personal concerns, with our sense of permanence, with our claims to power, there is no space left for God. We may be able to go along for a while like this, but eventually we will come up against a situation in which our presumptuousness is challenged. In our terror, we will feel as if God has hidden His face. But, it will be we who have hidden ourselves from God. The response is to turn to God, as did the psalmist: "I called to You, O Adonai; to Adonai I made appeal" (verse 9). The nature of that appeal is deep and transforming. It is not self-serving; it is not to return to the status quo ante. "What is to be gained from my death, from my descent in the Pit? Can dust praise You? Can it declare Your truth? Hear, O Adonai, and have mercy on me . . . that [my] whole being might sing hymns to You endlessly; O Adonai my God, I will praise You forever" (verses 10, 11, 13). The psalmist pleads: Help me, God, to clear my heart and mind; help me to live without pretense, rising above my ego, which will eventually die, so that I can open my heart to You in joy and in praise always.

This is the work of mindfulness practice. We find in a moment of surprise, of panic, of anger, of covetousness, or of self-satisfaction that we are overwhelmed. We cannot discern what has gone wrong in our lives, and we cannot see our way out. It is as if we have been cut off from all contact with others—we are alone in our suffering. But if we pay close attention to the truth of the moment, we may be able to see the source of our pain. We will be able to identify how suffering arises—in our thoughts, in response to others, out of fear or pride or ignorance or shame. In the choice to let go of the story, to relinquish our hold on our righteousness or our expectations, to "come down from our mountain," we open ourselves to the truth. We come alive again in the moment. We experience liberation and redemption. Even when the source of our pain is still present, even in the face of ongoing challenge, we can experience, with the psalmist: "You turned my lament into dancing; You undid my sackcloth and girded me with joy" (verse 12).

Pesukei Dezimra

Mizmor Letodah (Psalm 100)

The superscription of this psalm is *mizmor letodah,* "a psalm for thanksgiving." The word *todah* (thanksgiving) is related to the word *modeh,* the opening word of the siddur, the first word we are to speak upon waking. Now, however, we hope not only to orient ourselves toward an attitude of gratitude, but we want to root it in our hearts. Or better, we want to reveal that it is present in our hearts all the time. We want to learn to see clearly, to recognize the truth of our existence, overcoming pride and possessiveness, fear and fecklessness, to become one with the Holy One.

One way to prune away husks of obtuseness and insensitivity is to recognize blessing and to offer thanks. That is the theme of this psalm. We are first invited to serve God with joy. Whenever we come before God, it is to be in gladness and with shouts of joy. That is easy to do when things are going well. We naturally feel happy then, and we are inclined toward thankfulness and ease of spirit. That may be what the psalmist had in mind when he reminded us that we are God's "people, the flock He tends" (verse 3). When God is our Shepherd, how can we not be satisfied? How can we not be at ease when we are led to lie down in green pastures, to rest by still waters? That is the general sense of what it means for God to be our Shepherd.

But consider also what it means to be a sheep, what the actual experience is to be part of the flock. It is not all gamboling in the greenery in security and peace. There is also danger. Remember Jacob's complaint to Laban: "These twenty years I have spent in your service; your ewes and she-goats never miscarried, nor did I feast on rams from your flock. That which was torn by beasts I never brought to you; I myself made good the loss; you exacted it of me, whether snatched by day or snatched by night. Often, scorching heat ravaged me by day and frost by night; and sleep fled from my eyes" (Genesis 31:38–40). To be a sheep is still to experience miscarriage, and also to risk becoming dinner. However devoted the shepherd may be, there are dangers night and day. Pasturage is not always verdant: "Now Moses, tending the flock of his father-in-law Jethro, the priest of Midian, drove the flock into the wilderness" (Exodus 3:1). And life is not always dignified, but subject annually to rough treatment at the hands of the shearers.

The image of being God's flock is meant to reinforce the joy with which we respond to God. Yet we must be able to do so in the full awareness of ovine experiences. We, too, are subject to the vicissitudes of life in all of their forms—miscarriage in birth and in justice; random acts of violence from which no one can defend us; the vagaries of the weather and the variation in climate and scenery that shape our lives. There are times in our lives when we are "fleeced," and there are moments in which we are tossed on our backs, and left naked before the world. The psalm invites us to see the reality of life in all of its coarseness, in its harshness—and still to respond with thanks, in joy.

The psalmist offers an insight that is like a mindfulness teaching: "Acknowledge that Adonai is God; He made us and we are His" (verse 3). This is not a command to believe in God. Rather, we are told to acknowledge that we are not God. It is an invitation to recognize a fundamental truth: we did not create ourselves, we do not own ourselves. We tend to think that what we do creates the world. We believe that we have control over our lives, that we can discern all of the myriad lines of force and cause-and-effect, so that we can experience only blessing and never suffer loss. The psalmist would have us look again. We are subject, and not master. No matter how much we may see, we cannot see it all. No matter how much influence we may wield, our lives are determined by much greater forces. When we see this clearly, we open ourselves to a deep sense of humility. We cannot be haughty in the face of this truth: "He made us and we are His."

This is deepened further when we note that the consonantal text *(ketiv,* but not the read text, *kerei)* actually says: "He made us and not we ourselves." This reinforces the impetus to humility. We are the product of billions of years of life emerging in the universe, a process over which we have no control and of which we are not even the end result. That we exist at all is an amazing occurrence; that we share this moment in time with the whole of the rest of Creation is awe-inspiring.

The psalm continues: "Enter His gates with praise, His courts with acclamation" (verse 4). It is not sufficient merely to come to the above realization. Awareness demands response, action. In the biblical idiom, it is to move closer to God's dwelling, to come into "His court." What we mean is to clear out a space in our hearts and minds in which we can retain our awareness of the greatness of Creation and the wonder of our place in it. We want to be able to return, over and over, to the place from which we can see all of our experience in the light of Creation's unfolding—that even that which troubles us or leaves us broken can be present in God's house. In that light we will still want to respond with the psalmist: "Thank Him! Bless His name! For Adonai is good; His steadfast love is eternal; His faithfulness is for all generations" (verses 4–5). Even in our brokenness, even when we feel lost or fleeced, we want to be able to thank and praise God. We want to be able to know that this moment is also part of the wondrous, awesome, and awe-inspiring emergence of Creation. And indeed, God's steadfast love is eternal—that is, it is known throughout time, through time.

> *Hit-hallelu beshem kodsho, yismaḥ lev mevakshei Adonai.*
> *Dirshu Adonai ve'uzo, bakshu fanav tamid.*
> *Yehi khevod Adonai le'olam, yismaḥ Adonai bema'asav.*

Exult in His holy name; let all who seek Adonai rejoice. Turn to Adonai, to His might; seek His presence constantly (I Chronicles 16:10–11/Psalm 105:3–4). "May the Glory of Adonai endure forever; may Adonai rejoice in His works" (Psalm 104:31).

Early on in *Pesukei Dezimra*, surrounding Psalm 100, are extended passages composed of selections from the Book of Psalms. In a sense, the collected verses are meant to create new psalms. These two sets of verses create an interesting frame for this section of the service. At the start we are enjoined to seek God's presence always, and we are assured that those who do so will ultimately rejoice. Joy comes as a result of devoting our energies to finding God in all that we do. In response to a world in which that is our goal and passion, God rejoices as well. There is reciprocity between our joy when seeking God's presence and God's joy in us, as Rabbi Levi Yitzḥak writes:

> "This is what their father said to them" (Genesis 49:28). Understand this according to the following teaching: "the consort (*sheigal*—a term that also suggests sexual activity) stands at your right hand, decked in gold of Ophir" (Psalm 45:10), about which the sages said, "Because the Torah is as dear to Israel as *sheigal* is to the heathens, you have earned as your reward the gold of Ophir" (Rosh Hashanah 4a). Now, this presents a difficulty—why is it that the Jews alone merit (divine) love from this; don't they also prize other attractions and desires? This is what it means: When a particular desire enters a Jew's thoughts, like the desire for sex (*mishgal)* or some other physical delight, they begin to think: "Now, this thing was created by God, and 'All that the Holy One created in this world He only created for His glory' (Avot 6:11)—that is its ultimate purpose and reason for existence. Since its ultimate purpose and reason is greater than this thing itself—why should I lust after something small that will dissipate and be lost? Would it not be better to serve God as a faithful servant, loving the Holy Creator who is the ultimate end of all Creation? Moreover, even if I were to desire some thing and actually attain it, I would still have only that one thing at that one moment, and then I would discover that I desire another thing at another moment. But, when I serve the Blessed Creator, with the same enthusiasm I can attain at one moment all possible delights, for He is the sum total of all delights." . . . Now, even though this is a good path to follow, it is still not the best mode of divine service, since the person still has a personal stake in it, finding his own joy and delight in this service. The ultimate goal of divine service is to bring delight and ease of spirit to the Holy Creator, that the Creator will receive delight

from worshipers and their deeds. God will then enjoy them with the enjoyment that a parent takes in a wise child, as it says: "My child, if your mind gets wisdom, my mind, too, will rejoice" (Proverbs 23:15), and "May Adonai rejoice in His works" (Psalm 104:31).

(KEDUSHAT LEVI, VAYEḤI,
S.V. VEZOT ASHER DIBBER LAHEM)

In this text I see the dynamic of our rejoicing in seeking God, and God's rejoicing in our endeavors. The way in which we seek God is an inquiry into the nature and behavior of our minds. That is: What is it that attracts us? What is the nature of our response to the given moment, and what is its truth? When we investigate carefully, we learn to recognize when our minds and hearts latch onto things— jealousies, resentments, delights, attractions, anxieties over the past, or aspirations for the future. When we realize that we have begun to clutch at the present moment, to hold onto its pleasure or to control its discomfort, we can begin to ask the questions of the seeker in the passage above. Is this real? How am I trapped? What can I do to liberate my mind and heart so that I can serve God fully and in truth? As we uncover the truth more and more, we experience a lightening of the heart, an increase in joy. The world becomes fuller for us. God rejoices in our endeavors and responds in joy.

In the following passage, the starting assumption is that prayers of praise are directed to and affect the upper realms of the divine emanations, the *sefirot (Keter, Ḥokhmah, Binah)*. In this upper realm, there is no division, no contention, and essentially no sense of "otherness." In that place, where all is seen as a whole and all is known at one time and without comparison or priority, prayers are answered immediately. Everything, in all of its manifold manifestations, is perfect there. The following text, by Rabbi Elimelekh of Lyzhensk (a disciple of the Maggid of Mezritch), is a powerful instruction for "pruning" the husks that separate us from our true selves, from knowledge of the truth, from other people, and from God.

> This is the meaning of "Exult in His holy name"—that is, in the supernal realms in which there is only praise and exultation. In that realm, of itself "the hearts of those who seek Adonai will rejoice" (Psalm 105:3), immediately, even before any petitions can be voiced. This is the true meaning of the verse "the time approached for Israel to die" (Genesis 47:29). Our father Jacob, peace be on him, held in his mind at all times that the day of his death was near, that perhaps he might die this very day. Each and every day was in his eyes close to his death. In this manner he refined his physical self so that all of his thoughts were directed toward the upper realms.
>
> (No'am Elimelekh, Vayeḥi,
> s.v. vayikrevu yemei yisrael etc. [end])

We learn in this text that the fundamental source of our anxieties and our appetites is our awareness of our mortality—our fear of it, our resentment of it. We experience this fear and resentment sometimes as an emptiness, a hunger, and we try to fill it with things and experiences. The ultimate loss of our egos—that is, the end of our personal life-stories and our ownership of our possessions—makes us angry and impatient with people or events that inhibit our freedom of action, that take up our time. We think that because we are mortal we cannot know eternity, we cannot live in God's full presence. This text suggests that in this frame of mind we can never truly praise God. We will always experience duality and contention. We will never sense that our prayers, particularly those of petition, have been answered, since we still intuit our ultimate limit. And so, surely we will never experience the joy that comes with seeking God's face, or being in God's presence.

When we let our attention rest in the truth of the moment, we come to realize that it is eternal. It is the only moment we have. There is no guarantee of a tomorrow, or even of a next breath. That is what Jacob modeled for us. If every moment is potentially the only moment we have, it becomes more precious. We will not grieve that which we do not yet possess, nor will we resent what we have lost. In that instant we will be complete. The truth will indeed liberate us from anxiety, fear, anger, resentment. We will rejoice in that moment, and our joy will be God's joy, as well.

Halleluyah! Halleli nafshi et Adonai ahallelah Adonai behayai azamerah lelohai be'odi

"Halleluyah! Praise Adonai, O my soul! I will praise Adonai with my life, I will sing hymns to Adonai with my very being" (Psalm 146:1–2).

There is no separation between the realm of spiritual practice and the realm of daily living. We do not discharge our duties to God or satisfy the needs of our souls in the performance of ritual, nor do we fulfill our responsibility to our bodies and minds solely through exercise, proper diet, and satisfying work. The work of the spirit and the care of the body are one and the same. When we give mindful attention to our lives, we note not only our inner dispositions—our emotional, psychic, and spiritual states—but we also observe carefully our physical states—fatigue, energy, aches, disabilities. To dismiss one or the other of these aspects of our being would be to cut off a limb, to deny our wholeness. More, we would limit our capacity to know the whole of the truth of our lives. These verses remind us that our spiritual lives can only be lived fully to the extent that they embrace our physical beings and are expressed through them. Further, they remind us that our spiritual life should flow forth from us as a song. This is the force of the following teaching from *Tiferet Shelomo*.

> At this season (approaching the New Year), God's will and desire is aroused toward His special people and God generates understanding and yearning in them to ignite their hearts in service of the Holy One. This is the meaning of the verse, "You open Your hand and satisfy desire in all life" (Psalm 145:16). That is, You open Your hand (*yadkha*), that is Your *yods* (the smallest Hebrew letter, barely more than a dot, which is the point from which all Creation emanates), the openings of the supernal worlds, by which You satisfy and arouse in all life the will and holiness to serve God wholeheartedly. What is the meaning of "all life"? It is incumbent on every Jew to devote his very being and vital forces to the service of the Holy One, and to sanctifying the Blessed Name. . . . Thus, we must determine in our hearts, with full will and desire, to devote all of our vital energies and life force to the glory of the Holy One. As it says, "Praise Adonai, O my soul! I will praise Adonai with my life, I will sing hymns to Adonai with my very being." . . . That is, I will praise Adonai, with all of my vital force and with all of my soul and being. What David the psalmist meant was that he wished to praise the Holy One with all of his power and all of his soul.

> (TIFERET SHELOMO, NITZAVIM, S.V. O YOMAR ATEM NITZAVIM
> HAYOM KULKHEM LIFNEI H'ELOHEIKHEM)

I have worked at developing my soul so that it can sing praises to God. I would like to think that I could make the whole of my life a song of praise to God. The psalm, especially as the text above understands it, comes at this from two directions. One is that we are to experience the vital force that sustains us, that moves in us, that expresses our being-aliveness, and then devote it to serving God. The other is that all that we have, and all that we are and do, should be devoted to the service of God. When we succeed in bringing these two approaches together, they play off of each other and harmonize with each other, helping us to sense that all of our being is unified and directed toward a higher purpose.

That has been my experience, supported by my practice of mindfulness. I have a fair amount of stamina—I don't seem to need a lot of sleep, and I can stay on my feet for a long time. I do not tire easily when hiking, and I can cook all day for a large party and still have energy to enjoy the event. But I know the difference between what it feels like to engage in any of these activities willingly and when I do them without wholehearted engagement. In the latter instance I feel empty and edgy, and I become less communicative. I am not fully present. On the other hand, when I am fully engaged, when my heart and body are in concert, I am full of energy, I feel at ease around other people, and I sense that all of my being is present. I find that music spontaneously rises in my head, in my heart, and in my spirit.

The practice of mindfulness is the habit of attempting to experience the whole truth of the moment, from moment to moment. That is, we open ourselves to discerning as much as possible what we are feeling—physically, emotionally, psychically, and spiritually. The more clearly we can see each of those realms and can identify how we feel, the more we are able to bring our whole being into concert. We will be more able to accomplish our intention, since the whole of our being will be directed toward its fulfillment. In addition, greater awareness of our inner states and physical status helps us to experience each moment more fully. Each moment can be complete in itself, since whatever we are doing will have integrity in itself.

The text above subtly hints at a deeper message. The author hears in these verses from Psalm 146 an echo of the first paragraph of the *Shema*. There, in response to our testifying to (and, we hope, experiencing) God's Oneness, we are enjoined to love God with all of our heart, with all of our soul, and with all of our might. These same elements are present here as well. We praise Adonai with our souls. We praise Adonai with our very beings *(me'odekha)*, with all we have and possess *(be'odi)*. Offering God our whole being can only be through song, as King David knew. The psalmist said, *"va'ani tefilati,"* I am my prayer (Psalm 69:14).

Boneh yerushalayim Adonai nidhei yisrael yekhannes. Harofeh lishevurei lev umehabesh l'atzvotam. Moneh mispar lakokhavim lekhulam shemot yikra. Gadol Adoneinu verav ko'ah litevunato ein mispar.

Yehallelu et shem Adonai ki hu tzivah venivra'u. Vaya'amidem la'ad le'olam hok natan velo ya'avor.

"Adonai rebuilds Jerusalem; He gathers in the exiles of Israel. He heals their broken hearts, and binds up their wounds. He reckoned the number of stars; to each one He gave its name. Great is Adonai and full of power; His wisdom is beyond reckoning" (Psalm 147:3–4).

"Let them praise the name of Adonai, for it was He who commanded that they be created. He made them endure forever, establishing an order that shall never change" (Psalm 148:5–6).

One of the habits of mind that blocks the experience of oneness with God is the habit of egocentricity, the habit of setting our personal concerns above those of others. It is this sort of habit that we can understand, metaphorically, as a husk that covers our hearts and souls, a shell that we would want to remove to truly serve God. Often our first response to the accidents of our lives is, "Why me?" That is, why did this happen to me? But, seemingly just as often we ask, "Why not me?" Why did this happen to someone else instead of me? We don't want the cancer, but we do want the surprise party. Then again, should our child or a loved one suffer an illness or struggle with a life crisis, we might indeed ask, "Why not me?" And should some windfall blessing come our way unexpectedly, we might respond, in surprise, "Why me?" In all of these cases, whether we are responding selfishly or generously, we are still situated in a world that revolves around ourselves. We are the center of concern—what happens to us, what we wish had happened to us, how we would like the world to work according to our wishes and desires.

The verses cited above help us to shift our perspective from our self-centered view to that of the infinite universe. God numbers the stars—all of them—and gives each one a name. Whenever I read this verse, "God numbers the stars," I am challenged to do the impossible. I sense that their number is infinite, and it is therefore impossible for me to count them. If I were to focus only on infinity beyond my comprehension, I might well feel powerless, anxious, desperate. I might, as I think we all might, fear that our lives are pointless, that there is nothing that we can do that will help us to feel better or that can improve our own lives, let alone the lives of others. Our anxiety over our own suffering—our question, "Why?"—causes even deeper distress.

I am consoled by the knowledge that, in fact, there is a finite number of stars, and God, indeed, can count them, noting each one individually. And I experience that that same attention is being given to me, to each of us. I sense that nothing, then, exists or happens outside of God's awareness, and this is reassuring. At the same time that all of the stars in their courses in the sky are known and counted, so, too, am I noted in the course of my life. The possibility that God knows us in some way, that we are a significant part of a larger whole, of a finite known Creation, is what heals our broken hearts.

The verses from Psalm 148 deepen this sense. The universe that is known by God is also one that is orderly; it follows God's commands. The nature of these commands is not that one person should succeed and another suffer. Rather, the law is that nothing happens without some connection to everything else. There is a relationship among the stars in the heavens, the people on earth, and all aspects of Creation above, below, and around them all. Nothing has happened since the beginning of time whose effect is not still felt today. Everything our ancestors did changed the world into which we were born. Jerusalem stood, and then was destroyed. We are the "exiles of Israel" because of our ancestors' actions. Over the generations, Jews have striven to live by Torah, to survive, to provide for their children, and to sustain the world. We may not yet have been gathered into Jerusalem, but we know that our legacy makes us responsible to help to make that happen in the future. Everything that we do will change the world in which we live, and which we will bequeath to our descendants. They, too, will be responsible for helping to rebuild Jerusalem.

The laws of cause and effect interpenetrate the whole of Creation, from the beginning of time to the end of time. All that we do and all that we refrain from doing, all that we embrace joyfully and all that we avoid in fear or frustration, all that we do intentionally and all that we do without paying attention—all of our lives contribute to the immense whole that is cosmic existence. It is immense, but it is not infinite. It is known by God and it is connected together; it is a whole that follows God's will. The more we embrace that perspective, the greater our solace, the deeper our joy. The author of *Tiferet Shelomo* weaves these themes together.

These passages from *Pesukei Dezimra* are for the sake of the holy sparks. That is, when they are released from the control of the husks, where they had been lost, they begin to praise and glorify God's great name. . . . In this psalm (147) they sing, "Halleluyah, it is good to chant hymns to our God, etc. Adonai builds Jerusalem; He gathers in the exiles of Israel." And we also read, "and the strayed who are in the land of Assyria and the expelled who are in the land of Egypt shall come and worship Adonai on the holy mount, Jerusalem" (Isaiah 27:13). In this we see that the meaning of the ingathering of the exiles is actually that of the holy sparks that are scattered about the world. When they are gathered, they are brought to the heavenly Jerusalem, which will exist on the day "when Adonai binds up His people's wounds and heals the injuries it has suffered" (Isaiah 30:26)—that is, at the time of the Messiah (may he come soon). Therefore, it says, "Halleluyah, it is good to chant hymns to our God; it is pleasant to sing glorious praise"—when is this true? When "Adonai rebuilds Jerusalem" by means of "gather(ing) in the exiles of Israel," that is, the holy sparks that have been scattered throughout Creation. This is what we read in the Talmud: "When will it be that 'Lord rebuilds Jerusalem'? At the time that 'He gathers in the exiles of Israel'" (Berakhot 49a). The ingathering of these exiles (that is, the scattered sparks) is the rebuilding of Jerusalem.

(Tiferet Shelomo, Rimzei Purim,
drush al kabbalat hatorah [end])

We see here that the ingathering of the divine sparks is a way of speaking about the messianic experience. We have a role to play in bringing that about: we are charged with identifying and raising up these sparks everywhere we are, whatever we are doing. They are present in every moment—in every being, in every thing, in every event—and they seem to be our contemporaries, existent only in this moment. These sparks, however, have existed in the cosmos since the first moments of existence. They were all present in the first emanation of divine light into Creation. Ultimately, each spark is part of the larger light of Creation, and in any one is the whole. There is no past or present for them, no here or there. Each spark that we identify and raise up is like another stone in the walls of the "rebuilt Jerusalem." Each one is a mini-redemption.

At the same time, we exist in time and space. We encounter the sparks one by one. The challenge for us is to learn to discern the larger whole, beyond each individual spark in each individual being or event. When we consider the seemingly infinite number of previous steps it took to bring us to this particular moment, to see and raise up this particular spark, we will begin to open to that larger perspective. The more we hold that view, the more each individual redemption becomes the actual ultimate redemption. That the world is not transformed by our deeds testifies to the complexity of the whole. We can only do our part. Our intentions and actions may influence all others in ways that we cannot perceive in the moment, which may then actually bring the Messiah. Or they may not. We cannot see the whole, and the complexity of the system approaches the infinite for us. But it is a whole, governed by a divine law, and whatever we do, we hasten or hinder that final redemption.

The more closely we pay attention to the fullest truth of each moment, the clearer it becomes that our sense of control over the course of our lives and the world around us is the height of haughtiness. How did we arrive at this moment? What other forces were at work to bring us here? How clearly can we discern the intentions or motivations of those around us, to know if they are truly supportive, antagonistic, or neutral toward us? How clearly can we perceive our own intentions or motivations, to know if we have acted purely for the good of all? How can we know what the outcome of our actions will be—ultimately? All of these questions arise when we seek to know the truth of our lives from a calm and balanced perspective. The answers to them tend to lead us to greater humility. We come to recognize that we cannot know anything ultimate —and we hardly know antecedents any better. What we are left with is "Who knows?" and "There is just this." The outcome of this awareness is an expanding commitment to do the best that we can in any given moment, acting with justice, compassion, and a deepening apprehension of our need for forgiveness. The product of this process, of a mindful life, can be solace, joy, and a sense that ultimately, redemption of all Creation is possible.

Kol haneshamah tehallel Yah, Halleluyah!

"Let all that breathes praise the Lord, Halleluyah" (Psalm 150:6).

With these words we conclude the central, primary portion of *Pesukei Dezimra.* They are, as well, the last words of the Book of Psalms: a double summation, a double conclusion. In both cases, the intention is that this last line should communicate completeness. Everything that has preceded it, all aspects of Creation that had sung praises of God in the Book of Psalms, and all the words and intentions of the worshiper during *Pesukei Dezimra,* should join together in one rousing acclamation of God. "Let all that breathes praise Adonai." All the breath that had been used in praise thus far, and all the rest that may come, shall yet be devoted to the service of God. "Rabbi Levi said in the name of Rabbi Ḥanina: With each and every breath (*neshimah uneshimah*) that one breathes (*noshem*), one is obliged to praise the Creator. What is the scriptural support? 'Let all that breathes praise Adonai,' let each and every breath praise Adonai" (Genesis Rabbah 14:9).

In mindfulness meditation, a common starting point is attention to the breath. Both as a means of quieting the mind, as well as a phenomenon from which it is possible to learn important truths of life, the breath offers an easy and easily accessible point of focus. An early lesson from this practice is that just as the breath rises and passes away, so do all things. From the breath it is possible to learn how transitory all things—physical, emotional, psychological—actually are. In addition, we can learn how much we depend on in life without being actively aware of our dependence. That is, from our first breath at birth (unless our respiration has been compromised by illness) we have not thought about breathing. It just happens. Our autonomic nervous system takes care of that—just as it does our heartbeat, our digestion, and the release of the myriad hormones and chemicals that control our growth, our emotions, and so on. It is almost completely out of our control. Beyond that, we are sustained by the atmosphere that is shared by all people on earth, by the cycles of the oceans, and by the workings of the weather. The rotation of the earth on its axis and the revolution of the earth around the sun also happen without our intervention, without our even thinking about them—yet our lives depend on them. Watching our breath, we can easily learn gratitude.

The following text invites us to sense an even deeper gratitude, and in turn to offer our praises to God.

> We must always try to raise our thoughts upward (toward the spiritual), since from moment to moment the Blessed Creator, in great love and mercy, instills in us new vital force; from moment to moment the Blessed Creator renews our very beings. This is what the rabbis meant when they said, "Let each and every breath praise Adonai." That is, at each moment the breath seeks to leave us, and the Holy One, in great mercy, watches over us from moment to moment and has compassion for us, and does not let the breath depart. In this manner, when we raise up our thoughts, from

moment to moment we are actually created anew as new creatures. This generates a sense of enthusiasm in the service of the Blessed Creator, since everything that is new or renewed burns more powerfully. And, since we are created anew from moment to moment, we can burn with that same enthusiasm in the service of the Holy Creator.

(Kedushat Levi, Rosh Hashanah,
inyan perishah lekhohen gadol)

It seems to me that this passage turns the teaching from the Talmud on its head. That is, the implication in the Talmud is that every breath we take is a gift of the Creator. In response, that same breath, when exhaled, should become a praise of God. Here, instead, the breath that leaves the body could possibly be the last one—the breath is always seeking to leave us. That it does not, that we do not die at each exhalation, is cause for us to glorify and thank God.

The teaching from the Talmud makes sense intuitively. That is, we are formed in such a manner that we produce sound—the way we express our prayers of thanksgiving—when we exhale. Thus, "'Let all that breathes praise Adonai,' let each and every breath praise Adonai" by making sound. But, Levi Yitzḥak comes at it from another point of view. That which we breathe in is the breath of God, the renewed and renewing initial lungful of air that brought life to the first human being, and that we took at birth. With every inhalation we are brought back to life by the pure, holy breath of God. But, that breath does not remain with us. We do not own it. Perhaps, it is even foreign to us, and so it seeks to depart. It is only God's ongoing intervention, creating us anew with each inhalation, that keeps us alive. When we use that out-breath to voice blessings and praise of God, we also raise up what otherwise might be a source of suffering or evil.

When we pay attention to our breath, noticing its mechanics, sensing each element of the process of respiration, we come to appreciate Levi Yitzḥak 's teaching. That is, we tend to think that we breathe in, that it is our efforts that claim a lungful of air for ourselves. This is consonant with our tendency toward a self-centered worldview. We assert our power over the world; we take possession of the air; we breathe in what we need. The mechanics of breathing, however, suggest something quite different. Our inhalation begins when we contract our diaphragms. As this muscle moves, it "opens up" the chest cavity, creating negative pressure. Air enters our lungs not so much because we "pull" it in, but because it is forced in by the greater air pressure on the outside. When our diaphragms relax, the force of the outer air pressure forces our chest cavities to return to their natural, resting states. Air is forced out of our lungs, returning them to a state of equilibrium—a balanced state of air pressure inside and out. The natural state of our lungs is to be in balance with the outside air pressure. We breathe because air is first forced into our lungs, and then excess air rushes out, allowing the lungs to return to their natural resting state.

We do not breathe; we are breathed. Our egos lead us to think that we are in control, that we make breath happen—and that is true to the extent that our diaphragms contract. But we do not pull breath into our lungs, asserting our control over the world and claiming air for ourselves. We are blessed with air being forced into our lungs, and our lives are renewed over and over. Just as this is true for our breath, we learn that it is also thus with much of the rest of our lives. Our lives, on their most basic level, simply happen—and they happen without our direct control or manipulation. We may control our immediate surroundings, but so much of what happens around us is the result of myriad interactions among countless myriad people, animals, the inanimate world, and forces beyond our control. There is no malevolence directed at us in these interactions; they simply are. What happens just happens.

Thus, just as "with each and every breath that we breathe, we are obliged to praise the Creator," so, too, must we thank God for each and every instant of our lives. Each breath is given to us new, and we are made new. Each moment is given to us new, and we can become new in it. There is nothing more glorious, more miraculous, or more wondrous than that. Halleluyah!

From the passages that we have presented above, we can see how the prayers and psalms of *Pesukei Dezimra* can serve us in the process of dispelling confusion (pruning away the husks) that keeps us separate from the Holy One. Over and over they challenge our egos, our sense of being separate selves. They remind us that our ambitions and accomplishments are passing phenomena, empty of significance before, and outside of, the infinite and eternal God. We are God's, not the other way around, and all that happens to us happens within the totality of God's Being. We sense an orderliness, a law that shall never be changed. We are bound together with all other beings. What happens to us also happens to them, and what they do impacts on us. We cannot escape our creatureliness, our being bound up in the bond of all life. Our breaths, our lives, our very beings belong to God. As these words and ideas make their way into our hearts and we feel them and come to know them deeply, we experience the truth of our identity within God. Our hearts open and we become ready to recite the *Shema,* to bind ourselves to God, to celebrate that oneness.

The Recitation of the *Shema*

The section of the service that centers on the *Shema* is built to reinforce the intention to experience the sense of oneness with God. The *Shema* itself is framed by two descriptions of worship experiences in which the participants witness God's dramatic appearance in their lives. The first describes the collective, interactive song of the ministering angels in response to Creation renewed. Each day God revives the world, creating it anew. For this beneficence and gracious goodness the angels sing out their lives. The second scene is that of the redeemed Israelites at the shores of the Reed Sea. They had witnessed miracles in Egypt, but now have seen the ultimate divine intervention: the Sea opened to let them pass to safety and closed over their enemies. In response they sing praises.

The unfolding of Creation, as laid out in the siddur, starts with the appearance of light—both the light of the first day of Creation, but more significantly, the dawning of the great luminary, our sun. The return of the sun to the heavens each morning is viewed, and experienced, as an act of God's goodness, evidence of God's work in renewing Creation each day. Following hard on the heels of the sun, however, is the appearance of the rest of the physical world—including the ministering angels. All of them are God's creations, and all sing praises of thanks to Adonai. The uniform gratitude of all Creation for God's goodness is first hinted at in a brief alphabetical acrostic, *El barukh gedol de'ah:* "The blessed God of vast understanding prepared and created the radiant sun, forming this good light and all others as a glorious tribute ranged round His mighty throne. His distant holy hosts, those who exalt the Almighty always . . ." The use of the alphabet suggests a wholeness found both in Creation (as we have seen before, the letters of the words of Creation are still present in all things) and also in the fullness of the praise that the sun, the other luminaries, and the ministering angels sing to God. This is experienced even more powerfully when we notice that the poem itself does not speak the words of their praise, but rather sets up that next move. The poem ends with the words *"romemei shaddai tamid*—those who exalt the Almighty always." Always what? *"mesapperim kevod el ukedushato*—they tell of God's glory and holiness." Everything points to and leads to praise of God, with a common intent, with a singular purpose.

Rabbinic texts (and the siddur is a prime example of one) are fairly precise in their language. It is noteworthy that this poem ends with the word *tamid,* "always." While the sense of God's eternity, and of the continuing, ongoing response of Creation in praise, fills this part of the prayer service, the word *tamid* appears only three times. One is at the conclusion of our poem. The other is in a phrase that appears at the beginning and end of this first section preceding the *Shema: "uvtuvo mehadesh/hamehadesh betuvo bekhol yom tamid ma'aseh bereshit*—in goodness each day He renews the acts of Creation *always.*" God's daily, and eternal, expression of goodwill and blessing—the renewal of Creation—is echoed eternally by the song of thanks of the celestial bodies.

Further, this poem allows the siddur to move from concern with the celestial lights to ministering angels in particular. Following the above passage, we read of the angels, "Your servants all stand at the heights of the universe and give voice **together** (*yahad*) in reverence the words of the living God, eternal Sovereign." There is a unity of purpose among the divine servants: to sing praises to God. In reverence and love they actively, intentionally, and willingly fulfill the divine will. "They all take on themselves the yoke of divine service one from the other, and in turn, in love, grant permission to one another to sanctify their Creator" until "they all **as one** respond and sing forth: 'Holy, holy, holy is Adonai of Hosts; the whole of Creation is filled with His glory.'" This call of praise elicits an echo among other classes of ministering angels, and they, too, offer an equal and wholehearted response: "Equivalent to them they give praise saying: 'Blessed be the glory of Adonai from His place.'"

There is a long and complex history to this sort of description of the heavenly realms. What is important for us is the way in which the ministering angels, as well as all of Creation, join together with singularity of purpose and will to worship the Creator. As we read through this section of the morning service, envisioning the world slowly coming into view in the growing sunlight as a new Creation, accompanied by these heavenly choirs united in purpose, we are inspired as well. I recall an overnight outing at camp years ago. I stayed up all night, first watching the embers of the fire in the darkness. Then I became aware of the stirring of the world around me. Birds and animals began to move and make sounds. Slowly the sky lightened without any clear source. Except for my immediate surroundings I could perceive nothing of the world around me. The sky lightened, yet everything remained unclear, shrouded in the mist of morning. Over the lake the mist hovered and shifted, revealing the smooth surface here and there, now and again. As it slowly lifted, I could see the shoreline, and in turn, the trees at the edge were revealed to me. As sunrise approached, the sounds of the animals became more distinct, more profound. The sun's rays finally broke over the horizon and my companions stirred and came to life. In that short period I experienced the whole of the process of Creation. I saw how, indeed, in His goodness, God renews Creation every day.

My eyes were opened to the wonder of the morning, witnessing the return of the physical world to my perception and grateful to find myself in it, prepared to work in it another day. My thoughts went to the unselfishness of the angels and their joyful acceptance of their roles and their equally joyful invitation to others to join in praise of God. It is inspiring to think that we, too, can live that way. The attitude that will support such behavior is to "love and revere" the Holy One. It is engendered when we realize, in the words concluding this section preceding the *Shema,* that "God is unique—doing mighty deeds, creating new life, championing justice, sowing righteousness, reaping victory, bringing healing, awesome in praise, sovereign in wonders."

We read in the section immediately preceding the *Shema:* "Bring light to our eyes through Your Torah, cause our heart to cleave to Your commandments, and help us to unify our heart in love and reverence for Your Name." We want to be one with God; we want our intention to be God's intention. The study of Torah may reveal the light of God's presence in all things to our eyes. We may come, in this manner, to see the world differently—to remember in every instance that there is no place devoid of God. There is no event, no circumstance in which God cannot be found. Our hearts will thus be prepared to cleave to God. We will notice how, in everything that we do—particularly those acts that are *mitzvot*—God is present. There is a classical hasidic pun on the word *mitzvah:* it is connected to the word *tzavta,* "to be connected, attached; to be in community." To perform the *mitzvot* is to connect ourselves with the Holy One, to deepen our sense of partnership, of companionship. Thus, study of Torah, and the enlightenment that may come with it, helps us cleave to God, to sense a connection.

"Help us to unify our heart to love and revere Your Name." Why do we need our hearts to be made one? How will that deepen further the unity of purpose that comes through the study of Torah and observance of the commandments? The word for "heart" in this phrase is *levav* (as contrasted with the more common word *lev*). This form of the noun repeats the letter *vet,* leading to the following talmudic teaching: "'Love Adonai your God with all of your heart' (Deuteronomy 6:5, the second verse of the *Shema;* again the word for "heart" is *levav*)—with your two inclinations: your inclination for good and your inclination for bad" (Berakhot 54a). That is, this form of "heart," *levav,* suggests that our hearts are often divided. Our attention is scattered, our intention unclear. Our inclination for good is in tension with our frequent blindness to avarice or anxiety, and we swing between them. Our prayer here is that from the study of Torah and through companionship with God in the performance of *mitzvot* we might find balance, as well as unity of purpose, in our love and reverence for God. Our desire to do good flows not only out of love of God, but also out of awe for God's greatness and generous graciousness to us. We might avoid transgression and iniquity out of fear of God's response, but we will be more resolute in our intention when it is grounded in awareness of contrition in the face of God's great love for us.

These two sections preceding the *Shema* rely on the nakedness of our hearts, the depth of our mindfulness, to move us toward oneness with God. Over and over, in diverse images and powerful reminders, the paragraphs preceding the *Shema* move us toward an openness and a desire to join in with those around us—the ministering angels, the celestial bodies, all of Creation, our fellow worshipers—in a unison praise of God. The experience of oneness with all of Creation is the stepping-stone to unity with God. We are prepared in this way to proclaim God's uniqueness and unity in the *Shema*. We know that God is one, that all of Creation is one, and we are also part of that oneness. We cry out *"eḥad,"* we are one with God who is One, Alone, and there is nothing else.

It is hard to hold onto this awareness. As much as we delight in clear vision, in balanced, awakened attention to the truth of the moment, our minds tend to wander. This is a great challenge. It is what undermines our attempts at *deveikut,* deep consciousness of our attachment to the Holy One. It is what distracts us from remembering the ultimate unity of all things. Almost as a response to this reality we find that the second paragraph of the *Shema*

(Deuteronomy 11:13–21) brings a reminder, a message to aid us in holding ourselves in the One. The following teaching from the *Me'or Einayim* echoes one we met previously.

> A saying of the Baal Shem Tov (may his soul rest in celestial repose and may his merit protect us) was based on the verse, "lest you turn away (from God) and worship other gods" (Deuteronomy 11:16). That is, at the moment that you allow your awareness to wander from the Holy One, immediately it will be as if you are worshiping other gods. This is the ultimate goal of understanding: to know that all of your powers and your very essence are from the Holy Creator—that He is the power, the capacity, and the force in all things, that He makes all things move, even you. When you let your mind wander from this thought, you become like an idolater, worshiping forces other than the Holy One, since you no longer hold fast to the thought that all of your power and essence are from the Holy One.
>
> (ME'OR EINAYIM, SHEMOT,
> S.V. AKH DENODA SOD GALUT MITZRAYIM)

This text reminds us that in the midst of our inner experience of unity with God, we are constantly at risk of leaving that awareness. As much as attaining that state is the product of mindfulness practice, we also depend on that practice to help us sustain our attachment to God in the moment. Over and over as we practice, we look carefully to see what is happening, what our inner state is, what our physical state is, what prompts distracting or discursive thoughts. Out of that experience we are able to bring ourselves back to full awareness of the truth of the moment. We can then act to sustain our concentration, bringing our attention back to the moment—to sensing our oneness with God.

The process of preparing for and attaining some sense of unity with God is still not the final step in the work of divine service. Removing the husks—opening our eyes and hearts to a fuller awareness of our lives—helps us to strip away the barriers that separate us from God. In preparing for and reciting the *Shema* we experience our true oneness with God. Our interest, however, is not in that experience itself, in simply satisfying our personal desire to unite with God and be embraced in the oneness of all existence. Rather, it is to help us become proper vessels through which divine blessings can flow to all Creation. It is for that reason that the text of the siddur moves us out again from our inner experiences to connect with the world—further deepening our understanding of what it means to enter into unity with God.

The third paragraph of the *Shema* (Numbers 15:37–41) was included by the rabbis not only because it mentions the practice of wearing *tzitzit,* but also because it refers to the Exodus from Egypt. That event is the paradigm for all redemptions. It is the reminder of God's concern for the physical and emotional lives of all beings, as well as their spiritual experiences. The reference to the Exodus in this passage also leads us toward a deeper sense of oneness with God, one that may open our inner gates further to the flow of divine blessing. The Exodus, and particularly the crossing of the Reed Sea, was a moment not only of miraculous acts by God, but also of a prophetic revelation of God to all of Israel.

> Rabbi Yishmael asked, "How do we know that even a handmaid saw more at the shore of the Sea than even Ezekiel and all the rest of the prophets, of whom it was said, 'I appeared to the prophets' (Hosea 12:11) and 'I saw the appearance of God' (Ezekiel 1:1)?" . . . [The people sang,] "This is my God and I will exalt Him" (Exodus 15:2).
>
> (Mekhilta, Shira 3, Horowitz, pp. 126–127)

At that moment, not only did the people see God's power, but they actually saw God and were able to point and say, "This is my God!" It is that immediacy of experience toward which the prayer following the *Shema* moves us:

> God's words live and abide, they are faithful and pleasant through-out all time. For our ancestors and us, for our children and all generations past and future of the seed of Jacob, they are good and true, faithful and never disappoint, a law that never fails. It is true that You are Adonai our God, even as You were the God of our ancestors.

We hear echoes of the psalms, of the intricate, seemingly infinite way that all beings affect one another, all within God, all expressing God's intent. Our salvation at the Sea was a moment in which that larger intent was revealed, and which stands for us as a model to which we can return over and over again, as reminder and source of inspiration.

The siddur leads us to that moment just before the recitation of the *Amidah*.

> For all this, Your beloved sang praises and exaltations to You, Your dear ones offered psalms and songs, hymns and exaltations, bless-ings and thanksgivings to the Ever-living Sovereign. . . . Moses and the Children of Israel joyfully sang this song to You.

In response to the miracle at the Sea, the people responded in song. Their "psalms of adoration" echo other songs we heard earlier in the morning service, those of the ministering angels. The repeated acclamation of God's praiseworthiness and supremacy over all things and beings in this passage reiterates the lesson of the celestial beings. Not only do the content and form of praise repeat here, but so does the manner in which it is sung:

> The redeemed sang a new song to You on the shore of the Sea. **Together** (*yaḥad*) they all acknowledged You and proclaimed You Ruler: "Adonai will reign for ever and ever" (Exodus 15:18).

True songs of praise and acknowledgement of God's sovereignty can only be sung in community, when the participants experience a full oneness with each other. Only then are they able to sense oneness with God.

The Amidah

With this, the siddur moves us from our personal sense of unity with God, developed in response to the unison chorus of celestial beings, to a oneness that flows from our connection to and communion with our fellow worshipers. Had we remained in our private reverie, focused on the ministering angels and the divine realm, we might have attained a sense of oneness with God, but it would not have been complete. We need to expand our field of attention to include all of those around us. The poetic image of divine beings engages me, and it may even generate a sense of "love and reverence for God." But I am even more inspired when I can see God through God's work in the world, for our ancestors and for us, for all beings. That is when I sense that my union with God is whole. Only then am I able to remove the last threads of ego and self-service, truly becoming a vessel prepared to receive the divine flow, to be a conduit for divine blessing.

The pure openness, selflessness, and awareness of God that we attain in this manner prepare us to recite the *Amidah*. It is traditional to recite the verse "Adonai, open my lips and my mouth will tell your praise" (Psalm 51:17) immediately preceding the start of this prayer. It is a fitting sentiment, an expression of our intention to pray, and of our awareness of our dependence on God to do anything, even to pray. The hasidic tradition took this one step further:

> When a person begins to pray, immediately upon saying the words, "Adonai, open my lips," the *Shekhinah* clothes Herself in him and speaks through him. In addition, when he fully believes that She is speaking these words, then certainly fear and reverence will flow over him, and even the Holy One, as it were, will contract Himself to dwell in him.
>
> (Maggid Devarav Leyaakov,
> Likkutei Amarim, No. 3)

This teaching suggests that when we are truly open and one with God, our prayers actually become God's prayers. We do not only say, "God, if You open my lips then I will praise You." Rather, we now declare, "God, I give myself over to You. Open my lips and let Your words become Your praise." This teaching reinforces the degree to which this process demands that we relinquish our personal concerns and our ego expectations. Our prayer is not ours to give. Rather, it is an expression of the universal divine speech, the ever-flowing voice of the Holy One.

The wakeful attention established in our hearts when reciting *Pesukei Dezimra* helps to remove the barriers of confusion that separate us from God. When we enter into an awareness of our deep unity with God, when we experience fully the oneness of all Creation in God, we are prepared truly to pray. Our prayers will no longer be our own private affairs, our personal concerns alone. Rather, we will find a voice that echoes the will of God, that expresses something much closer to the intent of the divine heart.

God's words will flow through us and become our prayers. As the Maggid of Mezritch teaches:

> If your prayer becomes pure and transparent, then certainly the holy breath that leaves your mouth will cleave to and be bound up with the supernal breath, that which is always connected, which flows unceasingly into you. This is what the rabbis meant when they taught regarding the verse "Let all that breathes praise Adonai": "with each and every breath *(neshimah uneshimah)* that one breathes *(noshem)*" (Genesis Rabbah 14:10). Each and every breath that leaves you rises from lower to higher realms, and then returns from higher to lower. When you enter into that process fully, then certainly it will be easier to connect the divine portion in you to its source in the Holy One.
>
> (LIKKUTIM YEKARIM, NO. 136)

I sense that the flow of breath in and out, particularly when I use that breath in prayer, connects me directly to the Holy One. Our breath is God's breath; God's breath is our breath. There is no distinction in the moment of true connection. Our being is fully tied to God's being and our intention follows God's intention.

It is in this sense that the opening blessings of the *Amidah* serve as praises of God (and as an introduction to "asking for our own needs"). They are filled with descriptions of God's merciful, compassionate, and righteous dealings with our ancestors and with us. God acted lovingly for the Patriarchs (and Matriarchs) and so, also, will bring redemption to us, their descendants. The mercy that flows from the divine source is sometimes constricted, hidden from us. But it is always there, and when it appears, when we experience the renewal of our vigor or awareness, it is as if we have been revived, brought back from the dead. In this moment of openness and awareness of God's oneness, we sense ourselves made new and we experience true living.

For this reason, the tradition has expanded the third blessing of the *Amidah,* the *Kedushah,* when it is recited in public. Here we once again turn to the scene of celestial beings praising God. The oneness of purpose that we witnessed among them (in the section preceding the *Shema*) turned our hearts to seek oneness with God. That, in turn, moved us closer to our fellows, to share with them a transforming moment of divine revelation. Together we saw God at the Sea, and as one acclaimed God Sovereign of the Universe. Now it is as if we have actually become the celestial beings. "We sanctify Your name on earth as it is proclaimed Holy in the highest heavens. As recorded by Your prophet: The angels call one to another: 'Holy, holy, holy. *Adonai Tzeva'ot,* the whole earth is filled with His glory.'" This prayer puts the words of the angels in our own mouths, such that our voices become the angelic choir. Our prayers and praises are as pure, as willing, as unself-conscious, and as unselfish as theirs. Again we demonstrate that our will has become God's will, our intention to do only that which is in consonance with the divine law of Creation.

This level of devotion inspires further aid from God. The more complete we are with the divine, the clearer our vision of the intricate connection between all things and actions, the deeper will be our awareness of what is necessary to bring about the reunion of the *Shekhinah* and the Holy One. This, in turn, inspires us to greater devotion, to serving God with one heart and mind, as the following text suggests.

> The essential element in fully accepting the Torah and the *mitzvot* is committed devotion to sanctifying the divine Name, as the rabbis taught regarding the verse, "[You shall not profane My holy name] that I may be sanctified in the midst of the Israelite people—I am Adonai who sanctifies you" (Leviticus 22:32). That is,

first one must take upon himself the yoke of divine service and complete devotion to God's service, and only then will holiness descend on the Jewish people, which is the import of "I am Adonai who sanctifies you" (cf. Sifra, Emor 9:4). It is for that reason that first we recite the *Kedushah*, declaring God holy, and only then the following blessings: "You graciously endow mortals with understanding" and "Return us, our Father, to Your Torah."

(Tiferet Shelomo, Mo'adim, Shavuot,
s.v. le'olam lo eshkaḥ pekudekha ki vam ḥayyenu)

As I understand this text, it outlines a clear process. First we declare God's holiness, taking upon ourselves the commitment to divine service. Only then will we have created the conditions in which God can be sanctified in the world, in which God can do that which will reveal His holiness in the world. Even the exalted state of reciting the *Kedushah* and sensing a deep connection and attachment to God is not the final step of our prayer. Rather, the *Kedushah* enables us to discern what we still need to do to make our service more whole, our behavior more consonant with the divine will. This focus allows us to begin to supplicate God, to ask for help for all Israel.

It is for this reason that the first of the intermediate petitionary prayers begins not with a request, but with a statement: "You graciously endow mortals with understanding, teaching humans wisdom." We acknowledge that our capacity to clarify our awareness of the truth, to reach toward divine understanding, comes from God. And, still, it is not on the basis of our merits or accomplishments that we receive this help. Rather we rely on God's graciousness, so that we might further remove the habits that cloud our minds and lead us to act thoughtlessly toward others and ourselves. Thus, out of deep awareness of our human limits relative to God's infinite nature, we then ask for help in changing ourselves: "Return us, our Father, to Your Torah, and draw us near, our Sovereign, to Your service, and turn us fully toward You in repentance *(teshuvah)* and wholeness." The result of this movement—return, drawing near, and turning—is that we become more deeply aware of our need for forgiveness, from God and from others. Naturally, then, in the third intermediate blessing we recite, "Forgive us, our Father, for we have sinned; pardon us, our King, for we have transgressed."

In this manner, the movement of the recitation of the *Amidah* follows that of mindfulness practice. That is, just as there is no moment in prayer in which one has "made it," gotten to the end of a process, knowing all, so too with mindfulness. We pay attention from moment to moment. Our capacity to attend to the truth of the moment may deepen, we may be able to see more clearly the insubstantiality of being and lose our sense of ego, but all things change. And we will need to attend with equal dedication to the next moment and the next with all that they bring. Further, as we see more clearly how our attachment to our personal story causes us suffering—begrudging loss, fearing change—we have compassion for ourselves, and then for others. Out of our awareness, we open our hearts toward them. We seek to do all we can to ease their suffering, to offer them compassion, to do righteousness and justice. Further, we see with greater clarity how we must change, to seek amends with those we have harmed. Awareness, transformation, and atonement—the same movement that marks the opening of our prayers of petition—signal a balanced and attentive mind. The experience of this balance is liberation, freedom from habit, and ease of action.

One of the consequences of approaching God in prayer, in seeking to come close to God's awareness of the ultimate nature of the universe, in awakening our attention to its widest potential awareness, is that we come to realize that there is no way that we can know the final consequence of any of our actions. We may expand our horizons, include more people and other factors in our assessment of the situation, and deepen our intention to do the best possible for all concerned. Nevertheless, the permutations of connections and interactions beyond our vision and ken are too great for us to analyze them all. Thus, we ask in the prayer announcing the coming of the New Month that God "fulfill all the wishes of our hearts for good," since we cannot know if what we pray for is truly for the good of all.

The tenth of the intermediate petitions is our response to this truth:

> Let Your tender mercies, Adonai our God, be stirred for the right-eous, the pious, the elders of the House of Israel and its remaining scholars, for faithful proselytes, and for us. Reward all who fully trust in You, and cast our lot with them. May we never despair, for our trust is in You.

We appeal to God to include us among all those whom we deem deserving of God's mercy—those whose devotion to God seems deeper than ours, even if it appears so only to us. That is fine, since our actions for good affect other people, and that merit can be shared and extended to others. But we do not stop there. We realize that our capacity to truly evaluate what constitutes full and holy devotion to God may be flawed. We recognize that what is apparent to our eyes may not reflect what is happening below the surface, and those whom we consider pious and worthy may be struggling with sin and failure just as we are. So we continue, stepping beyond the traditional categories of piety, asking that God's full attention be turned toward those who fully trust in Him. Further, we ask that we be included in that group.

In this we confess our true intention. It is not to be righteous or pious or an elder per se, but rather that we be counted among those who fully trust in God. Those who trust in God, who acknowledge that only God can know the full truth of any act, interaction, or event, do not despair of their own finitude and ignorance. Rather, having extended themselves in prayer, in mindful attention to the moment, they attain a sense of acceptance. What is true in this moment could not be other than what it is, since it is the complete, absolute, and truthful culmination of all acts, interactions, and events preceding that instant. We may accept the perfection of this moment, that it could not be otherwise—even when it is disappointing or unfulfilled. Still, as a consequence of our actions and of those who devote themselves to trusting service of God, we may also look forward to a change that will bring even more peace, compassion, and justice to all beings.

And so, as the blessings continue, we may pray for the rebuilding of Jerusalem and the time of the Messiah. Our intention is to turn our hearts and devote our spirits to serving God in truth and to trusting in God's truth. We have faith that the ultimate outcome will be peace for all beings, justice for all humankind. That, too, is God's prayer. The Talmud offers this as a version of God's own prayer: "May it be My will that My mercy may suppress My anger, and that My mercy may prevail over My [other] attributes, so that I may deal with My children with the attribute of mercy and, on their behalf, stop short of the limit of strict justice" (Berakhot 7a). Inasmuch as that is God's prayer, it is only fitting that our concluding petition be that God hear our prayers.

> Hear our voice, Adonai our God. Have compassion upon us; pity us. Accept our prayer with loving favor. You listen to entreaty and prayer. Do not turn us away unanswered, our Sovereign, for You mercifully hear the prayer of all mouths. Praised are You, Adonai, who listens to prayer.

We do not ask that our prayers be answered or fulfilled in their particular detail. Rather, we plead that God hear our prayers: Accept the offerings of our mouths, hold them in the fullness of Your knowledge, and let the outcome of all prayer be compassion, mercy, and goodness. In our petitions we hold fast, as best we can, to the infinite understanding and awareness of God. We do not pray for ourselves alone, but rather we pray for the good of all humankind, of all Creation. The oneness that we experience in our moment of prayer is the oneness that we desire for all beings; for the *Shekhinah* and the Holy One.

As the *Amidah* moves toward its conclusion, these themes are sustained in praise of God. We ask first that God accept our prayers—not answer them, but hold them, receive them, acknowledge their source in our intention to sanctify God's Name. We then acknowledge and thank God for "our lives that are in Your hand, for our souls that are in Your charge, for Your miracles that daily attend us, for Your wonders and gifts that accompany us, evening, morning, and noon." Again, nothing is outside of God's awareness. Fully attentive prayer awakens us to the awareness of those miracles, so that we can rejoice in them. Secure, for the moment, in that trust, filled with awe and joy in the sense of participation in the oneness of God and the whole of Creation, we can offer nothing but our hope and desire that we will witness—contribute to and participate in—a time of peace for all people.

It may not be possible, or proper, for one to pray formal prayers all day. Still, participating in the formal prayer service opens up the possibility that we might maintain a prayerful attitude throughout the day. Having given attention to removing the husks, the confusion, that separate us from God, we can strive during the day to prevent others from growing over our hearts, from thickening and closing us off from God. We can preserve an awareness of the experience of oneness with God, of the shift in our awareness and perspective from this encounter. The presence of that spirit in our hearts will be manifest in our interactions with others. We will be transformed, and from our actions they may be as well.

So, too, with mindfulness. We cannot sit in meditation all day. Yet, having taken some time to pay close attention to the truth of the moment, to learn to see clearly how our egos separate us from our own best interests, from other people, and from a sense of belonging to the whole of Creation, we are able to bring that habit of attentiveness into our daily interactions. We will be more adept at catching ourselves in moments of fear, selfishness, jealousy, pique. We will be able to look past those feelings to discern what is really true, to offer ourselves, and others, compassion and love. We will be transformed, and from our actions they may be as well.

Opening to God lifts our hearts, opens our eyes, and brings us to share in God's concern for the whole of Creation. Our prayers for peace reflect our commitment to devoted service of God and our intention to live mindful of the truth, committed to treating all people with compassion, justice, and peace. Our prayers, even when phrased as petition, do not seek to change the order of nature. Electric train sets, healing from disease, prosperity, and wholeheartedness are not given to us; we have to attain them. When we turn in prayer to God we locate ourselves in the grand unity that is God's being, that is the whole of the cosmos. We place our lives in the web of interconnection that is the whole of the unfolding of Creation. We confess the truth of our lives. Held in God's awareness and secure in that clear knowledge we find solace, hope, and joy.

Chapter Seven

Mindfulness and Jewish Holidays

As we seek to become increasingly aware from moment to moment of the truth of our experience, we find that we can wake up in any circumstance. We can pay close attention to one phenomenon—our breath—or to one activity—prayer. Those moments of focused concentration can create circumstances in which our hearts and minds open up to an awareness that embraces the whole of the cosmos. From our private, inner attention, we can move outward to connect in a deeper, more heartfelt manner with our families, our communities, and all of Creation. This sort of focused attention is best sustained in an ongoing format, and this practice constitutes a spiritual discipline. The ritual of daily prayer, like daily meditation, creates a context in which we can practice paying attention.

Sometimes, however, we can hold our attention in too tight a focus. While it is possible to become aware of and open to all of Creation in a single breath, it is also appropriate, even necessary, to open our hearts and minds to the vast openness of the cosmos to remind us that our personal spiritual quest is only that—one person's striving. For our hearts to be balanced, we need to balance our awareness as well, bringing our personal lives, our daily affairs, into a fuller relationship with the interconnected web of all existence. While the ritual of daily prayer provides a practice of intimate focus, the yearly cycle of the holidays opens up our awareness to the larger systems and communities in which we live. As we move through the year, we have to lift our eyes from the day before us to see what is approaching. We are invited, at times commanded, to prepare for each holiday as it draws near. The unique rituals of each holiday— whether home- or synagogue-based, whether liturgical or culinary— demand that we pay attention ahead of time to what the holiday will bring. This practice helps us to broaden our perspective and keep our minds and hearts open and receptive.

Moreover, the holidays carry their own messages, and they insert their particular concerns and values into our individual lives. We are challenged to think through, to experience that which the holidays bring. In that way, we are offered new opportunities to examine our lives, to see what is true, to experience more deeply how connected we are to others—and also remind ourselves how easily we lose sight of that when our vision is clouded with pain, fear, self-satisfaction, or fatigue. The holidays break our routine to open us up again, to wake us up in our lives. In this chapter we will examine a number of the cyclical holy days (Passover, Shabbat, the High Holy Days of Rosh Hashanah and Yom Kippur, Purim, and Tu B'Shevat) as examples of how the holidays broaden our perspective and keep our hearts, minds, and eyes open to the truth of our lives.

Passover

Passover, celebrating the Exodus from Egyptian slavery by our ancestors in antiquity, plays a central role in Jewish religious thought and practice. It testifies to God's direct interest and involvement in the world. It serves as the model for fundamental social values: recognition of human dignity, responsibility for the powerless, humility, the importance of both freedom from oppression and freedom of choice, the significance of work and rest to human expression, the insidious danger of worship of false gods. In the Jewish mystical tradition it gained another aspect: Passover marked the process by which—and serves as the model for which—awareness and God-consciousness can be liberated from servitude to selfishness, blindness, and ignorance. Consider this passage from the *Me'or Einayim*:

> It is well known that the mystery of the Exodus is that consciousness was in exile and contracted. No one knew how to serve God with joy and an expansive mind, which is the fullest consciousness. This is taught in the verse: "Know the God of your father [and serve Him with single mind and fervent heart, for Adonai searches all minds and discerns the design of every thought; if you seek Him He will be available to you]" (I Chonicles 28:9). Further, it is known that knowledge implies union and delight, as it says, "And Adam knew [his wife]" (Genesis 4:25).
>
> But, in the Egyptian exile, the peoples' consciousness was constrained, which is like *metzar yam*, the narrow sea. For the stream of awareness that flows from the sea of wisdom was constricted and diminished, and they had not yet achieved an expansive consciousness. But, with *Yetziat Mitzrayim* (the Exodus from Egypt), when they came out of *metzar yam* (the narrow sea), consciousness of God grew and expanded. The verse says, "And he (Israel) knew God" (Exodus 2:25), meaning that God-consciousness increased. Further it says, "You continued to grow and expand" (Ezekiel 16:7), meaning that Israel's awareness and consciousness continued to expand and grow, so that they could serve the Holy Creator with the pure, effulgent joy of delight in performing a *mitzvah* and serving God. Israel's capacity to worship the Holy One in joy had expanded so fully since their consciousness had grown out of its constriction that "a handmaid saw at the Sea

more than even Ezekiel saw [in his vision]" (Mekkilta Beshallaḥ 15:3).

(Me'or Einayim, Devarim,

s.v. bemidrash tanḥuma)

In this text we see that the experience of Egyptian bondage was not only an historical event; it is understood as an ongoing possibility. Whenever our eyes and hearts close against the truth of our experience, we deny the interconnectedness of all beings, and so we deny God's reality and subject ourselves once again to Egyptian bondage. Pharaoh denied God's reality and power, made himself a god, and so was able to deny the humanity of the Israelites. The undeniable truth of all that has conspired to bring all of Creation to this pass is God's signet: "The seal of the Holy One is Truth." When we wake up to that reality, realizing how we have made ourselves gods, closing off all others from our hearts and rejecting their claims on our humanity, we are released from exile.

Our experience of liberation is from moment to moment. It does not happen once and for all. The Bible reminds us over and over to "Remember the day you came out of the land of Egypt." And we can experience the Exodus over and over. Each time we open our hearts to the truth of our existence, we acknowledge God's reality and we come out of Egypt, bringing more awareness with us. This awareness makes it possible for us to engage with the world for the benefit of all beings, and not simply to satisfy our personal needs or desires. This is how we connect the *middot*—the divine qualities that are the source of our personal qualities as well—to their source, to God.

When we are subject to our habitual reactions to the events of our lives, we are not free. When we cannot see how our hearts are closed, how our vision is clouded, or how our minds are confused, then we are unable to act with wisdom. As a consequence, we are slaves to our passions (for good and for ill), dragged and compelled to act without awareness. When we are able to experience the truth of our lives, to witness and step back from the habitual movements of our hearts and minds, we become free to make choices. Slaves are not free to make independent choices. We become free when the clouds of confusion clear from our hearts and minds, and this liberation is expressed in our capacity to make thoughtful, informed, mindful choices of how to act, and to react, in our lives. Over and over, from moment to moment, we are reminded—and given the choice—to come out of Egypt, to be liberated in the fullness of awareness.

Shabbat

Shabbat is one of the most distinctive practices of Jewish spiritual life. It is a day set apart from all others. It is a time of stepping back from daily endeavors, from the distractions of weekday engagements, to reconnect with our soul, with our ground. Through the various Shabbat observances, we learn to perceive the beauty of the moment.

Shabbat is a day of rest. In the cessation of daily labors we imitate God, who rested on the seventh day, sanctifying and blessing it, thus completing Creation. Each week we enter into that holy time; the time is holy whether or not we recognize or acknowledge it. By taking on Shabbat observance we provide ourselves with tools by which we can experience "holiness in time" (as Rabbi Abraham Joshua Heschel put it), and taste the blessing of Shabbat. The labors that we put aside are those that in some manner demonstrate our mastery over nature. The rabbis of antiquity identified thirty-nine types of labor, which can be grouped into these four categories: baking (and all that is required to prepare bread, and so, all of our civilized sustenance); preparing fabric (and all that is required to produce cloth, and so, being civilized by being clothed); preparing a scroll (and all that is involved in writing, and so, being civilized by producing permanent records of our ideas and imaginings); constructing a building (and every sort of completion and destruction of objects, and so, being civilized by controlling space and separating ourselves from the wildness and chaos of nature). When we refrain from doing these things, we attest to our true status: we are creatures, not Creator.

It is also true that on Shabbat we do not retreat to a cave, sit in the dark, or remain motionless in bed all day. We do not cease being human—creatures who are social, joyous, inquisitive, assertive, reflective, and sensitive to the holy. It is just that by limiting the realm of our activities, we open up the opportunity to experience our lives more deeply. When the car, the television, the phone, correspondence and "business/busyness" are put aside, we find that we are not bored, but stunned. When meals can be eaten at leisure, we find that food tastes better, conversation expands, our hearts open to others. We discover that there is time to read, to reflect, to observe. There is silence. There is stillness. There is beauty to be found in every moment, in all that merely exists without our additional comment.

All of this is enhanced by the attention we give to making Shabbat a delight. Along with changing our behavior to affect our inner experience, we seek to change our environment. Many people prepare the dinner table with a special tablecloth or with special dishes. Others transform the meal by cooking something special, something other than what would seem "everyday." Many people change their clothes from what they wear on Friday to something unique for Shabbat—and many also bathe before Shabbat to deepen that sense of transition. Whereas weekday meals are often rushed, and in many instances not eaten together as a family or in the company of other people, Shabbat is a time for leisurely eating with the companionship of guests. Along with these physical changes, the rituals associated with the beginning and ending of Shabbat enhance the sense of the holiness and blessedness of the day.

Shabbat observance can generate an experience much like a mindfulness retreat. Retreat practice strips daily living down to its most minimal: care for bodily functions, eating, and sleeping. When not sleeping, all action is devoted to deepening our awareness of the moment. Even when eating, we can bring our attention solely to the food and the experience of each mouthful. Rather than mindlessly consuming our food ignorant of its taste, quality, or texture, on a retreat we give all of our attention to just those things. We seek to sense every part of the food, to experience it fully in the mouth, on the tongue, in the throat, in the belly. We become witnesses to the miracle of nature, what it provides for us, and its capacity to sustain us. And we rejoice in being sustained, celebrating every mouthful, every taste.

Shabbat opens up the opportunity to experience every moment in that manner—not only in the delicious meals that we may consume, but also in the quiet of conversation, in the beauty of Shabbat candles, in the ease of unfettered time. Even synagogue services can be like a retreat, especially if they are long. Without our cell phones, we are out of touch with the rest of the world. We cannot be found, yet we need not worry. We can let go and begin to pay attention to what is going on around us. We become aware of the people in synagogue with us. Our minds at ease, we begin to pay attention to the content of our thoughts: Are we critical of others, the way they pray, their clothing, hairdos, expressions? Are we carrying on a conversation with them in our minds, bringing old grudges, irritations, or gossip with us into synagogue? Are we generous with our thoughts, seeing the goodness and loveliness of the people around us? As the congregation continues with the service we have the luxury of leisure, of extended time, to pay close attention to the prayers themselves. Our minds and consciousness open up, and words that we have merely voiced before jump off the page and claim our attention. "What does this mean? What do I mean when I say it? How can I understand this prayer such that it will make me more compassionate, more just?" Further, we discover that we have our own prayers that well up in the silence, which we add to those of the congregation. Time in synagogue is like a mini-retreat, geared to helping us settle our minds, open our hearts, and see more clearly. Shabbat helps us to wake up to our lives, to experience holiness in time, and to commit our lives to increasing blessing in the world around us.

Shabbat is central to the Jewish system of thought, practice, belief, and spirituality, yet one might ask: "If this is so, why was it not created first among all the works of Creation?" One answer might be that all of the first week of Creation was directed toward the moment of Shabbat, toward its completion in God's rest and blessing. Yet, the rabbis did not miss the opportunity to teach a different lesson: "If a person does well, they say, 'You preceded all the works of Creation,' and if not, they say, 'A gnat preceded you, a snail preceded you'" (Leviticus Rabbah 14:1). This saying is based on the fact that there are apparently two stories of Creation. In the first, human beings were created on the sixth day, following all the other creatures. But in the second story, human beings seemingly precede all other creatures. But Shabbat does not appear in the second story; it is only found at the conclusion of the first. If it is possible to read the order of Creation as descending rather than ascending, it might suggest that Shabbat is not all that important!

Instead, our tradition claims that although Shabbat was created last in the order of Creation, God had thought of it first, and it was the goal toward which all of Creation was directed. This idea is found, for instance, in the popular hymn *Lekha Dodi,* chanted in the synagogue at the start of Shabbat. There, this idea is expressed as, *"Sof ma'aseh bemahshavah tehilah,"* what was last in the doing was the first in thought (or, the final deed was in thought from the first). This is a useful idea for the rabbis, allowing them to give Shabbat priority in their value system. Further, that Shabbat was thought of before Creation and then sealed its completion gives Shabbat the quality of totality, of encompassing all of Creation. Creation rests between the original thought and its completion; embraced by Shabbat, it is given purpose and made holy by it.

Shabbat, and mindfulness practice, offer us the opportunity to emulate God's intention in creating Shabbat. That is, on Shabbat (as in mindfulness practice) our thinking can become clearer, our intentions purer, and we can strengthen our capacity to bring our actions in line with our intentions. I have found that when I first sit to meditate, my thoughts are scattered. I think about a dozen things at a time. And, often, the things that I think about are not always admirable. I may experience critical thoughts, angry thoughts, distracting thoughts, planning thoughts, licentious thoughts, escapist thoughts. As each thought arises I react differently: sometimes I follow it into a reverie or a long discursive train; sometimes I react to the thought, criticizing myself for having it, condemning myself—for self-aggrandizement or for self-denigration. Out of this roiling pot of thought and response, it is hard to imagine how I can come to do anything positive and with intention. But, the longer I sit and work to calm my thoughts, directing my attention toward one phenomenon like my breath, the more I find that my mind settles down. I am no longer plagued by random, radically shifting thoughts. As thoughts arise, I am more able to choose how to respond. I can pay attention to their content, to the feelings attached to them, to the history that they call up, and determine whether I want to investigate that line of thought and feeling now, or later. Alternatively, I can acknowledge their presence but return to my breath. I regain some choice in my inner life. I bring intention and action closer together, my desire to see clearly, to experience the truth of the moment and my capacity to do so. What I intended at the beginning, when I first sat down, comes into actuality in the end.

This is what I also experience on Shabbat. My refraining from productive activities is for the sake of preparing space—in my mind, in my heart, in my soul—to see more clearly. When I see more clearly, I can make better choices. I want to participate in the process of *sof ma'aseh bemahshavah tehilah,* I want my actions to match my intentions. While this does take work, this is the work that makes us most human. Our capacity to see the truth, and to free ourselves to choose the good, is our highest calling. This is illustrated in the following text from *Avodat Yisrael.* It situates the concept of *sof ma'aseh* in the unfolding of Creation, placing human free will in the very nature of the universe. That God created the *rakia* (the firmament separating the waters above from the waters below) is suggestive also of how God created the room for human free will.

> God set the realms of above and below apart, set a curtain and spread out clouds to cover the holy realm. This was to make it possible for humans to imagine that the Holy One removed His providence from the world, that the world just follows its natural course. God did so, even though that meant that people's sins might even push away the *Shekhinah,* that they might even have the audacity to say, "Make way for me!" God made this curtain so that people would not be able to perceive God's Unique Oneness, even saying that the Holy One does not oversee this world (Heaven forefend!). God's vision encompasses the whole of the earth; nevertheless, this is imperceptible to people—and this is the function of the *rakia* (firmament).

The Zohar teaches that when you reverse the letters of the word *rakia* you will find *ikar* (essence, fundamental meaning), and this is the essence and objective of Creation, in the nature of *sof ma'aseh bemaḥshavah teḥilah.* For, in the end, the whole of the system of moral accountability derives from the function of the *rakia,* which separates between the upper waters—which are holy thoughts—and the lower—the evil, malevolent waters (cf. Psalm 124:5). It is our human choice whether to rise up to the loving waters, above or below the "thread of love" (cf. Tamid 28a; Ḥagigah 12b).

We praise God in our (Shabbat) morning prayers, announcing that He is "God who opens each day the gates of the east, who breaks open the windows of the *rakia.*" The word "east" is *mizraḥ,* and when we remove the initial *mem* we can find the word *ḥazar,* meaning "return." The Holy One opens the way for us to return, for every day the announcement goes forth ["return you wayward children" (Jeremiah 3:22), cf. Ḥagigah 15a]. And we, who serve the Holy One, are then the ones who bring about return *(teshuvah)* and who break things open, just as we say of the one who prays with *kavanah,* "He breaks open the windows of the *rakia.*" This process of return flows from our obligation to bring back to God all of our senses, our powers of sight and hearing, as is suggested in the verse, "All is from You, and it is Your gift that we have given to You" (1 Chronicles 29:14).

(Avodat Yisrael, Avot 5:1, s.v. ve'al)

Follow the progression in the argument of this text. The division that made possible the appearance of dry land and the emergence of terrestrial life was the separation between the upper and lower waters. This helps us to find our place in the world, to orient ourselves. We extrapolate from that initial separation and accustom ourselves to seeing the world in terms of oppositions and dichotomies. That, too, is helpful in that it allows us to discern between pure and impure, proper and improper, good and evil. Nevertheless, should we allow ourselves to think that this division is the true nature of existence, we would make a fatal mistake. We will begin to think that only our reasoning, only our discernment, only our prejudices and preferences matter. Yet the dichotomies that orient us in the world are ultimately only a covering, a curtain behind which stands the True Actor, the One of True Oneness. Only in our choice to look beyond the curtain of division, to seek out the unifying holiness in Creation, will we succeed in living a Godly life.

Shabbat is considered "a taste of the world to come," a hint of that ultimate unity. That world is called "the world that is all good" (Kiddushin 39b), the world in which all of our terrestrial and mundane distinctions fall away. By means of Shabbat rest, in stepping away from weekday endeavors, in returning to our position as creature and not Creator, we establish enough space that we might see beyond the *rakia,* that we might learn the *ikar* of the ultimate unity of all things in the Holy One.

This is the work of mindfulness. We work to quiet the mind so that we can pay close attention to the truth of our lives. We step back from our habitual responses so that we can create the space in which we might choose freely the right and proper way to behave. We come to recognize the passing nature of our responses. We realize how often we are trapped in habit. We seek to look beyond, to see the ultimate. In this we seek to move beyond our egos, beyond that which claims all and says, "Make way for me!" Mindfulness moves us to an awareness of our part in the unfolding of Creation, our role in bringing all things into line with God's unique unity and the oneness of all Creation. Mindfulness and Shabbat practice lead us to connect our actions to our truest intentions, to bring about the final fulfillment of the initial thought: let all things find their right place, in the One.

The High Holy Days: Rosh Hashanah and Yom Kippur

The New Year (Rosh Hashanah) and the Day of Atonement (Yom Kippur) are commonly known as the High Holy Days. They mark the beginning of the spiritual year in the Jewish calendar. The Ten Days of Repentance from Rosh Hashanah through Yom Kippur are actually the core of a much longer period, stretching from the start of the month of Elul (immediately preceding Tishrei, the month of the New Year) through the end of the holiday of Sukkot (the Festival of Booths). The whole of this time is one that is devoted to introspection, self-evaluation, and personal transformation.

While repentance for sins or misdeeds is a central concern of the High Holy Days, too limited an emphasis on failures of ritual observance or legal principles would obscure the larger concern of these days, which is personal transformation. If we are truly to change our behavior (even if to recommit to halakhic observance, which is no small undertaking), we must be able to see ourselves clearly. Our change will flow from our capacity to understand how we have come to this particular pass, to see what it is that stands in the way of our living as truly as we would wish, to express our intention in our deeds. We begin this process in the month of Elul, when we add Psalm 27 to the daily prayer services. This psalm invites us to join the author in facing the truth of his life, his anxieties, his self-delusions, and his egocentric bravado.

Preparation: Psalm 27

The psalm starts out on a note of confidence: "Adonai is my light and my help; whom should I fear? Adonai is the stronghold of my life; whom should I dread? When evil men assail me to devour my flesh—it is they, my foes and my enemies, who stumble and fall" (verses 1–2). The speaker has no doubt of his place in God's favor, demonstrated by his self-assurance before his foes. That certainty blinds him to fear or dread, even if those sentiments might be warranted, even if they actually exist in his heart. In that spirit, the psalmist moves even further, asking more than just security: "One thing I ask of Adonai, only that do I seek: to live in the house of Adonai all the days of my life, to gaze upon the beauty of Adonai, to frequent His temple" (verse 4). The author wants more than just God's protection; he wants God's company, to live always in God's presence. Confident of God's favor, he ventures to ask for more, yet we sense a note of uncertainty. "He will shelter me in His pavilion on an evil day, grant me the protection of His tent, raise me high upon a rock. Now is my head high over my enemies roundabout; I sacrifice in His tent with shouts of joy, singing and chanting a hymn to Adonai" (verse 5–6). If enemies stumble and fall, if they have no power over the speaker, why does he suddenly suspect that an evil day may come on which he will need protection? Although he first sought to dwell in Adonai's house, communing with and gazing upon Adonai always, he now suggests that there may actually be another, deeper reason for staying there—one that even he is not prepared to articulate. He is, in fact, still afraid. He hides that fear, and imagines himself more firmly ensconced in God's house, raised up even higher, away from his enemies and foes. Only when he can imagine himself secure and sheltered in God's tent does he envision himself fully celebrating his thanks to God.

What has been so far a poem of praise and thanks, of seemingly unequivocal security in God's presence, breaks down at this point. The subtle appearance in these last verses of doubt and uncertainty now fractures the façade of assurance in a cry for help. "Hear, O Adonai, when I cry aloud, have mercy on me, answer me. To You my heart says, '(You say,) "Seek My face!" O Adonai, I do seek Your face!'

Do not hide Your face from me; do not thrust aside Your servant in anger; You have ever been my help. Do not forsake me, do not abandon me, O God, my deliverer" (verses 7–9). What the psalmist had felt to be God's ongoing, immediate saving power—Light and Help and Stronghold—now is obscured. The bravado he had expressed in the face of adversity is now completely gone, and gone along with it is his sense of God's presence. Where the psalmist had felt God projected into his life—light shining on him—he now has to seek God out. He pleads that he has always sought out God, that he has moved toward God and not relied on God's gifts and beneficence. He cries in terror that God might have abandoned him.

Yet we begin to sense the emergence of subtle self-awareness. The poet begins to sense that God's hiding His face is not merely a happenstance, without precedent. Rather, the psalmist seems to understand that he himself may have something to do with this situation. He reasons that God may hide "in anger"—and if so, that it is in response to something he has done. In such a moment of realization, of self-evaluation and stock taking, we might expect the poet to begin to ruminate on what it was that may have angered God, on what it is that he will have to change in order to return to God's good graces, to truly merit God's attention.

But that does not happen. Instead, we hear the psalmist following a different tack: "Though my father and mother abandon me, Adonai will take me in" (verse 10). Another diversion, another protestation of reassurance. Rather than consider why he now feels abandoned by God, he protests emptily that God would not do so; his pain could only be because his family and friends, even his parents, are not trustworthy. He hides his inner unease, his awareness that his early bravado was overstated, misplaced. He claims God's attention; he asserts a special relationship.

This cannot hold, and the psalmist begins to reconsider his situation. Perhaps there is something that he has to do to merit

God's attention. Perhaps he has to change his behavior. So he pleads, "Show me Your way, O Adonai, and lead me on a level path, because of my watchful foes. Do not subject me to the will of my foes, for false witnesses and unjust accusers have appeared against me" (verses 11–12). The psalmist recognizes that he needs help, that his earlier assurance was overblown. So he turns to God for direction. Yet he is still not out of the woods. He has not yet stripped away all pretense. His interest in walking God's path is not for the sake of following God's ways, but so that he will be saved from his foes. His devotion to God is still conditional. God's place in his life is still measured in its utility.

Unanswered, broken, almost given over to despair, the psalmist realizes that his selfish needs cannot be the basis for his faith. He is moving, slowly, in fits and starts of awareness, toward serving God out of love, out of devotion, and without hope of reward. He begins to frame this new awareness: "Had I not the assurance that I would enjoy the goodness of Adonai in the land of the living . . ." (verse 13). The ellipsis is in the original text. The sentence begins with the conditional "were it not," but there is no conclusion, no next step, no "then." It is as if, in mid-sentence, in mid-thought, the poet realizes that once again he is placing his faith in a reward, in a boon—in seeing God's goodness. He stops, finally, mouth open, terrified and abashed at his audacity. He looks carefully at the truth of his life, and at the truth of existence. He sees clearly what it truly means to claim that Adonai is his light and that therefore he need not fear. He understands, in the end, that all that is left to him is to "Hope in Adonai; be strong and of good courage! O hope in Adonai" (verse 14).

As we approach the High Holy Days, this psalm helps us to prepare spiritually. As we follow the drama of the psalm, we come to recognize how much we share with the speaker. We too would like to have faith. We want to be able to face life with courage, with strength, with certainty. When we pay attention to the truth of our existence—that nothing is permanent, that all things change, and therefore we are constantly pulled by our spontaneous reactions of joy or dejection, that we place our dependence on things to help us feel secure—we find ourselves, like the poet, aghast at the myriad ways in which we hide from our terror and cling to our delusions of permanence.

When we come to the last line of the psalm, we are prepared to follow the instructions: Hope in Adonai. This does not mean that we halt all action and wait; this is not a retreat from engagement in the world. Nor does it mean that we may act without thought or concern, leaving God to sort out the end results. Rather, to hope in Adonai is to strive to see as clearly as possible what is true and real. It is to be as mindful as possible of our inner lives, of our fears and attachments, of our egos and egotism. To hope in Adonai is to commit to action that flows—as much as possible—from mindful intention, from the desire to do the best for the most. It is to acknowledge personal need and desire, to strive to attain comfort or satisfaction, without being overcome by them, without becoming blind to the needs of others. To hope in Adonai is to be open to the possibility of finding blessing even in the moments of greatest pain or deepest despair. It is to be fully present in every moment, willing and grateful.

To hope in Adonai is to also acknowledge our limits. We may strive to become as aware as possible of our inner struggles, to take responsibility for our habitual responses and our reactions to the events of our lives, yet we are still neither omniscient nor omnipotent. We cannot see all of the antecedents of any given moment—the desires, fears, or greed of other people; the larger social, political, economic, geologic, psychic, or spiritual forces—that may have brought us to this instant. We can hardly see clearly the inner forces that bring us to do what we do. To hope in Adonai is also to trust that when we do our best to wake up to our lives, to see the truth of the moment as clearly as possible, we will act with the most honest and generous of intentions. We trust that, whatever our success or failure, God will know our hearts. Having set our intention to act mindfully, we trust that our actions will contribute to approximating the best of God's intention for the perfection of the world.

Rosh Hashanah

This double meaning of "hoping in Adonai" is echoed throughout the High Holy Day liturgy. On Rosh Hashanah we celebrate the Creation of the world. The rabbis identified three themes reflecting three implications of the fundamental idea of Creation:

1. There is a Creator, who, by virtue of having the power and the will to create, and also then created the world, is Sovereign.
2. The Sovereign God desires that this world become perfect, and He has acted in history to make that evident and to inspire us to participate in attaining that goal.
3. God, who existed even before Creation, knows all that goes on in the world, holding all acts and events of the past and present in mind, so that nothing will be lost, so that everything that has and will exist can participate in that final perfection.

Each of these three themes are expressed in the course of the *Musaf* (Additional) service on Rosh Hashanah in prose presentations, further illustrated by ten selections from Scripture: *Malkhuyot* (God's Sovereignty), *Zikhronot* (God's Remembrances), and *Shofarot* (God's intervention in history accompanied by the *shofar*).

Of these three sections, the *Zikhronot* section speaks most directly of mindfulness. I am challenged by the idea that what I have forgotten (especially that which I have chosen to forget, that which I would prefer to forget) is not completely forgotten or gone from the world. I am comforted that what I have forgotten (lost from my memory, obscured by years of inattention or crusty resentment or pain) may yet be brought back to mind, still exists in God's remembrance. When I confront these two experiences of memory on Rosh Hashanah I find them to be extremely powerful. They help me to do the work of the holiday: deepening my focus in self-examination, in self-awareness, and in waking up in my life.

The central passage in the High Holy Day liturgy introducing *Zikhronot* says:

> You remember the work of Creation, noting all creatures from the beginning. All hidden thoughts are revealed before You, and all of the infinite secrets from the beginning of time. There is no forgetting before Your glorious throne, and nothing is hidden from Your gaze. You remember every deed; no creature is so remote as to be hidden from You. It is apparent and well-known that You, Adonai our God, foresee and observe everything to the end of time, for You will bring to bear all memories when You note the doings of every living thing, bringing to mind all the countless acts of Your myriad creatures.

Before God, there is no fudging the truth. As I think over what I have done, how I have behaved and treated other people, I find that I can always contextualize my actions; there is always some extenuation. When I read this passage, I realize that however much I may see reasons and explanations for my behavior, my reasons and explanations are really excuses and obfuscations. In the light of God's complete knowledge and memory, I stop even before

I start. My mouth opens to explain, and the words freeze in my mouth. I am culpable. I did what I did; I said what I said. And, if I want to live in truth, if I wish finally to hope in Adonai alone, then I had better learn to admit the truth of my life. Facing the full force of the whole truth and nothing but the truth—truth beyond my immediate perception, truth beyond my desire to know—I am laid bare. I am stripped of pretext, made dumb. I can only admit the truth, and with new eyes and a new heart turn myself to doing better later. And, then, I hope in Adonai.

And again, when I read these words, I am heartened. Is it possible that I have done things that I have forgotten that are to my credit? Is it possible that a casual smile, a friendly glance, a small courtesy, an act of generosity that I hardly noticed and didn't consider significant, actually made a difference to another person? Could I have saved a life without even knowing it? I may not remember; I may not know. But God does. And God remembers, as well, all the many deeds that were done for me, all of the good that my parents, grandparents, siblings, and friends have done on my behalf; all of the ways that I have been helped along the way. When I stop to consider all that God remembers, I am more able to remember, myself.

I remember my father. He is not alive, and cannot know—in person—what I have made of my life. Yet when I remember him, it is as if he comes alive in me. He is present to me, and so he knows me. And as he comes alive in me, I know him better. His life, his joys, his values, his quirks, and his failures are all present to me. When I remember them, in a flash, all at once, the whole of his life as I experienced it comes together. I sense it again, yet also in a new manner. In remembering him now, incorporating all that I knew, all that I have since learned about him and about myself as a father, a husband, a son, I retrieve him and he is new. My sense of who he was is enlivened. And as I remember him in this new manner, I, too, become new. I am changed.

That God remembers everything that has happened since the first moment of Creation means that nothing is ever lost. Everything is available to us, so that we may know the truth more clearly and live our lives more honestly. Whatever is hidden is not gone forever. It is possible, if I hope in Adonai, that I will be able to uncover that which has been obscured. I can face my past. I can embrace my past. God's remembrance makes possible my wholeness, and thus also the possibility that the world itself can be made whole.

The text of *Zikhronot* continues:

> This, today, is the beginning of Your work, a reminder of the first day. "This is a law for Israel, a ruling of the God of Jacob" (Psalm 81:5). Yet, it is also for the nations that on this day it is decreed: war or peace; famine or plenty. All creatures are noted on it, that they be remembered for life or for death. Who is not called to account on a day like this, when the memory of all Creation comes before You: how we behave and how it is noted, the thoughts that lead our every step, our plans, and our stratagems, the inclinations of our hearts?

Present, but not overstated, in this passage is an awareness that what happens on Rosh Hashanah is not limited to that one day a year. "This, today" is the day on which God's remembrance embraces our lives. "Who is not called to account on a day like this?" What day is a day like this? Every day. Over and over we confront moments of choice: war or peace with our neighbors, our families, our hearts; famine or plenty for our spirits, our communities, the struggling masses of the world; life or death in this moment or the next. In each moment we can wake up to the truth, see the world (our actions, our intentions, our successes, and our failures), and remember that God remembers everything. We can stop in the moment and take stock, considering our lives in the light of God's memory. That moment can be both challenging and heartening, possibly opening a new path for our lives. We will be able to choose for peace, for plenty, and for life. It is for this reason that it makes sense that Rosh Hashanah is known in the liturgy as *Yom Hazikaron*, the Day of Remembrance.

This is the work of mindfulness. The practices of prayer and reflection, as well as the texts of the day, support us in looking closely at the truth of our lives. That God knows and remembers all supports us in our attempts to become as aware as possible of our habitual responses, to understand the habits of mind that prevent us from seeing clearly. Our desire to wake up in our lives, to know each moment in its fullness, is sustained when we recognize that each day is a day of accounting, a day of evaluation. On any day, in any moment, we can move aside the veil that obscures our view of ourselves and of others. Our capacity to remember as much as possible supports our will to be as honest as possible in our interactions. Rosh Hashanah observance is an invitation to realize that everything happens "on a day like this," on this day, in this moment.

Yom Kippur

As we have seen in the liturgy, the theme of God's remembrance, that God takes note and recalls each and every act of every being, is tied to the theme of judgment. We understand that, as well, in our own experience. When we confront our lives with clear vision and honest assessment, we come to judge ourselves. As my teacher Sylvia Boorstein teaches, seeing the truth through a calm and balanced heart sparks a spontaneous moral inventory. And just as this is the work of Rosh Hashanah, so too, is it the experience of Yom

Kippur. Much of the traditional liturgy is made up of prayers for forgiveness of sin, that we might merit acquittal in the divine court.

This image is captured in one of the central prayers of the High Holy Days, recited on both Rosh Hashanah and Yom Kippur. It is the prayer known as *Unetaneh Tokef.* Its central image is captured in the following passage:

> All who have come into this world pass before You as a flock of sheep. And, as a shepherd numbers his flock, causing his sheep to pass under his staff, so will You move us along, numbering, counting, noting every living being—and allotting the time of all creatures, writing down their final judgment.

God knows and remembers everything. This means not only that we might come to know the truth of our lives more clearly (as on Rosh Hashanah). This prayer also suggests that on the basis of God's complete knowledge and memory, we are judged. Indeed, the most famous section of this prayer follows:

> On Rosh Hashanah it is written and on Yom Kippur it is sealed: How many shall pass from life and how many shall be born into it; who shall live and who shall die; who in the fullness of life and who with life foreshortened; who by fire and who by water; who by sword and who by beast; who by hunger and who by thirst; who by earthquake and who by plague; who by strangulation and who by stoning; who shall have rest and who shall wander; who shall experience quiet and who shall be tormented; who shall be at ease and who shall be afflicted; who shall be poor and who shall become rich; who shall be cast down and who shall be exalted.

It is nearly impossible to read this passage without inner turmoil. It does not comport with our experience of the world. That is, we know too many people whose lives have been cut short, yet whose conduct has been exemplary; we know too many mean, unscrupulous, and evil people whose lives seem easy and blessed. We cannot see the connection between behavior and punishment, and we find it difficult to believe that anything would justify an untimely or difficult death. Moreover, we find it difficult to accept that God plans out each and every individual occurrence, down to the details of every individual's death. It is hard to connect the vagaries of life, the happenstances and mischances of the everyday, to the will and judgment of God. It is impossible for us to reckon the calculus of judgment that this prayer seems to suggest.

As difficult as it seems to understand this prayer, it may still be possible to read it as a mindfulness teaching. For that, we will turn to the sections that precede and follow what we have already read.

> *"Unetaneh tokef"*—We acknowledge the full sanctity of this day, for it is awesome and awful. On this day Your sovereignty is raised up, Your throne is established in mercy, yet You also sit on it in truth. In truth, You are Judge and Prosecutor, knowing all factors and bearing witness to all actions; You transcribe and affirm the testimony, having numbered and counted all deeds, remembering even the forgotten things. You then open that Book of Remembrance, and it speaks for itself, for each of us has signed it with our deeds.

God may act as judge and prosecutor, but in the end, we are the prime witnesses. It is our testimony that seals the case—our own deeds. God does not read a charge that He has made up, nor does He arraign us for deeds unknown to us or hidden from us. The docket is written in our own hand. We, in the presence of

God—who reigns in mercy and truth—find that we cannot but give voice to the truth. We tell it all. We pour out the truth of our lives.

In the presence of God, who remembers all and who is the fount of Truth, we cannot wriggle free. We can no longer make excuses, we cannot hide from what is before us: "How many people pass away each year?! How many are born?!" The suffering of the world is incalculable, as its joy. How can we absorb it, take it all in, witness it? We are challenged to look beyond our own suffering, our own losses, our own fears, our personal experiences of "injustice." We may read the obituaries, and we certainly know when relatives and friends die. We take every opportunity to joyously celebrate births within the circle of our acquaintances. But do we really see what is happening around us? How many thousands of children die of starvation or of preventable diseases each day? How many thousands are born who will never see the age of five years? How many people die on the streets of our cities for lack of food or shelter? How many more die in bloodshed and violence? Have we truly seen that truth? Have we truly paid attention to the suffering of the world, to the rise and fall of individuals, communities, states? Have we looked closely enough that our hearts have broken, that we have seen ourselves in the eyes of the starving child, in the face of the villain, in the mouth that cries "O"?

In the presence of God, who reigns in mercy and truth, we find that we cannot but give voice to the truth. We tell it all. We pour out the truth of our lives. The truth is that we are alive in a world of suffering and we usually hide from it. When we are presented with our own actions, when we see our lives laid out in truth, we suddenly see all that we have hidden from. How many people! How much struggle! What suffering! Our personal losses and victories suddenly pale in significance; our self-justifications sound hollow. How can we abide living in this world without doing all that we can to alleviate that suffering? And, how shall we go on living, when we see that for all our efforts we will not improve the lot of so many people?

And suddenly we are brought up short. We realize that this suffering does not merely go on "out there," among the downtrodden, the poor, the forgotten. It is our suffering as well. The Mahabharata says, "What is the most wondrous thing in the entire world? . . . That all around us people can be dying and we don't believe it can happen to us. That no man, though he sees others dying all around him, believes that he himself will die."[2] We are that man. We make our way through life observing but not really understanding the nature of the human condition, the full extent of the suffering. But, through the words of the *Unetaneh Tokef*, we are brought face to face with the reality and magnitude of human suffering—along with our own suffering and our own mortality.

In this moment of crisis, the prayer reaches its conclusion: "But penitence (*teshuvah*), prayer (*tefillah*), and good deeds (*tzedakah*) can annul the severity of the decree." When we see clearly the nature of human existence, when we feel deeply our mortality and imperfections, we then realize that there is nothing more for us to do than to devote our energies to serving the Truth and caring for other people. Penitence is the process of stock-taking, requiring that we submit to the charge and challenge of Yom Kippur in some manner every day. "Rabbi Eliezer said: 'Repent one day before your death.' His disciples asked him, 'Does anyone know on what day he will die?' He said to them, 'Then all the more reason that he repent today, lest he die tomorrow, and thus all one's days will be spent in repentance'" (Shabbat 153a). It is not only on Yom Kippur that we are to take stock, that we are to wake up to our lives and to the lives of others. Yom Kippur brings us face to face with our mortality. When we pay

[2]Sharon Salzberg, *Lovingkindness: The Revolutionary Art of Happiness* (Boston: Shambhala Press, 2002), p. 106.

attention to the truth of our lives, we face our mortality as well, and we begin the process of opening ourselves to others.

Prayer is our confession of the truth. We acknowledge our mortality, we announce our awareness of responsibility for our actions, and we express our intention to live closer to our consciousness. We put our lives on the line, seeking to know the truth and to speak the truth, so that we will be able to act in truth. "There are those whose concentration and *kavanah* is so intense, that according to the nature of things they might die after just two or three words [of prayer]" (*Likkutim Yekarim,* No. 31). When we have clarified our intention through *teshuvah,* our prayers can become the whole of our lives. Our every act can be an expression of our intention, a word of prayer.

At the conclusion of the *Unetaneh Tokef* prayer, we acknowledge the limits of our abilities. We are mortal: "like fragile pottery, withering grass, fading flowers, a passing shadow, a dissipating cloud, a fleeting breeze, scattering dust, a fleeting dream." Whatever we may set out to do, it will be limited. We will not, we cannot, accomplish all that we intend. For all that we desire to live fully in the light of the truth, over and over again we will have to make ourselves right, we will have to rediscover the path. And we will never reach the end. "But You are Sovereign, God who lives and endures." God's eternity offers a moment of hope. We may not fulfill all of our intentions. We may not succeed in "curing" the human condition. But there is yet hope. In God's eternal awareness and memory, our intention counts. Our efforts make a difference. "Your years have no limit, Your days have no end . . . Your mysterious name is beyond explanation. Yet Your name befits You as You befit Your name. And You have named us in Your name." Our efforts have worth in that they are linked to God's efforts. Our intention, when aligned with the truth, is God's intention. Our actions, in the light of the truth, can be God's actions. Our good deeds establish *tzedakah,* righteousness in the world. They may be imperfect and they may be ephemeral, yet we touch eternity through our shared intention with God.

We are indeed judged on Yom Kippur. But we are judged every other day as well. Every day may be our last, so we cannot take a day off, we cannot rest on our laurels, nor can we rely on others to do what we know is right. Our fates are sealed in every moment—not by decree but by our choices, and by the seemingly infinite actions of all other beings in Creation. We, along with all others, will either live or die in the next year. When we choose to look clearly in the face of the truth, we may be overwhelmed by the immensity of the demand—that we act impeccably. Yet when we acknowledge the truth, we no longer fear a judging, punishing God. Rather, we enter into an intimate relationship, in which we realize that we share intention and action, and so are strengthened and heartened. In that moment, indeed, we can be sealed for life in God's eternity.

Purim

Yom Kippur is considered by many to be the most significant, the most powerful day in the Jewish calendar. Purim, on the other hand, could be the silliest, the least significant. Yet, consider these two texts:

> In the future, all of the festivals will be annulled, but Purim (*yemei purim*) will never be annulled, as it says, "And these days of Purim shall never cease among the Jews, and the memory of them shall never perish among their descendants" (Esther 9:28). Indeed, also, the days of Atonement (*yemei hakippurim*) will never be annulled, as it says, "This shall be to you a law for all time" (Leviticus 16:34).

> (MIDRASH PROVERBS 9:1)

Purim is named for Yom Ha-kippurim, for in the future we will delight on it (i.e., Yom Kippur), changing it from affliction to delight. And, so, as the *Shekhinah* [and we] are forbidden to wear leather-soled shoes on that day, in that future time we will say of her, "How lovely are your feet in sandals, O daughter of the Noble One" (Song of Songs 7:2). Delight, joy, and many boons are prepared for her. . . .

(Tikkunei Zohar 57b)

There is a connection between Yom Kippur and Purim that extends beyond their homonymity, an eternal association that extends beyond the demands of scriptural proof. This connection rests in the question: What are the consequences of our actions?

That seems like a simple question. When we do something, we see what happens next: I hit my brother and he cries (if he is smaller than I) or he runs after me to beat me up (if he is bigger); I douse my eggs in hot sauce and my tongue and mouth burn up; I write with my pen, or press on the keyboard, and letters appear that communicate my thoughts. Even when we can't quite see all of the steps in the process, we usually have some understanding of the results that follow from our acts: I push the buttons on my telephone and in another home the phone rings; I donate blood and someone later is helped; I hit the "send" icon, and my email message is relayed to someone on the other side of the world.

There are times, however, when we cannot determine what the outcome of our acts will be. In a moment of anger or frustration I yell at my son. I may see the immediate result: he may cry, or hide, or run away. If I then reach out to him and apologize, he may calm down and we may get along. But, I cannot be sure how my anger has affected him. I cannot know (and, quite possibly, neither can he) how the hurt might remain with him, might make him cautious around me, holding back out of fear or resentment.

I had an apple tree, a gift from a congregant. I planted it, and I liked the idea that it might someday provide fruit. One year, it was covered with bugs and its leaves crumpled, and I sought advice from the local nursery about how to care for it. I was told to spray the tree each spring with some chemical. And I did. The bugs did not return, and the tree produced prodigiously. But I do not know what consequences may result from the dispersal of the spray in the neighborhood, of the residue on the ground at the base of the tree, of its presence in the fruit I consumed and shared with others.

I smile at other drivers. I even let them merge in front of me. I wave "thank you" to others who let me into traffic. I let people with fewer groceries go ahead of me in the checkout line. I open doors for other people. I have no idea what this means to them—if I'm just a sucker and a pushover or if they appreciate a small act of courtesy. And certainly, I have no way of knowing if there is any long-term outcome.

I once had a bar mitzvah student who was one of the least interested and least motivated of all of the youngsters I have ever dealt with. I was frustrated with his lack of interest, but even more with the dismissive attitude he brought to the whole endeavor. My frustration with him was deepened by the lack of interest his parents showed in his studies, in the programs that we ran for the parents of the bar/bat mitzvah class, and with the religious and spiritual life of the congregation in general. I was sure, once he was finished, that he would be done with Judaism and Jewish life forever. Years later I ran into his mother in the hospital, attending to her father who was dying. When I entered the hospital room and identified myself, the grandmother grew very excited. "You were the rabbi who bar mitzvahed my grandson? Oh, rabbi, you wouldn't believe it. He just got married. And you know, the girl he married— well, she wasn't Jewish, but they took classes together, and she converted, and they had the most traditional wedding I've ever seen. And, they keep *shabbos,* and kosher, and he's very happy." I do not take credit for the course his life has taken—but I ask myself: do I know the consequences of my actions?

Each of us is responsible, alone, for our actions, yet we cannot dissociate ourselves from others. We are caught up in webs of interconnections, moved by wave upon wave of intersecting circles of consequences. We all stand at a single point: the intersection of the horizontal axis, comprised of all the actors at this very moment, and the vertical axis, comprised of the events of the past moving forward into the future. We suffer and benefit from the actions of others, just as our actions affect others. The righteous are caught up in the punishment of the wicked, just as the wicked seem to benefit from the blessings of the righteous.

When we pay careful attention to our lives, we come to see that we cannot deny that actions have consequences. Nor can we draw clear, unequivocal, or definitive links between actions as causes and suffering (or blessing) as an effect. Our intuition tells us that we cannot avoid "doing" anything—our mere existence affects the whole of the world. We breathe, we need space and sustenance, we seek companionship, and we exercise our wills. Even to withdraw from society as a hermit or recluse will not end our claim on Creation; our actions will still have consequences.

When we look closely at what is true, separating out the story from what actually happened, we see how little our intentions and our perceptions of our actions have to do with what actually happens. A moment of inattention, a mistaken inflection in our speech, a startled response—each can affect others in ways that we cannot foresee, and of which we may not be immediately aware. Only later might we be able to discern how we went wrong, and try to make up for unintended consequences. And even then, there remain myriad, if not infinite, ways that our actions have impacted the world, creating outcomes we can neither know nor control.

If we cannot see everything clearly all at once, how can we know what is just? We have an intuitive sense, it is true, yet our intuition is ultimately founded on our perceptions, and often reflects our expectations of how things should be, of what we would like them to be. Our interests, our fears, our needs, our jealousies, and our compassion all affect our perception of the moment. We act on the basis of those perceptions. But, does that mean that our actions will be just? To see justice in its fullest, truest form we would need to expand our view, to see more of the scene, to visualize fully the totality of all interactions leading up to our actions. Further, we would need to see the consequences of our actions played out in all their fullness to know if they are just. But our vision is limited: we cannot know the full scope of the past or future, and we are left with a vague feeling that what happens to us and the outcome of our actions are not quite just; things are "not fair."

Mindfulness practice is useful in this regard. In the spaciousness of heart that we experience when we see the truth clearly, we can begin to see connections and possibilities that suggest deeper causes and more subtle effects. We learn to distinguish between our perceptions of events and the larger field of the totality of actions shaping those events. We learn to tell the difference between our actions and the stories that we tell about how and why we acted in a particular manner—why we responded to someone else just as we did, why we are justified in feeling harmed or in feeling righteous. Once outside the story, we are able to disengage from self-interest. At a distance we become aware, again, of our own need for compassion—regarding our own fears, anxieties, insecurities, or needs. Moreover, this awareness, standing outside our need for self-justification, does not generate new accusations of the other. Rather, it helps us to open our hearts to the other, to recognize their fears, anxieties, insecurities, or needs, as well. They, too, are in need of compassion.

When we are able to hold the truth of our own experiences with compassion, we are better able to see a way toward a just resolution that will result neither in the destruction of the other nor in self-denigration. That is, when our responses are severed from the impulse for vengeance and are clear of self-justification, they are more likely to lead toward truth. We will be able to approach the other with understanding, and offer a solution (which may yet include compensation or other punishment) that still affirms the other's being and innate value. "Say to them: As I live—declares Adonai God—it is not My desire that the wicked shall die, but that the wicked turn from his evil ways and live. Turn back, turn back from your evil ways, that you may not die, O House of Israel!" (Ezekiel 33:11). The outcome of our calm, open attention to the truth brings us to the same conclusion. We first recognize that we may need to "turn back" from our own perceptions, from our biases and assumptions about the intentions of the other and about our self-justifying righteousness. Then it becomes clear to us that we do not desire the annihilation of the other, but that they be reconciled with us and we with them, and so we seek a way toward restitution and accord.

The rabbis understood that a desire for absolute justice (at least in the instant)—even on God's part—would only lead to destruction. They recited these verses, and learned from them: "If You keep account of sins, O Adonai, Adonai, who will survive? Yours is the power to forgive so that You may be held in awe" (Psalm 130:3–4). For them, this text resonated with Abraham's challenge to God regarding the impending destruction of Sodom and Gomorrah. They understood the need for the God of Justice to do justice, and they balanced it with our need for justice to be tempered with mercy.

> [Abraham] said before Him: "'Far be it from You! Shall the Judge of the earth not do justly?' (Genesis 18:25). If it is justice that You

ask for, there can be no world here. And if it is a world that You ask for, there can be no justice here. You are trying to hold a cord at both of its ends—You want the world and You want true justice. If You don't give up just a little, Your world will not survive."

Said the Holy One to him: "'You love righteousness and hate wickedness' (Psalm 45:8). You love to justify My creatures and you hate to indict them. 'Therefore has God, your God, chosen to anoint you with oil of gladness over all your peers' (ibid.)."

(Leviticus Rabbah 10:1)

Even the God of Justice cannot execute absolute justice. Mercy, some space in which there is room to acknowledge human frailty and imperfect understanding, must be inserted into the process. It is as if Abraham offered God this mindfulness instruction: "Take a breath. Consider: What is the truth? It may be that absolute justice is the Truth, but do You, God, want that absolute—and absolutely destructive—truth? Are You, will You be, the God who also loves mercy, who created the world that it might be inhabited by human beings, that they might hold You in awe?" God's response in this text seems to flow from a mindful perspective. God comes to see that absolute justice may be too much for the world to bear. But, more, God seems to be relieved, and in the expansiveness of a more balanced heart, more loving.

Nothing is quite so simple, however, when dealing with rabbinic thought—or when thinking through the consequences of actions. The text above does not suggest that God did not ultimately punish the people of Sodom and Gomorrah. God did, and in a devastating and terrible way! Rather, the rabbis teach here that in God's heart of hearts, He desires mercy and not punishment. But justice must still be executed.

It is difficult to communicate in translation, but embedded in the text above, there are at least two layers of tradition. There is a sense of repetition: the double juxtaposition of justice and the survival of the world. The passage, "You are trying to hold a cord at both of its ends—You want the world and You want true justice. If You don't give up just a little, Your world will not survive" is distinguished from what precedes it in that it is in Aramaic, and not Hebrew. It jumps out a bit in the original, as if the compiler of the passage were saying, "Pay attention here!" This may have been a popular saying, one that could have circulated in the vernacular. The statement "You are trying to hold a cord at both of its ends" has the sense of a folk-saying, and it helps to bring to life the dilemma with which Abraham confronts God.

But there is more to this. In the first section of the text, the one in Hebrew, the tension between justice and the world was simply stated: "If You want the one, You can't have the other." There is no distinction made between one choice and the other. It is balanced: "If X, then not Y; if Y, then not X." In the second section in Aramaic, however, the speaker has a bias: he wants the world to endure! The problem is presented with some urgency, and the outcome stated with concern: "If You don't give up just a little, Your world will not survive." The speaker wants the world to continue to exist, and suggests that the way to get there is for God to give up just a little—to give up on absolute justice, on absolute truth.

What does it mean for God to give up on absolute, truthful justice? In a sense, it would be to betray the Truth (which is, ultimately, God). The consequence of God not exacting punishment in a perfect, visible manner would be to undermine God's identity as "the Judge of all the earth." This is the situation facing the psalmist:

> God of retribution, Adonai, God of retribution, appear!
> Rise up, Judge of the earth, give the arrogant their desserts!
> How long shall the wicked, O Adonai, how long shall the wicked
>   exult,

shall they utter insolent speech, shall all evildoers vaunt
themselves?
They crush Your people, O Adonai, they afflict Your very own;
they kill the widow and stranger; they murder the fatherless,
thinking, "Adonai does not see it, the God of Jacob does not pay
heed."

(PSALM 94:1–7)

The wicked think that the absence of response to their evil deeds means that there is no God—or, at the very least, that God does not see or care about what goes on in the world. This problem troubles the author of Ecclesiastes as well.

And here is another frustration: the fact that the sentence imposed for evil deeds is not executed swiftly, which is why men are emboldened to do evil—the fact that a sinner may do evil a hundred times and his [punishment will] still be delayed. For although I am aware that "It will be well with those who revere God since they revere Him, and it will not be well with the scoundrel, and he will not live long, because he does not revere God"—here is a frustration that occurs in the world: sometimes an upright man is requited according to the conduct of the scoundrel, and sometimes the scoundrel is requited according to the conduct of the upright. I say all that is frustration.

(ECCLESIASTES 8:11–14)

Not only does the absence of evident justice undermine right thinking—that is, that there is a God who values justice and executes judgment on wrongdoers—but it also undermines civil society. When people see miscreants going unpunished, they are emboldened to break the law as well. Ecclesiastes' frustration is compounded by the fact that not only do scoundrels escape punishment, but they often are seen to prosper (while the righteous suffer unjustly). This too emboldens those who would defy God's laws, and undermines religious sentiment and social order.

The rabbis took this to heart. As much as they wished for God's mercy (even at the cost of absolute, truthful justice), they recognized that they could not afford to undermine God's justice fully. In the rabbinic text cited above, the Aramaic voice suggested that if God did not "give up (*mevatter*) just a little," the world could not stand. The verbal root of the words "give up" is related to the word that means "to loosen, unbind." Abraham calls upon God, in this passage, to "loosen up" somewhat, letting some miscreants go.

A word with the same root shows up in another text. There Rabbi Ḥanina introduces his teaching saying, "Anyone who says that the Holy One is lax in executing justice (*vatran*), let his bowels go loose (*yitvatroon*). Rather, God is long-suffering, but does collect His due." Clearly the audacity of the claim (that God is lax in executing justice) and its punishment (loose bowels) are meant measure for measure, at least on the level of the wordplay (*vatran/yitvatroon*). The earlier midrash had Abraham confront God saying, "Let loose (*mevatter*)," an act that here is considered blasphemy, worthy of great suffering. What is the point of this text? It is to suggest that God's justice is not "loose," that actions do have consequences, even when one cannot see them. Rabbi Ḥanina continues:

[Jacob deceived his father Isaac, and received his blessing, leaving none for the firstborn Esau.] "When Esau heard his father's words, he cried out an exceedingly great and bitter cry" (Genesis 27:34). Jacob caused Esau to cry out bitterly. But, where do we find that he paid for that deed? In Shushan, as it says: "and [Mordecai] cried out a great and bitter cry" (Esther 4:1).

(GENESIS RABBAH 67:4)

Jacob was the ancestor of the Jews of Persia, and Haman was the descendant of his brother Esau. When Haman's plan to destroy the Jews was publicized, Mordecai suffered great emotional pain— measure for measure, commensurate with the pain that Jacob had inflicted on Esau generations earlier.

What is striking here is that Jacob and Esau lived over a thousand years before the events of the time of Mordecai and Haman, yet they are still intimately connected. Rabbi Ḥanina suggests that while Jacob's sin (namely, the suffering he caused his brother in stealing his blessing) may not have been punished in his own time, justice was not ignored. Rather, it was deferred, simply held off until a later date. Moreover, justice in this case does not consist of the guilty party suffering punishment. Justice can play itself out in the lives of family members and associates long after the original event. Did Mordecai do anything to merit this suffering? Had he personally, sinned against Haman (or Esau, for that matter), that he should have had to suffer and cry out as Esau had done so long ago? The answer, both in the Bible and in this rabbinic text, is, "No." But truthful justice (which Rabbi Ḥanina insists cannot be "loosened") flows through generations, finally being played out measure for measure.

This text is terrifying on the one hand, and fascinating on the other. The horror that we feel is twofold. We are terrified that we will suffer and not know why. The deeds of those who preceded us—people of whom we may not even know, and actions of which we can have absolutely no knowledge—those deeds may lead to our own suffering. This midrash does not suggest that Mordecai knew that his bitter wailing was intended to discharge a debt to the descendants of Esau—that it would clear the slate, as it were, so that Haman could be defeated. He simply experienced his own terror, fear at the approaching conflict and possible annihilation. We also sense horror when we realize that our actions may be faulty in some way, yet we may not actually know of them or sufficiently pay for them. (After all, the Torah itself suggests that Jacob had paid somewhat already: Isaac informs Esau, "Your brother came with guile" [*bemirmah,* Genesis 27:35] and later, when Laban substitutes Leah for Rachel in the wedding bed, Jacob complains, "Why did you deceive me?" [*rimitani,* 29:25]. But while Jacob suffered for his action, measure for measure, the compensation was not paid to Esau directly.) How will our deeds come back to us? And more frightening to consider, how will our actions play out in the lives of our children and our children's children?

What is fascinating about this midrashic text is that it undermines the larger conflict driving the story in the Book of Esther: God's eternal battle against Amalek. Soon after the crossing of the Sea of Reeds, the Israelites were attacked by a tribe known as Amalek. The assault was perfidious: "He surprised you on the march, when you were famished and weary, and cut down all the stragglers in your rear" (Deuteronomy 25:18). The people of Israel were hardly prepared for battle, and a successful outcome was not to be assumed. After the defeat of Amalek God declares, "I will utterly blot out the memory of Amalek from under heaven," and Moses elaborates, declaring, "Adonai will be at war with Amalek throughout the ages" (Exodus 17:14, 16). Despite God's declaration of personal intent, in Deuteronomy Moses interprets: "When Adonai your God grants you safety from all your enemies around you, in the land that Adonai your God is giving you as hereditary portion, you shall blot out the memory of Amalek from under heaven. Do not forget!" (Deuteronomy 25:19). It may be God's war, but we are charged with fighting the battle. Whatever our ancestors may have done to incite or invite Amalek to attack, or however innocent they may have been and his assault unprovoked, we are responsible for fulfilling God's intention to wipe out Amalek. The play of the generations, for merit and for responsibility, runs up and down the line.

This generates the underlying dynamic of the Purim story. There, the villain is the wicked Haman. We know from the start that he is wicked, given his pedigree: Haman the son of Hammedatha the Agagite. Why is this telling? Because we also know that Haman's ancestor the Agagite is none other than "King Agag of Amalek" (1 Samuel 15:8). Haman is a descendant of the perfidious Amalek with whom Israel, as God's proxy, has an eternal battle. Nothing good will come from Haman, we are sure, and whatever else happens, he will have to be destroyed. The text explicitly tells us this, and its veracity is emphasized in that it is Haman's own wife who speaks it: "If Mordecai . . . is of Jewish stock, you will not overcome him; you will fall before him to your ruin" (Esther 6:13). The Jewish people and the family of Amalek are eternal enemies, and the former are bound to prevail in the end.

For all that the Book of Esther is based on this larger conflict (where the Jews are innocent, and the fall of Haman/Amalek is a given), the midrash above suggests that things are not so clear. First, we should not be seduced into thinking that, as victims, we are by definition innocent. Second, we cannot look exclusively at only one event, one interaction in the whole of history to determine guilt or innocence. This midrash invites us to look more closely at every aspect of the story, to look outside of its givens—in time, in space, in actions, and even in the dramatis personae. When we expand the field of our vision, we include more data than in our first assessment of the situation. When we begin to ask the question, "What is the story here?"—meaning, what is it that we are telling ourselves to hide from the Truth—we often gain a new perspective on our own behavior, and a new understanding of that of others.

The importance of this wider view to developing our own expansive hearts and generous spirits can be seen in some other rabbinic texts related to this midrash. In each, there is a lesson that

flows from the deep awareness of how justice—truthful justice—
may be unbearable at the moment, but its absence does not mean
that justice is not ultimately served. That awareness, in turn, pries
open our hearts and clears our eyes to see the need, always, for
compassion and mindful attention to the truth.

> "The couriers went out posthaste on the royal mission, and the
> decree was proclaimed in the fortress of Shushan. The king and
> Haman sat down to feast, but the city of Shushan was dumb-
> founded" (Esther 3:15). Said Rabbi Ḥanin, "Anyone who says that
> the Merciful One is lax in executing justice *(vatran)*, let his bowels
> go loose *(yitvatroon)*. Rather, God is long-suffering, but collects his
> due. [God] said to the Tribes (the sons of Jacob), 'You sold your
> brother (Joseph into slavery) while you sat to eat and drink (cf.
> Genesis 37:25ff). So, then, will I do to you,' as it says, 'The king and
> Haman sat down to feast'" . . . Rabbi Yissakhar of Kefar Mandi
> taught: "Now, considering that Joseph had already forgiven his
> brothers saying, 'It was not you who sent me here, but God' (Gen-
> esis 45:8), and still we see that the punishment for the sale of
> Joseph was set and extended even to the days of Mordecai, how
> much worse will the punishment be for someone who has not
> already been forgiven!"
>
> (ESTHER RABBAH 7:20)

Here the issue is not the tense interaction between Jacob and
Esau (finally acted out in the persons of Mordecai and Haman),
but rather the conflict among the sons of Jacob. The brothers'
action was vile, and it is a clear violation of a law in the Torah: "He
who kidnaps a man—whether he has sold him or is still holding
him—shall be put to death" (Exodus 21:16). Even without this
transgression, the relationship among the brothers was negative
and a cause of contention. Forgiveness would have been a good

outcome just on that level. But the brothers went beyond that, selling Joseph into slavery and suffering with guilt and anxiety ever after. They lived in dread of the consequences of their act. Yet at the moment when it was most likely that vengeance or punishment would come crashing down on their heads, when they stood forlorn before Joseph, they were forgiven. Nevertheless, their deed still stood unpunished.

The lesson taught by Rabbi Yissakhar reaches beyond the specific case of Joseph and his brothers, even beyond the story of Mordecai and Haman. He teaches us that even though we might not be able to undo our sins, that our actions set in motion unchangeable consequences, we must not become fatalists. We must not give up trying to affect the outcome. Implicit in his teaching is the insight that had Joseph not forgiven his brothers, there is a chance that Haman's plot might have been fulfilled, or perhaps the punishment for their crime might have been put off to a later time, and fulfilled in an even worse manifestation. The more we can train ourselves to awaken to the truth, the more we will be able to prevent mistakes, recover from them sooner, and recognize when we are trapped working through old stories—so that we can minimize the negative outcomes. We will then be able to seek and offer forgiveness.

Rabbi Ḥanina's teaching also appears in a pericope in the Palestinian Talmud that seeks to plumb the full depth of God's forgiveness—for both the righteous and the wicked.

> Rabbi Aḥa and Rabbi Tanḥum son of Rabbi Ḥiyya taught in the name of Rabbi Yoḥanan: It says of God that He is "slow to anger (literally, long in anger)"—the idiom is not *erekh af* (where the word for anger, *af,* is in the singular) but *erekh apayim* (in the plural). God lengthens His spirit before He calls one to account. Once He starts to collect [payment], He again lengthens His spirit and collects.

Rabbi Ḥanina taught: Anyone who says that the Merciful One is lax in executing justice *(vatran)*, let his bowels go loose *(yit-vatroon)*. Rather, God is long-suffering, but does collect His due.

Rabbi Levi taught: What does it mean that God is "long to anger"? God "distances anger." This can be likened to a king who commanded two tough legions. He reasoned, "If these soldiers remain stationed here with me, and my subjects anger me, they (the soldiers) will act against (punish) them. Let me instead send them far away, so that if my subjects anger me, it will take a while until I can send for my soldiers, and my people will seek to placate me, and I will accept their supplications." So, too, does the Holy One reason: "Anger *(af)* and fury *(ḥeimah)* are My destroying angels. Let me send them far away, so that if Israel angers me, it will take time until I can send for them, and Israel will then repent and I will accept their repentance."

(YERUSHALMI TA'ANIT 9A)

Rabbi Ḥanina's teaching stands sandwiched between two others here, and it is not connected to the story of Jacob or Joseph or Purim. Rather, it serves as a transition between the two surrounding teachings. The first lesson depicts God as executing judgment, but moderating it somewhat by "extending His spirit," that is, by being compassionate. Rabbi Ḥanina teaches that God is long-suffering: His anger may abate but He will ultimately punish transgressors. The lesson that follows includes a parable that suggests that God's anger is directly related to God's justice and the force of His punishment. If God can only hold off from acting on His anger, He will ultimately be ready to receive prayers of contrition and acts of transformation. People will repent and God will forgive them. Execution of judgment may be forestalled, perhaps prevented, but certainly lessened. So, too, can we affect the outcome of our interactions: by taking a breath and "lengthening" our spirits, by holding off from acting on our anger, and finally by waiting to consider what is a wise action; remaining open to and anticipating changed circumstances and new understandings will allow our responses to tend toward greater compassion and mercy.

Taken together, this series of texts offers us teachings that support our practice of mindfulness. What we hope is that in the process of waking up to the truth of the moment, of our lives, we will develop more compassionate hearts. As we work slowly, regularly, watching each moment to know its special character, we learn that nothing is permanent. All things change. When we sit in meditation, we frequently observe how thoughts arise and pass away, superseded by others, which, in turn, pass away as well. We learn to recognize that our emotions, too, are transitory. We can then look more dispassionately at our actions, and evaluate them with clearer vision and a more open heart. In turn, we often become aware, in a new way, from a different perspective, of the inner states of those around us. We begin to forgive without having been asked, as we realize that the one who has hurt us did not intend us harm, but acted out of fear, anxiety, or pain. We also find that we understand our own role in the conflict differently. We see more clearly how we played out a story, acting from avarice, terror, or jealousy.

The more clearly we can observe our own actions and interactions, the more aware we become of how precarious is the path of righteousness. No act can pass without scrutiny. Each word bears careful screening. We see how easy it is to hurt another person. We see how effortlessly we can create our own exile, and how far-reaching the consequences of our mistakes might be. Our desire for compassion—from ourselves, from others, from God—leads us to understand how much we must extend ourselves in compassion toward others. We will then be much quicker to forgive, anxious not to cause any further pain. We will develop the capacity to hold back from our first inclinations, aware of the danger of our initial, spontaneous reactions. We will take a breath or a break in time, creating emotional space and psychic distance from being startled—and allow ourselves to pause to consider what is the wisest course of action at this moment. And, who knows, in that instant, we may be surprised to hear the other person say, "I'm sorry."

Our discussion has revolved around the connection between Esau's and Mordecai's cries. One flows from the other, measure for measure. It is not only the similarity of the words in the two instances that caused Rabbi Ḥanina to teach about God's patience in exacting punishment. It also has to do with the actual terms themselves, and the meaning of this outcry. Esau cries out and the phrase is *vayitz'ak tza'akah;* when Mordecai echoes, the text says, *vayiz'ak za'akah.* The words are very similar, almost identical. Nahum Sarna suggests that they "are simply dialectical variants of each other."[3] Yet, there is a slight semantic difference between them. When Esau cries out *(tzadi-ayin-kof),* his cry emanates from the clear awareness that he has been harmed. He has lost his blessing through guile and trickery; he has suffered injustice. That cry demands justice, requires response. Mordecai cries out *(zayin-ayin-kof)* in anticipation of evil. Haman's plan has been announced, but it is yet months away from being fulfilled. He is the victim of an evil plot, but he has not yet been subject to its execution. The fullness of his oppression has yet to be confirmed.

In either case, however, these cries "connote the anguished cry of the oppressed, the agonized plea of the victim for help in the face of some great injustice. In the Bible these terms are suffused with poignancy and pathos, with moral outrage and soul-stirring passion."[4]

---

[3] Nahum Sarna, *The JPS Torah Commentary: Genesis* (Philadelphia: Jewish Publication Society, 1989), p. 132.
[4] Ibid.

The biblical response to these outcries is to hear *(shin-mem-ayin)* and to know *(yod-dalet-ayin)*. This is true both in the case of Sodom (Genesis 18:20–21) and of Egypt (Exodus 2:23–24; 3:7–10). The initial cry demands investigation, but once observed fully it leads to confirmed awareness, to knowledge. "In the biblical conception, knowledge is not essentially or even primarily rooted in the intellect and mental activity. Rather it is more experiential and is embedded in the emotions, so that it may encompass such qualities as contact, intimacy, concern, relatedness, and mutuality. Conversely, not to know is synonymous with dissociation, indifference, alienation, and estrangement; it culminates in callous disregard for another's humanity."[5] God could not remain deaf to Esau's suffering. He had to act, just as He could not refrain from responding to the cry in Sodom or in Egypt.

One of the more curious commandments related to Purim is "to drink so much that one cannot differentiate between 'cursed be Haman' and 'blessed be Mordecai'" (Megillah 7b). There is another way to understand this commandment. The original idiom for "cannot differentiate between" is *"ad delo yada,"* that is, "until he does not know between." But we would do better to translate it in light of the rabbinic Hebrew idiom *"ad shelo,"* simply meaning "before." The instruction may be understood: become intoxicated, or simply at ease from drink, before you can reach the conclusion that Haman is, in fact, cursed, or that Mordecai is, clearly, blessed.

Again, we might read this teaching from the Talmud as a moment of mindfulness at work. That is: A person is required to attain a sense of completeness, of sweet joy, through the contemplation of the objects of the sayings "cursed be Haman" and "blessed be Mordecai," coming to know the truth of their suffering,

---

[5]Nahum Sarna, *The JPS Torah Commentary: Exodus* (Philadelphia: Jewish Publication Society, 1991), p. 5.

each one in his own heart, each one from his own story. First, we must be able to see Haman and Mordecai simply as human beings: descendants, ancestors, and actors. They are shaped by all that preceded them, and by their perception of their places in life: who they are in this moment. As we enter the story, each stands at the intersection of the horizontal (contemporaneous) and vertical (historical) axes. At that moment of "right now," each confronts his sense of self and of his life course. In that very moment, neither is cursed nor blessed: each struggles to hide from the truth or to know it, to act out or to act from. When we look upon them in that moment of choice, in the immediacy of the now, we have compassion for them both.

Neither is victim or victor in that moment; that will only be known from their decisions. When we look upon them, attentive to their cries, their struggles to free themselves from their stories, from the inheritance of their ancestors, from their blindnesses and haughtiness, our hearts are touched. We hear, and then we know. When we know, fully, the truth of this moment, we are moved to "intimacy, concern, relatedness, and mutuality." We connect with them, we feel for them, and we desire only the best for them.

And, for ourselves. We realize that Haman and Mordecai are literary characters, but they depict people with hearts and souls, with families and work, with hopes and fears—just like us. Just like them, we struggle to face each moment with an open, awakened heart, seeking to know the truth and to be able to live by it. Listening to them, we hear our own inner cries, and we go down to look, to ascertain what is the truth: what is the oppression, what is the suffering, what is the slavery in which we are mired. And then, we know; and knowing, we can act. We can choose how to live—neither as oppressed nor as oppressor. Neither as cursed nor as blessed. With clarity of vision and openness of heart, we may be able to act in such a manner that we prevent doing injury to another, from creating dynamics of sin and retribution, of responsibility and guilt handed down from one minute to another, from one day to another, from one generation to the next.

Tu B'Shevat

I was to lead the first meditation session at MAKOM: The Center for Mindfulness at the new Jewish Community Center in Manhattan. The facility is unique in many ways. First, the room itself is oval in shape, open at both ends to allow entrance, with a window in one of the sweeping long walls. The cushions in a circle on the simple, highly polished hardwood floor seem embraced, sheltered, upheld. Second, this is the first JCC to have been built with space dedicated to spiritual practice. Third, the whole of the JCC has been conceived around this space. The intention is that all of the JCC programs will flow from and reinforce a mindful and Jewish sensibility: each moment is pregnant with the presence of God, and each moment, lived in truth, will be one of compassion and justice.

The opening of MAKOM had been long in coming. The JCC's pool was already in use, as was the gym. The nursery school was already in its second semester. Still, there were no doors to shield the room from noise in the hall outside, none to close off the storage rooms inside. Workmen were hammering, sawing, and doing their thing—making a racket in which it was difficult to concentrate and meditate. Nevertheless, it was time to start the daily morning and evening meditation sessions.

The day on which we started was the eve of Tu B'Shevat, the time in late winter known as Jewish Arbor Day. The rationale for this holiday is that, according to the rabbis, it establishes the separating point between generations of fruits. That is, fruits that flowered and budded previous to this date constituted one cohort, and those that flower and bud after it consitute another. The practical import is that the fruits in one cohort cannot be used in the calculation of the harvest to determine how much fruit must be segregated out as a tithe offering. This is similar to the way we often use different dates to group things: June 30 to end one fiscal year, July 1 to start the next; November 30 as the cut-off date by which a child must turn five years old to enter kindergarten; and the like. Tu B'Shevat, then, marks the cut-off date of the previous year. It marks the end of one year, the turning-point of the next. What we have in hand at that moment is the fruit of the year that has passed. It is that fruit that we will count as a cohort, which will be grouped together and tithed as one crop. We do not yet have any fruit from the new crop. Tu B'Shevat, then, brings the past to closure.

But it also marks the future. The classical commentator Rashi explains why this time is appropriate as a turning point. "Most of the rains of the year have passed. This time is the season of mating. The sap has begun to rise in the trees, and they will start to blossom from this point on" (Rosh Hashanah 14a, s.v. *ho'il veyatzu rov gishmei shanah*). From this perspective, Tu B'Shevat marks the beginning of something, the start of the process of blossoming and producing fruit. The actual process, however, is hidden. The sap that is flowing is only inside the tree; it is not visible in the outside world. Its product will not be seen for some time. Tu B'Shevat celebrates the future, the potential of the moment.

As we sat together in MAKOM on that first morning, it was evident how appropriate it was to be celebrating that holiday. That the building existed, that the space for our meditation was ready, rested on the endeavors of hundreds of people in the past: those people who had first imagined creating a JCC on the Upper West Side of Manhattan; the director and her staff who had helped to create the vision and execute the process; the funders and donors who had helped to make it possible; the architects, craftspeople, and laborers who had actually built the building and all that was in it. In that room, we were aware of all the people who had been involved in making it possible for us to gather at all.

At the same time, we were initiating a program that had only been imagined. We who gathered to sit knew why we were there, each with our own particular intention. But, we could also sense that something else was happening. From that moment on, morning and evening meditation sessions would take place. Different and various teachers would lead the sessions. Many and varied participants would come—some once, some regularly, some now, some later. We had no idea what the role of MAKOM would actually become in the life of the JCC, but we sensed its potential rising up in that moment. We were there in its heart, holding a space of heartfelt gratitude, love—and hope.

And all the while, the workmen were clanging and banging, continuing their endeavors to complete their tasks. Each time a saw whined, metal clanged against stone, a hammer banged against nail, or a voice called to another, we were challenged to maintain our concentration and composure. We were challenged to sense our own reactions, to see the truth of the situation, and to determine what would be the wise course of action in the moment. We could respond with contention or with compassion. Our first impulse was to inform the workers that we were holding a meditation session next door, and to ask them to be quieter. But, even when they tried to accommodate our needs, they could not stop their work. The needs of the larger JCC, their integrity as journeymen, and their responsibilities to themselves and their families for sustenance, precluded such a pause. In every moment, with each breath, we faced the next choice: will we hear the sounds as distractions, invasions of our domain (both where we sat and our inner space), or experience them simply as "sound"? We could allow our minds and hearts to create conflict ("How disrespectful they are!" "Those people are such a distraction!" "I wish that they would go away and leave me in peace!"), or we could celebrate our mutual contributions to the life of the JCC. And return to the breath, to the truth of that particular moment.

So there we sat. And we found the truth of that Tu B'Shevat in the JCC to be also the truth of our lives. In every moment we are the beneficiaries of the intentions and the work of myriad other people—both those around us and those who came before us. In that same moment, the seeds of the unfolding future are maturing and the sap of the flow of life is rising in us. We are about to move forward into the next moment, to reveal its particular flower, to bring forth its fruit. And we find ourselves balanced between the two. In fact, all that exists in this moment is this very moment. It is no longer the past and not yet the future. It is its own particular experience. We can meet its clanging and banging—from the outside or generated by our own hearts and minds—with wisdom, accepting "what is" in joy, or we can make up stories that create contention and unhappiness.

Given the blessing of the moment at which we have arrived, is it not more likely that the future that is about to flower will be fuller, happier, more blessed if we can learn to accept each moment as it is, in its fullness, in its truth?

Section Four

Ḥesed

Chapter Eight

Mindfulness, Love, Fear, and Faithful Living

Whial en I was a freshman in college I frequently attended the Orthodox *Kabbalat Shabbat* service at Hillel. A young graduate student in Chemistry, a rabbi and the son of a prominent rabbi, led the Orthodox community there. He was charismatic, and the early stirrings of the *ba'al teshuvah* movement (young Jews of non-Orthodox backgrounds taking on Orthodox practices and beliefs) could be felt among the students in his *minyan.*

One evening, before services, I found myself in the lobby while he was engaged in a conversation with a young woman. It seemed somewhat public, so I stood by, listening in. She asked, "But, what is it that God wants of us?" Something about the question grabbed me, perhaps because I was thinking about it, too. Spontaneously I responded with the words that had stuck in my mind, familiar from the daily service: "Adonai wants *(rotzeh)* those who revere Him, those who hope for His mercy" (Psalm 147:11). The rabbi brushed my answer aside and went on with his response—about doing *mitzvot,* keeping Shabbat, etc.

I was hurt and a little disappointed that he did not give my response much attention. And clearly, the event has stayed with me over several decades. As I reflect on that interaction and my response now, I have come to recognize two faults in my interjection. One is that I interrupted what was perceived to be a private—or at least a focused and impassioned—conversation in which the rabbi (and likely his questioner) had a particular "pastoral" interest or goal. My interjection was a distraction to him and may have prevented him from really reaching the soul of her inquiry. The other is that I have come to understand Hebrew and its idioms much better, and realize that while in colloquial Hebrew to say *rotzeh* is to say "want," in the biblical idiom it is closer to "desire, value, will"—even "love." Moreover, in the case of this verse, it is not so much "what" God wants as "whom" God desires, delights in, favors. So I concluded that I had misunderstood the verse altogether and consequently misrepresented its theological intention.

These days, though, I am not so sure. What does the psalm actually say?

> Sing to Adonai a song of praise; chant a hymn with a lyre to our God—who covers the heavens with clouds, provides rain for the earth, makes the mountains put forth grass; who gives the beasts their food, the raven's brood what they cry for. He does not prize the strength of horses, nor value the fleetness of men; but Adonai desires those who fear Him, those who depend on His faithful care.
>
> (PSALM 147:7–11)

God provides for all beings, from the beast to the raven's brood. The natural order is set to provide that which will satisfy our needs: clouds, rain, grass, food. What could God possibly need from us? Certainly not prideful assertions of *our* power!

What does God want from us? My answer now would be: our awareness that all we are, all that we have, all that sustains us, comes from God. In moments in which I am deeply aware of that truth I am humble, and I fear God. What else is that "fear" than appreciation of my, and our, powerlessness before the Eternal? After all, can we make rain? Do we cause the grass to grow? Is it in our hands to satisfy the needs of all the creatures of the world? How can we not be humble? How can we not fear the One who not only can, but does, do all those things?

But the fear of God does not stand alone; it is tied to the awareness of our dependence on God's faithful care. Those who sense God's overwhelming power to create and sustain all life understand also that Creation and our existence in it is an expression of God's overwhelming love. That aspect of God's concern is called *ḥesed*. It is love—covenantal love, that which is committed to another in relationship. In that sense it is faithful. God cares for us, out of love, and we respond with humility, reverence, fear—and love.

The psalm adds another layer to this dynamic relationship. God desires "those who depend" on God's love. The verb here translated "depend" (*yaḥel, hameyaḥalim*) might better be understood as "hope for, look forward to." To recognize our powerlessness relative to God's sustaining force leads us to recognize that we need God's care. We cannot do it alone. And so, we hope in God's lovingkindness. We look forward to receiving God's faithful care.

This theme is echoed in a number of other passages in Scripture.

> Kings are not delivered by a large force; warriors are not saved by great strength; horses are a false hope for deliverance—for all their great power, they provide no escape. Truly the eye of Adonai is on those who fear Him, who look forward to (*hameyaḥalim*) His faithful care to save them from death, to sustain them in famine. We set our hope in Adonai, He is our help and shield; in Him our hearts rejoice, for in His holy name we trust. May we enjoy, O Adonai, Your faithful care (*ḥasdekha*), as we have put our hope (*yiḥalnu*) in You.

(PSALM 33:16–22)

Again, we are presented with the vanity and hubris of those who confuse human power with ultimate power. Kings and warriors expect that large forces and strong horses will deliver them. But what is it that they hope to defeat with their forces, to escape with their horses? Death! Help against that enemy will come neither from political power nor from physical might. There is nothing that we can do to overpower that foe. The terror that moves kings and provokes warriors, however, can be overcome.

When we shift our consciousness from fear of death to fear of God, from anxiety over mortality to hope in lovingkindness, we can be saved. This transformation is heartening. When we let go of our fear of death and loss, we are freer to realize the fullness of life, to experience joy. "Put not your trust in the great, in mortal man who cannot save. His breath departs; he returns to dust; on that day his plans come to nothing. Happy is he who has the God of Jacob for his help, whose hope is in the Lord his God" (Psalm 146:3–5). Our struggle against mortality, our incapacity to overcome death, is a source of sadness and despair. But, trust in God's faithful love, in the truth of our mere existence in this moment, in the blessing of our very existence, is a source of joy. Hope in God is merely a "help and shield," but it is not a magic potion. It will not prevent death, but it will help us to endure it, to accept it, even in life. We are thus protected from the anguish of hopelessness, and aided in opening to joy.

The calm, balanced acknowledgement of the truth of the human condition, of the way the world works, is liberating. The mind, not struggling in any way to hide, is awake and present. This, then, leads to a deep awareness of God's immediate presence, and with this awareness, a sense of joy. This is reinforced in the last line of Psalm 33, which is a mindfulness instruction: "May Your lovingkindness, Adonai, be upon us when we place our hope in You" (verse 22). God's lovingkindness is always present; it is manifest in our existence, in Creation. Our capacity to perceive that as true is often obscured by our fear of death and our anxiety over loss and pain. When we place our hope in God we can escape the battle against death. Death does not disappear; loss is unavoidable. But we need not engage in an adversarial struggle with it. Deliverance comes when we trust in God, when we experience life without denying death. In those moments of clear vision and openness of heart, we are blessed with the awareness of God's lovingkindness, which transcends death. The experience of God's faithful care is the result of our capacity to realize that our only hope is in God, in accepting the truth of life. Our hope in God becomes the experience of God's loving care.

This moment of transcendence, this transforming hope, appears in the middle of the Book of Lamentations. The five chapters of this book are dirges read each year on Tishah B'Av, the anniversary of the destruction of Jerusalem by the Babylonians. While each chapter may stand alone, the whole of the book reveals a slow movement from abject suffering and loss, punishment for sin that results in alienation from God, to a claim against God and a call for His saving mercy. The turning point appears near the middle of the third chapter.

> My life was bereft of peace; I forgot what happiness was. I thought my strength and hope had perished before Adonai. To recall my distress and my misery was wormwood and poison; whenever I thought of them, I was bowed low. But this do I call to mind, and therefore I have hope (*oḥil*): the kindness (*ḥasdei*) of Adonai has not ended, His mercies are not spent. They are renewed every morning—ample is Your faithfulness. "Adonai is my portion," I say with full heart; therefore I hope in Him (*oḥil*).
>
> (LAMENTATIONS 3:17–24)

All that preceded this passage had been descriptions of Zion's suffering and of Israel's disgrace. God stood off, aloof, uncaring, sending destruction upon His beloved people for their transgressions. The poet could hardly raise his head for the pain and loss. Yet something happens in this moment. In the space between one verse and the next, memory and recollection shift from tasting like poison to offering redemption.

What is the source of this shift in tone and understanding? For all that the destruction of Jerusalem represents an ending, a kind of testimony that God has abandoned His people, the poet suddenly becomes aware of a new fact: as painful as it is to remember the past and recall his suffering, he is nevertheless alive to do so. He can think; he can bring things to mind. From the constricted vision of destruction, distress, misery, and alienation, the poet suddenly opens to an awareness of God's faithfulness—that it has indeed not ended. How does the poet know this? He becomes aware of the fact that he has seen new days. He realizes that for all of his suffering, he has not been destroyed. He understands that with each next breath, with each next moment, with each next day, he has been blessed by God's enduring love and mercy—even in the midst of his terrible suffering.

This realization allows the poet to shift his self-conception from abject sufferer, alienated from God, to a sufferer who is not alone. He finds room in his heart to think about God as the One who might yet draw near. His recollection of the past no longer brings only pain for its loss, but hope for a renewed loving relationship with God. Moreover, he can shift his vision from his suffering at the hands of a distant, punishing God to his relationship to a present, comforting God. Further, he can now more readily recognize his own responsibility in making that happen. "Of what shall a living man complain? Each one of his own sins! Let us search and examine our ways, and turn back to the Lord" (3:39–40). This shift in orientation, from a focus on God's punishing hand to the poet's own hand reaching out for connection, makes rapprochement possible.

Taking stock of his own deeds, of his own contribution to his suffering, the author of Lamentations is further emboldened to call upon God to act. Yes, God, he says, I have acted wrongly, and I have brought punishment upon my head. But, enough! I have suffered too much. I will do what is required on my part to return to our previous loving relationship, but You, too, God, must act. "I have called on Your name, O Adonai, from the depths of the Pit. Hear my plea. . . . You have seen, O Adonai, the wrong done me; Oh, vindicate my right!" (3:55,56,59). Your faithfulness, God, demands that the world be brought back into balance. My suffering—our suffering—has been too great. I deserved punishment; I acknowledge that. But You, God, have gone too far. I will change my ways, and let my suffering be recompense for my past misdeeds. But do not leave me here in misery. Redeem me, God, bring me back to You and Your love.

Who is it, then, that God will favor? Who is it that God desires? It is those who fear Him, who are honest about their actions, who are not haughty before the Eternal. Those very ones will also realize that they must take responsibility for their actions and the consequences of those actions. When we acknowledge the truth of our lives, of our actions and their consequences; when we seize the opportunity afforded by our ongoing existence to re-evaluate our lives and change our ways—we then experience a sudden turn of heart. Like the poet of Lamentations we find that we can hope in Adonai, in His lovingkindness and faithfulness. "May Your lovingkindness, Adonai, be upon us when we place our hope in You."

But what are we to do with Job, with the one who epitomizes the suffering that does not flow as a consequence of our actions? How can we hope in God, trust in God's faithful care, when we cannot explain the root of our suffering?

That was part of Job's experience. Early on in his dispute with God (more, with his supposed comforters), Job presses his argument: I suffer, yet I am innocent, and I wish to know why that is so! Job has experienced the onslaught of death and suffering like no other person in the Bible. Yet he does not hide from his predicament. He does not accept his visitors' various explanations for his suffering, their justifications of God's actions. He is unwilling to look away from the truth of his life, both the severity of his loss and his ignorance of any sin justifying such punishment. He struggles to square that truth with what he expected to be the reward for having been "blameless and upright, fearing God and shunning evil" (Job 1:1). It would seem impious to challenge God, to question His justice, yet that is precisely what Job does. He believes that to do otherwise would actually be to deny God, to lie about his life and his suffering.

He rejects Zophar the Naamatite's justification of God: "Will you speak unjustly on God's behalf? Will you speak deceitfully for Him? . . . Will it go well when He examines you? Will you fool Him as one fools men?" (13:7,9). Instead, Job insists on speaking his own truth, the truth of his life before God, rather than lie. "Keep quiet; I will have my say, come what may upon me. How long! I will take my flesh in my teeth; I will take my life in my hands" (13:13–14). We come now to the critical moment. Job recognizes that he can only present his own perception of the truth, and that it may be insufficient as an argument against God. Yet what can he do? His faith in God's justice, his trust in God's lovingkindness, will not permit him to let go of the truth. It may be dangerous, yet he must go forward.

Here the text of the Bible places before us two versions of what he says, of what is in his heart. We are presented with a virtual homophone, a word written one way that sounds like another with yet a different orthography and meaning. The written text has the word *lo* *(lamed alef)*, meaning "no, negation," yet the tradition would have us pronounce instead *lo* *(lamed vav)* meaning "in Him." In the first instance, Job says, "He may well slay me; I may have no hope *(lo ayaḥel)*; yet I will argue my case before Him. In this too is my salvation: That no impious man can come into His presence" (13:15–16). In the second instance we read, "Though He slay me, yet will I trust (hope) in Him *(lo ayaḥel)*; but I will argue my ways before Him. This also shall be my salvation, that a hypocrite cannot come before Him."

Is there a difference between these two readings? In the end, no. The first reading acknowledges the ultimate audacity of bringing a case against God. It may be more than God can bear, beyond acceptable behavior. God may yet lash out in anger at Job's impudence, and what hope would he have then? Nevertheless, Job persists in his argument, trusting still that there may be salvation for him. If he is pure of heart, if his intention and his challenge are not "impious," he may yet survive.

In the second reading, Job again acknowledges the danger in his protest. God may yet slay him—either in the ongoing unfolding of his suffering or for his impudence. Here, however, the suggested reading opens up to our theme. "Though He slay me": even though my children lie dead before me, my fortune is destroyed, my body is afflicted, even though death and loss are all I know and may yet overtake me, "yet I will hope in Him." My hope in God, my trust in His faithful care transcends even my own experience. My suffering does not stand alone, outside of the larger context of God's lovingkindness. It must fit; therefore, I seek the understanding to know how it fits. It is thus that I can "argue my ways before Him." If it were not for God's ultimate care and infinite attention to this world, and to me, I would not be able to go on. "I know that my Vindicator lives; in the end He will testify on earth" (19:25). Even if I die.

If there were anyone who might "curse God and die" (2:9), it would be Job. Yet he does not. He need not. His struggle is not solely to uncover the deepest levels of divine justice. It is to reestablish his hope in God, so that his suffering not overwhelm him, so that he might once again return to a full life. Job's affliction is great; greater, perhaps, than most any of us will ever know. To give in to the simple equation "I suffer, therefore I have sinned" would be to undermine his trust in God's ultimate justness and eviscerate the deep connection he feels with God, one that he assumes allows him to present his argument. More, when he presses his case, he does so not only for himself, but for all of us who cannot understand the nature or source of our suffering.

In the end, God does not share His reasons with Job. He does not explain the source of his suffering, nor its purpose. Still, Job is not beaten into silence by the end of the book. Rather, he releases his hand from his struggle because God has finally answered. God has assured him of His ultimate faithful care; not only for him personally, but for all Creation. Job's words come back to us: "Though He slay me, yet I will hope in Him." I can hold whatever comes my way, Job says, I can bear any loss or pain, God, so long as You are with me. I know You are with me because I hope in You. In the words of the psalmist, "May Your lovingkindness, Adonai, be upon us when we place our hope in You."

The flow of emotions and the shifting understandings of relationship with God illustrated in the examples above find their way into the thinking of the Jewish mystical and hasidic traditions. A fundamental belief is that God's initial and ultimate relationship to Creation is love (ḥesed). Before God brought the world into being, all of God's attributes remained only potential. There was nothing on which they might be brought to bear. It was only through Creation that the potential of God's love and justice could be actuated. God's highest desire was to love, and be loved by, His creatures—

particularly human beings, the only self-reflective, choosing creatures (cf. Zohar II 42b). The purity and power of that love was so great, however, that it precluded any separation. Nothing could exist independently from it. Therefore, God set in place limiting forces, stepping down and contracting the flow of that love into the lower, more material world. In order that humans might tolerate God's love and appreciate it, its power had to be limited, stepped-down.

Yet, any limitation of God's love, no matter what the motivation, would be experienced as a lessening of God's love, just as we know from our own interactions that less love is often experienced as antipathy. This constraining and limiting force is *gevurah,* God's governing power. It is often experienced as an expression of *dinim,* what we would translate as "judgments." It would be better, however, to understand *dinim* as the untoward events that we experience in our lives—loss, alienation, pain, and struggle. The goal of our *avodah,* service of the Divine, is that we might come to see beyond the immediate experience of the *dinim* to see God's ḥesed in its source. In hasidic terms, this is called *hamtakat hadinim beshorsham,* "sweetening the suffering in its source," through the process of following the appearance of all things back to their root in divine love.

Another way of understanding the dynamic of ḥesed and *gevurah* is to return to the view that there is a divine spark in all things. In that sense, all things are of God; all things participate in God's holiness, at least in their core. These sparks, however, are largely concealed from our view. They are hidden in the husks, the *kelipot,* that bind them in the material world. It is our job to learn to reveal these sparks, to raise them up to their source and redeem them. This is no easy task. Our very physicality, our participation in material existence, distracts us. We lose sight of our own inner sparks, and so we forget our intimate connection, our shared essence, with all that is. We tend to see ourselves as separate from other things, from other beings.

It is in claiming independent existence, in asserting an Other in the face of the One, that we conceal the divine spark in us and in other things even further. Indeed, when these divine sparks are mis-used—turned to mundane or hurtful ends—or when they are mis-appropriated—used for selfish ends and the satisfaction of ego-needs—their appearance changes. They no longer appear to us as divine sparks, evidence of God in all things. Rather, we find that they appear to us as lack, deficiency, competition, or conflict. Our misperception, obtuse to the presence of the Divine in all things, creates the experience of evil in the world. When we learn to sense the divine sparks in all things, when we experience God in all things, we then discover that God is present even in those difficult moments. In this manner evil is transformed: we remember that God is in all situations, and we yearn to perceive God's presence and goodness in everything.

In the end, there is nothing but God. Our actions—our own existence, our own behavior—will reveal that truth. In the end, our actions either create the conditions to perceive the blessing that God's glory fills all Creation, or we suffer its perceived absence. The following text attributed to the Baal Shem Tov expresses this very awareness.

> In each and every one of our gestures the Blessed Creator is pres-ent. It is actually impossible for us to move or to speak except for the energy of the Holy Creator (in us). This is the meaning of the phrase "God's glory fills the earth"—every word that we speak derives from the World of Speech, and any thought we think derives from the World of Thought. When our speech is directed toward the good, connecting thought to each word, we connect the two worlds and generate good. But, when we speak ill, we

bring about adversity (Heaven forbid!). There is great wisdom in this, in line with the verse, "Choose language craftily" (Job 15:5). That is, we should habituate ourselves so that nothing ill escapes our mouths, nothing that derives from the realm of judgment *(sitra dedina)*. Rather. our habit always should be to speak good, and to direct our thoughts to the good, the realm of *ḥesed,* and in this manner bring it about.

(KETER SHEM TOV, NO. 273)

I learn from this text that there is no independent evil, and there are no things that in and of themselves are bad. Rather, it is in our mouths and our hearts, our hands and our minds, to reveal God's presence in the world, or to conceal it.

The word of God brought the whole of Creation into being. The mystical tradition has conceived of speech as the production of the sounds of the letters of the Hebrew alphabet. The twenty-two letters produced in the original divine utterances combined, recombined, and reordered themselves over and over such that all aspects of Creation, in their manifest and manifold appearances, might come into being. The divine spark that enlivens all things, that connects Creation to the Creator and so connects all things together in God, is present in these letters, as we learn from this text from the *Me'or Einayim.*

The Holy One contracted Himself, as it were, in the letters of the *alef-bet,* such that each aspect of Creation was able to sustain the divine light and vitality outpouring from His very Being into it. The source point was in the letter *alef,* which has the quality of Torah in the world of Emanation (the highest, most spiritual/ ethereal level of Creation), but the other realms were not able to receive that light because of its intense clarity, so close was it to

God's very Being. Therefore, the Holy One contracted His divinity along with the letter *alef* into the letter *bet*, with which the Torah opens. *Bet* (like the word *bayit*, house) has the sense of "contraction," since in this letter the Holy One contracted Himself such that the lower worlds and all created things would be able to receive the light of God's vital force. And, after this He contracted Himself, as it were, with the letters *alef* and *bet* into the letter *gimmel*, and so from letter to letter, contraction after contraction. The closer an aspect of Creation and its letter is to the original *alef*, the brighter and purer is the divine light (in it), and it has a more spiritually refined quality. Nevertheless, the process of creation and contraction proceeded from *alef* to the letter *tav*, which represents the lowest level. At this level of Creation, human choice is fully operational: *tav* is for *tiḥyeh*, you shall live; *tav* is for *tamut*, you shall die. Control over all the worlds from *tav* to *bet*, the capacity to connect everything to its divine source, was given to the Jewish people, that they might raise all levels up to the *alef*, the *aluf* (Ruler) of the Universe, to unite all things in the Holy One. And, in raising all things up, they further energize the process of drawing down divine blessings to all the worlds and all creatures.

(ME'OR EINAYIM, ḤAYYEI SARAH,
S.V. V'AVRAHAM ZAKEN BA BAYAMIM, ETC.)

This text reminds us that God's very Being is present in all Creation, contracted in the letters of the *alef-bet*, combined and recombined to name and sustain all things. The letters are the building blocks of Creation, and the divine energy that sustains all things is thus present by means of the letters. We are able to access these letters, and raise them up to their source, when we speak words in holiness. The letters that make up the sounds of our speech, when we speak with intention and for the sake of connecting with God, can ascend to higher and higher levels. How we speak, what we speak about, when we speak, and with whom we speak, all affect this process. Even when we think that we are engaged in the most mundane conversation, we can still raise up the letters and the divine energy in them, discovering and revealing in the process that God is in that place, in those words, too. We can, in this way, transform every moment, every encounter, and every interaction, making them holy, discovering God's love and power in them.

Jews have been fascinated with the alphabet from early on. In the Book of Psalms there are numerous alphabetical acrostics, where each of the letters of the *alef-bet* is used as the initial letter of each verse (and, in Psalm 119, there are eight verses for each letter). In later times, the same practice shaped the poetic expression of liturgical composers. Perhaps the motivation to use each letter, and all the letters, was to be able to say everything that could be said. If all of the letters are in play, then everything that could possibly be said with them, symbolically, has been expressed. The psalms and liturgical poems, as praises of God, ought to express every possible sentiment, which is actually impossible. Using all of the letters, the poets acknowledge that it would otherwise be impossible to say all the praise that otherwise is due to God.

Contemporary poets struggle with the same concern. How can words fully express the totality of any moment—its emotional content, its historical antecedents, the physical phenomena that hold all of it together? Is there any way to compact everything into the limited, restricted forms of language and speech? Yet, not to try would be to cut ourselves off from fully experiencing and expressing our lives. A recent example of a poem that uses the alphabet as a means of acknowledging the limits of language while seeking to say it all is found in the collection *Jersey Rain* by Robert Pinsky, former poet laureate of the United States.

ABC

Any body can die, evidently. Few
Go happily, irradiating joy,

Knowledge, love. Many
Need oblivion, painkillers,
Quickest respite.

Sweet time unafflicted,
Various world:
X = your zenith.[6]

Pinsky's poem, while not directed as praise of God, struggles with the same issues before us: How shall we have hope in our short, often painful life on earth? How shall we live fully conscious, fully aware, in the face of death? He acknowledges that it is not easy. Many people do not succeed. Without denying that life may be painful, Pinsky also reminds us that it can also be sweet. We too often rush through those moments of "sweet time unafflicted"; we fail to notice their exceptionality. Too often, we take them for granted, only noticing the times of affliction. More, it is not only time that can be sweet. The world in its diverse and various manifestations is also wondrous, yet we often ignore it in favor of the routine, the expected. Pinsky urges us, as do our hasidic teachers, to look again, to see through the mask of the natural, to see the wonder in all of life's manifestations. In that, he turns us around from the initial orientation of the poem—death and suffering—and points us toward our "zenith": happiness, joy, knowledge, love. A

[6]Robert Pinsky, *Jersey Rain* (New York: Farrar, Straus and Giroux, 2000), p. 10.

true perception of the world, of time and existence, leads us upward, outward, toward a fullness, a wholeness.

What makes this poem so much like one of our hasidic meditations is that it recognizes a dynamic flow back and forth. The text from *Me'or Einayim* above suggested that the divine force comes into the world, stepped down in power, through the descent of the letters from *alef* to *tav*. But our capacity to recognize the divine power in the letters of the words we speak, inherent also in the very fabric of the things we use, raises up the letters, reversing the flow. We raise up the divine force from *tav* to *alef*, connecting the lower realms with the upper, and energizing the flow of divine blessing "downward" in return. Pinsky starts his poem with the letter A. The direction of the poem, its emotional flow, is, at first, downward: "Any body can die." We might expect that the force of this movement will lead all the way to the end of the alphabet, to zero, to nothingness. He shifts course, however, and we find that an honest consideration of the nature of life—that it includes both death and "sweet time unafflicted,/ various world"—leads us back up, toward the infinite "zenith."

The limitation of human existence in its embodied form, the contraction of divine vitality in Creation through the forces of *gevurah*, of necessity brings some suffering. Because we are created, made of finite, physical stuff, we suffer loss, illness, and pain; we must die. The true challenge is to recognize the blessing of being alive, to become aware of the presence of God in us and in all things. When we succeed in that endeavor, we find ourselves enlivened. Our particular suffering does not disappear. We carry it differently. We do not enjoy our pain, but we find that it need not diminish our capacity for joy, for love.

This is not to suggest that God sends us afflictions, or that there is some "good" in suffering. Pain is pain, and it is not good for anyone to endure pain. Rather, our challenge is not to remove God from our moments of affliction, nor to deny God's presence in the midst of our suffering. Job would not "curse God and die." He knew that God must be present for him, even in his perplexity, even in the injustice of the moment. It was his hope that God would respond to his challenge—that God was not deaf to his plea or absent from his life—which sustained him. And it is what we must learn to recognize as well—"sweet time unafflicted,/ various world."

Another piece of contemporary literature helps to illustrate and expand this theme. Jean-Dominique Bauby, the editor of the prestigious European edition of *Elle* magazine, suffered a massive stroke in the brain stem, leaving him in what is called "Locked-In Syndrome." That is, his mind continued to function, with memory, intelligence, and emotion. His body, however, was almost completely paralyzed, dependent on constant nursing help, connected to a respirator, a gastric feeding tube, and an intravenous drip. All that was under his direct control was the function of his left eyelid. In this condition, he found a way to write a short book, *The Diving-Bell and the Butterfly*. The diving-bell was what he called his experience of his body—inert, outside of his control, dependent on others for its sustenance and well-being. The butterfly was his mind—still agile, still beautiful, still seeking the sweetness of life.

How, locked in as he was, did he "write" a book? When his family and friends realized that he could voluntarily blink his eye, they devised a method for discerning his will and learning his thoughts. They would repeat the letters of the alphabet, with the most frequently used letters first, and he would blink to identify the right one. They would transcribe that letter, often then guessing (both correctly and, frustratingly, incorrectly) at the word. During long nights and days without change, weekends without a hospital's regular activities, he turned his mind to memory and reflection. He re-created menus for meals he had cooked, but would not again. He imagined the touch of his wife, the feel of holding his children.

He recalled visits to the shore with his parents, revisiting his child-hood relationships. He reflected on the nature of his life in the hospital, on the character of his caregivers, on how his life had been changed in an instant. Each of these memories and thoughts he developed into brief essays, which he edited in his head, over and over. And finally, letter by letter, over and over, he would "dictate" his chapter to a secretary. He completed the book; it was published and in the bookstores three days before he died.

Trapped in the "diving-bell," Bauby could have receded, giving up on a world he would never affect again, which he could only experience indirectly. The emotional and psychological pressure to give up, to close off, to fall into a perpetual sleep must have been great. Yet the "butterfly"—his mind, his imagination, his love of life, and his yearning to be connected to it no matter how tenuous the situation—stimulated him to write, to communicate. Bauby himself wrote:

> . . . when blessed silence returns, I can listen to the butterflies that flutter inside my head. To hear them, one must be calm and pay close attention, for their wingbeats are barely audible. Loud breathing is enough to drown them out. This is astonishing: my hearing does not improve, yet I hear them better and better. I must have the ear of a butterfly.[7]

The urgings of his soul, the rustle of swirling in his heart, are perceptible only in the silence. Locked in his body, cut off from active participation in the world of doing, Bauby discovers a new world in the silence. He plumbs it for its message: Live.

---

[7]Jean-Dominique Bauby, *The Diving Bell and the Butterfly,* translated by Jeremy Leggatt (New York: Knopf, 1997), p. 97.

In this extraordinary story, we witness at work the interplay of thought and speech, the emergence of the good in the midst of evil, life in the midst of suffering, the power of the letters of Creation to redeem and uplift the soul—indeed, all of life. Stripped of the capacities that identify a person as an actor in the world, denied the power to assert "Make way for me!" as if he were a god, Bauby discovers other sources of power. Love and fear, jealousy and compassion, longing and fullness mix and appear, together and separately. As they arise, he identifies them in his mind, in his heart, and he comes to cherish each one—for they are the fullness of his life, the only true things in his control, that which is most alive for him. That he asserts himself to reach out to others to communicate his discoveries and his awareness then brings them from silence to speech, from the darkness of his tragedy to the light of redemption in his book. Apparently Rabbi Menaḥem Naḥum knew this process and experienced it in his life as well, as we read below.

The source of Torah and the wellspring of wisdom, which we perceive in their revelation in speech, is in the World of Thought. This realm is that of *Ḥokhmah* and *Binah*, God's wisdom and understanding. In the World of Thought, Torah is completely ethereal and inscrutable, without any aspect of revelation. The mechanism by which it is brought out of this hidden and secret realm, where there are no words and there is no speech, to finally be expressed in speech is through the aspect of awareness *(da'at)*. *Da'at* is the vehicle by which Torah and wisdom are drawn from Thought to Speech, and it includes in it the *middot* (aspects of God) love, fear, compassion, and limitation. This helps to explain why, throughout the Torah, it says, "God spoke to Moses saying: Speak to the Children of Israel." That is, Moses embodies the fullness of *da'at*, awareness, and he is able to draw out of the secret realm of Torah in the World of Thought to reveal it to the Israelites in the form of speech. Thus, "God spoke to Moses": by means of *da'at* the revelation of Torah in speech is united with the source, the wellspring of Wisdom in its hiddenness. . . .

Therefore, someone who engages in the study of Torah and prayer, saying the letters of the words of Torah with fear and love, can attain to the mystery of *da'at*. That is, by means of fear and love (the mechanism of *da'at*) he can draw into his mind and his speech from the source of the World of Thought, and the upper realms of *Ḥokhmah* and *Binah* will pour through him. In turn, his words of Torah will be united with the supernal wellsprings of Wisdom.

(Me'or Einayim, Vayeitzei,
s.v. vehinei lehavin inyan zeh)

Love and fear, fear and love. These are not opposite emotions; they are complementary. They balance each other, and to hold one without the other is to diminish our emotional and spiritual capacities. When we face the truth of our lives, both the full compassion (*ḥesed*) that comes to us as well as the limitations (*gevurah*) that shape our every endeavor, we experience both love and fear. We experience God's love for us in our very existence, and we respond in gratitude and love—toward God and toward others. At the same time, we are awed, reverential, and even fearful before God when we recognize how tenuously we hold onto our lives, how short-lived our successes are, how our best plans sometimes produce perverse results. This fear does not lead us to cower in the corner, but rather awakens us to a deeper awareness of our responsibility for every outcome, a deeper commitment to live with great care. We shape our behavior to honor God and to respect and care for other people.

When we connect on a deep level with love and fear, when we touch the source of all wisdom, we open a channel through which that wisdom can flow. That channel is speech. What we say may not be different in terms of its content, but it will be different in terms of its intent. Had Bauby not dictated his book from within his locked-in state, his reminiscences would not have been quite so remarkable, nor his observations so powerful. The force of his words came from the unique level of awareness that he derived from his particular situation, from his exceptional awareness of the human condition, his connection with *da'at*. He was able to communicate the significance of being alive to those of us still blessed with mobility and the capacity to speak and respond. He opened a channel for us from the source of Wisdom so that we might travel with him back to that source, and be blessed by it.

Bauby's words, dictated letter by letter, opened a gate for us to the source of love and compassion. Although reading his book might be terrifying—that we, too, might suffer such a hemorrhage or some other horrible accident of life—his testimony helps us to see that it is possible to live in the face of death. More, his words invite us to quiet the clatter of thoughts that fill our minds and distract us from the truth, so that we can discern our own butterflies in the silence. As a consequence of his communication, yet without suffering our own trauma, we rise above the forces in our culture that would distract us from the fundamental truths of existence. We, in any moment, can wake up to what is going on in our hearts and minds, and we can choose to treat ourselves, and others, with love and compassion, with justice and righteousness. We can speak words made up of the letters of Creation with the intent of returning them to their divine source. We can engage with others, seeing in them letters clothed in flesh, and find in others the echoes of divine utterances. In moments of adversity, we can remember that even then God is present.

The source of all Creation is Love, *ḥesed*. For the divine energy to find its way from its pure source to coarse physicality, it must be limited, reshaped, and repackaged in such a manner that created matter can hold it. That process requires a degree of contraction, of rigor, of limitation, which we might experience as love withheld, or the absence of God's presence. What the hasidic tradition comes to remind us, what Pinsky and Bauby exemplify, is that even in the limitation God is still present; there is still love.

This is, indeed, the work of mindfulness. Over and over again we are reminded—directly or indirectly—of our mortality. We hear bad news. We are frustrated in our endeavors. We are challenged by a loved one. We lose something—a possession, a person, our honor. In every instance, we fear that this event may somehow be our undoing. In shame we wish we could fall through the floor and disappear. We hide our faces in our grief. We fear that our lives are coming to an end, or are threatened, in every moment. Our spontaneous reaction is to lash out, to defend ourselves, to hold onto the status quo at all costs. And rightly, we should protect ourselves. But we must be sure that our lives are indeed threatened. So often it is only our perception of threat, our fear of loss, our anxiety in the face of mortality. When we stop to consider what is actually going on, what is the truth of the moment, we discover that our ego is bruised; our sense of self is exposed. But our lives are not at risk.

And then there will come a moment when in fact our lives are at risk. We will, eventually, face death. As that time approaches we will sense its advance and, in a way much more legitimate, we may fear death. In that instance, how we have lived our lives will shape how we respond to our end, how we deal with our decline and death.

A woman I know has a form of dementia, what we now identify as Alzheimer's disease. While she functions well some of the time, there are moments when she exhibits great frustration and anger. I am tempted, at times, to think that this reflects her inner awareness of the losses she has experienced and her frustration and anger at her more limited life. But her daughter has an additional perspective: what frustrates and angers this woman now is precisely what did so earlier in her life. Then, she would complain when something was out of place in the house, when someone behaved in a manner that did not fit her sense of proper order or timing, when she was not the center of attention. And, so too, now. There are ways in which she is just as she was before, only more so—exaggerated by her inner fears and the lack of control brought on by the disease.

We carry into our old age and our illnesses much of who we have been throughout our lives. We respond out of habit, out of the worldview that we have adopted and utilized throughout our lives. The challenge of our lives is to live so that when the end of our days approach, whether from disease or simply as a matter of age, we will be able to respond with a full heart, without falling into debilitating reactions.

> As a comment to the words in the psalm, "I shall not die by live" (Psalm 118:17), Rabbi Yitzhak said: "In order really to live, a man must give himself to death. But when he has done so, he discovers that he is not to die—but to live.[8]
>
> When Rabbi Bunam lay dying, his wife burst into tears. He said, "What are you crying for? My whole life was only that I might learn how to die."[9]

When I first learned these teachings they did not frighten me. I did not think that they urged me to deny life in this world, to give

---

[8]Martin Buber, *Tales of the Hasidim* (two volumes), translated by Olga Marx (New York: Schocken Books, 1947), vol. 2, p. 291.

[9]Ibid., vol. 2, p. 268.

myself over to melancholy, to ruminate on death and my mortality. Rather, they made me mindful of how much I wanted to live so that, when my time to die arrived, I would not be overcome by fear or frustration, but that I would be able to live fully to the end. I know that I may not be able to exercise conscious control over my life—I may also suffer from Alzheimer's or some other affliction of the mind. Nevertheless, I hope that the manner in which I live now—in my relations with other people, in my response to each day's frustrations and disappointments, successes and joys—will prepare me to respond to that greater frustration and disappointment with fullness and grace.

When I recognize the truth of my mortality, when I see in each moment of frustration a rehearsal of my ultimate annihilation, I may now be able to prepare. Rabbi Yitzḥak instructs us to die— not physically, not even emotionally. Rather, we are to allow our expectations to die. I can still hope, I can plan and imagine—without mistaking hopes for realities. Thus, when "what is supposed to be" and "what I need to have" and "what I wish would continue" fall away, I am left with joy in the present moment. This is what it means to come alive: "I shall not die but live." To prepare all my life to die is to live fully in life with the intention of welcoming all that there is to life—including loss, frustration, change, aging . . . and death.

And so, we must learn to recognize those moments when we are likely to act in fear, and we must then hold back, waiting before we respond. Once our vision has cleared, once our assessment of our situation is brought into line with reality, we can respond in truth. The more we learn to do this in the moment, in the small interactions that make up the cloth of our everyday life, the more we will be able to bring the same ability to bear on the larger injuries of life. When our lives are truly threatened, when we face moments of life-and-death, we will be more able to react with grace, compassion, and love. We will learn to give up fighting the "diving-bell" and learn to listen for the "butterfly" in our lives. And the fluttering of those wings will bring us joy, and carry us away on our last breath.

This is what God wants of us. This is what it means to "hope in the Lord." Our hopes, our attempts to see the truth of our lives, to hold both love and fear, help to open a channel to the Source of Creation. To hope is to recognize God's presence in every instant, in every thing. In return, we will be blessed with the capacity to perceive even more clearly the love that lies behind all Creation, that love sustains us and all things. We will see that there is no separation between us and God, between us and all things, between life-in-the-moment and life-eternal. Eternity is here with us in each moment. Each moment, then, will be full, rich, promising. Each day will teach us how to live, so that if it were our last day, we will be satisfied.

Chapter Nine

Mindfulness and Appetite

Mindfulness practice helps us develop the awareness that there is nothing but God, and that our ego-responses separate and cut us off from God. Our capacity to observe our habitual reactions provides the tools necessary to prevent our egos from taking over, our fears of annihilation and death from controlling us. But as we move our egos out of the way, as we diminish the boundary between us and God, do we become invisible? That is, what happens to "me"? Do I disappear? Does this being, this body, just move along without will, without purpose, accepting everything as it is? Do I float along without emotion, without passion, without intention? Do I give up feeling good or bad about what happens around me—to my family, friends, and community?

If God can be found in every aspect of Creation, and a divine spark is hidden in everything—even in the ugly or obnoxious behavior of another person, in the food I eat, and in the deeds I do, in the body of the earth even when it quakes and in the spirit of the atmosphere even when it churns—then must I consider everything "good"? Is everything that happens to me "good"? Is everything that I do "good"?

When we wake up to the truth of the moment, peeling from our eyes and hearts the intervening veils of habitual reactions and ego needs, we are better able to discern what would be a wise and compassionate response. Indeed, the reason to try to see clearly is to know what to do. The product of wisdom—awareness of God's presence in all things and the attendant responsibility to preserve and sustain the divine spark in all things—is morality. When we see clearly and discern a wise course of action, we are more able to undertake that action without contention. Having moved our ego needs out of the way (as best we can), we can act with purity of purpose and clear intent. We will be present to our circumstances with balanced hearts, and so will not need to embellish our actions with self-justifying stories. We need not impute evil motives to opponents, nor burden ourselves with shame and guilt—or worse, with pride or self-righteousness. So, although we may sometimes need to say "no"—to ourselves and to others—we do so out of compassion, both for ourselves and for others. We act without creating new ego conflicts; our deeds will be "for the sake of Heaven."

The goal of mindfulness is to "purify our hearts," to see the truth so clearly that we break open to the wonder of Creation and the presence of the Divine in everything. The more clearly we see, the more "transparent" we can become. The flurries of emotions that trap us in anger or fear, in desire or want, will not catch on anything in our hearts, and God's light will shine more brightly through us. Then, rather than responding out of habit, we can choose a course of behavior: to do that which brings us closer to fulfilling God's intention, God's will. Our hearts will be pure, and God's presence in each moment will be more evident. So moved by God's presence and our desire to be close to God, we will have to act: "When a ram's horn is sounded in a town, do the people not take alarm? . . . A lion has roared, who can but fear? Adonai God has spoken, who can but prophesy?" (Amos 3:6,8). Our response, however, will not be habitual or instinctive, but reflective, intentional, and compassionate.

It is in the moment of choosing that we exercise our most human faculty. It is in the capacity to choose that which will be most compassionate and most just that we display our most God-like quality. This is the lesson in this text from the *Me'or Einayim*.

"Know therefore this day and keep in mind that Adonai alone is God *(YHWH hu ha'elohim)* in heaven above and on earth below; there is no other" (Deuteronomy 4:39). . . . The Holy One created the world with light and darkness, and a whole day is made up of both darkness and light, starting with night and then daylight; they are combined together (even though they are opposites) to constitute a full day. Note: First there is darkness and then there is light, and the Holy One makes peace between them, as it says, "Who forms light and creates darkness, making peace" (Isaiah 45:7). And, indeed, people were created in the same manner. Dimness of awareness is the presence of the *yetzer hara* and is called darkness, while the appearance of the *yetzer hatov* is like the break of day. In this way, we start out in darkness, before we are endowed with the light of understanding; we are constricted, our minds are small, and this darkness is the place of adversity. That good and evil are naturally imprinted in us is so that we will then have to make choices. . . . This will help us to realize that "darkness" is merely the appearance of "God *(Elohim)*" in a constricted mode, which appears as "adversity," and we will be able, through our understanding, to bring this darkness to its ultimate source *(YHVH:* God's loving Oneness). . . .

Thus, also, when in the course of our daily endeavors, making a living or fulfilling other needs, we find that we feel "constrained," limited in our accomplishments, we will be moved to then hold tightly to God. We will begin to pray, bringing into ourselves the quality of compassion, which is the quality of "Adonai *(YHVH)."* This will energize and move the divine realms. Just as we

bring evil into good to form complete Oneness, in the same manner that darkness is combined with light to make one whole day,
so too this unity will appear in the divine realms, since it is in our
hands to effect this ultimate unity.

(ME'OR EINAYIM, VA'ETHANAN, S.V. BAPASUK 'VEYADATA HAYOM
VAHASHEIVOTA EL LEVAVEKHA KI H' HU HA'ELOHIM,' ETC.)

According to this text, we will have a complete understanding
of ourselves and our lives only when we acknowledge the ultimate
unity (in its source and in its meaning) of both good and evil. We
are most in the dark when we are unaware of this. We experience
the events of our lives as "adversity"; we are troubled, enraged, cap-
tivated, jealous, etc. We suffer, and must find a way to bring our
understanding to bear, to bring light into our situation, so that we
can be whole. This text suggests that the first step in this process is
to admit what is happening: "I am in a 'constrained' place, and I
need help." That, in itself, is a prayer. By acknowledging our tight
spots, how hurt we are or how pained we feel that we are hurting
others, we open ourselves to God's "quality of compassion." The
way to experience God's compassion is to let go of our sense of
"adversity," of contention and opposition, and to embrace the whole
as the totality of Creation that it reflects. In this moment, in the
act of making a choice and exercising our free will, we overcome
the divisions in our own hearts—between "adversity" and "happiness," between us and the other, between what we want and what
is—and we thus invite in God's compassion. As God turns to us in
compassion, helping us to experience wholeness, so too will we be
able to turn to others with compassion.

I spent a period of time working as a chaplain following the
attack on the World Trade Center. Early on, I met a man waiting
for financial support. From his appearance I would have thought he

was an artist (and this, itself, would be worth a whole chapter on how we make up stories). He had short-cropped dyed hair, a small goatee, and earrings. I found out that I was wrong. He was an electrician, and he had lost thirty union brothers in the tragedy. He had been injured as well. As we spoke, I learned more about his life. He had had aspirations of being a dancer, which were dashed in a motorcycle accident years ago. The doctors had not expected him to walk again, but he pushed himself through physical therapy and exceeded all hopes. He had a girlfriend and, even though his relationship with his family was strained, he maintained contact with his sisters and his parents.

What made this meeting so meaningful to me was that, beyond his story of perseverance and determination, he also was a recovering alcoholic. He had gone through some heavy bouts of drinking in his earlier years—so bad, in fact, that he had been homeless several times. He had worked hard to get clean and sober, failing and trying again. Yet here he was—in the aftermath of the worst disaster to have struck his community, suffering the loss of dozens of friends and hundreds of acquaintances, dealing with new injuries on top of those ongoing from his earlier accident—and he was still sober. And he knew it. And he knew that it was only through his dedicated commitment to see each moment clearly, to choose in each moment not to drink, that he was able to survive, to function, to have any hope of a future. It would have been so easy for him to sink into the darkness of depression, pain, and fear. He could easily have cried, "Why me?" and crawled into a bottle—and who would have blamed him? But he didn't. And from what I could hear, he was not likely to. He understood how important it was to see clearly ("I'm not the only one suffering here; this didn't happen only to me, and at least I am alive"); to recognize the truth of the moment ("One day at a time"); to choose light over darkness, life over death ("If I can make it through today without a drink, that is one more day sober"). What kept him alive, and what brought light into his darkness and made him a whole person, was his capacity to make a choice in each moment. He recognized the workings of his *yetzer hara* (namely, his habitual, addictive response), yet he chose to exercise his will to act with wisdom, to follow his *yetzer hatov*. This is "understanding," wisdom, insight—light that includes darkness, awareness of the oneness of all things.

Having survived this great a tragedy, he could have sunk into a self-centered depression. He could have made himself into a victim, seeing only his personal loss, and making his happiness dependent on having others make him whole. In this manner he would have been responding from a deep emotional motivator: the emptiness of hunger. We find that inner sickness modeled in the narratives of the Torah. It is expressed in one of the constant complaints of the Israelites in the desert: "Who will feed us meat?" (Numbers 11:4). In the wilderness God provided the Israelites with manna each day—a miraculous display of God's compassion and concern. Nevertheless, they complain. They want something else, but express their desire by denying the truth of God's providence: "We remember the fish that we used to eat free in Egypt, the cucumbers, the melons, the leeks, the onions, and the garlic. Now our souls are wasted, our gullets are shriveled. There is nothing at all! Nothing but this manna to look to!" (11:5–6). The needs of the ego, the fears that drive the heart and mind, produced in the Israelites (and so also now in us) feelings and perceived needs based on an incorrect assessment of reality.

The behavior of the Israelites reflects the nature of our habitual minds. They look for stimulation; they are not easily satisfied. Of whatever seems good they want more; of whatever they find repulsive they want less. Thus, that which is routine frequently appears dull, boring, "shriveled," passé; we want more. Always more. "Take this away and bring me something else! I like this, so bring me more!" But no matter how much "more" we might have, we are still left with our selves—with the fact that we cannot be other than who we are, where we are at this very moment. Our constant striving for ways to avoid the truth of our lives—that breath arises and passes away, that one day dawns and then sinks into darkness, that death follows birth—leaves us always hungry.

In another passage, however, the Torah provides us with training against this folly. Leviticus 25 contains instructions regarding the Sabbatical year and the Jubilee. Every seven years the land is be left alone—a year of Sabbath rest for the earth: "But in the seventh year the land shall have a sabbath of complete rest, a sabbath of Adonai: you shall not sow your field or prune your vineyard. . . . But you may eat whatever the land during its Sabbath will produce" (25:4,6). Beyond that,

> You shall count off seven weeks of years—seven times seven years—so that the period of seven weeks of years gives you a total of forty-nine years. Then you shall sound the horn loud . . . and you shall hallow the fiftieth year. You shall proclaim release throughout the land for all its inhabitants . . . each of you shall return to his holding and each of you shall return to his family. That fiftieth year shall be a Jubilee for you: you shall not sow, neither shall you reap the aftergrowth or harvest the untrimmed vines . . . you may only eat the growth direct from the field.
>
> (VERSES 8–12)

These two practices—the Sabbatical year and the Jubilee—present a landed, agricultural community with a significant problem: how will the people survive without tilling the land? It is conceivable, if people are careful, that they will be able to get along, and perhaps even thrive during the course of the Sabbatical year.

But they will have to hope that their hard work will produce a rich yield in the sixth year, so that they will retain enough to eat during the seventh. The Jubilee makes even that plan very difficult to achieve, since it requires two years in a row of inactivity—nearly three years from the end of the harvest in the sixth year to the harvest of the ninth.

The Torah anticipates the natural concern this would raise in the hearts of the Israelites:

> You shall observe My law and faithfully keep My rules, that you may live upon the land in security; the land shall yield its fruit and you shall eat your fill, and you shall live upon it in security. And should you ask, "What are we to eat in the seventh year, if we may neither sow nor gather in crops?" I will ordain My blessing for you in the sixth year, so that it shall yield a crop sufficient for three years. When you sow in the eighth year, you will still be eating old grain of that crop; you will be eating the old until the ninth year, until its crops come in.
>
> (VERSES 18–22)

The flow of this passage is instructive. At first God declares, clearly and comfortingly, that there will be enough food. But the human heart, despite this assurance, succumbs to fear and uncertainty, to hunger and doubt: "What are we to eat?" God's response to this impudent challenge is calm and not punitive. Rather, expanding on the original promise, God reassures the Israelites, repeating the promise that they will have enough food. This passage echoes our own ongoing struggles to maintain clear vision, so that we will not get trapped in habitual responses. When we can see the truth, we will be able to see the blessings before us, even when the situation seems precarious. But when we give in to nagging doubt, when we allow hunger to overwhelm us with the "What if?" questions, we become blind to what is. We will grasp at everything around us to fill our hunger and to slake our doubt, in a futile attempt to manage the future, to control all "ifs," to keep uncertainty at bay. It takes work, then, to recover our composure, to once again see the truth.

We are challenged in this passage to find a way to combine darkness and light, to find the larger wholeness in the moment of our uncertainty. We can understand that the Sabbatical year, and even more the additional Jubilee year, might be seen as a form of darkness. It is natural to be concerned about "what are we to eat." The Torah hopes that we will seek to connect these practices to the greater light, to see this as an invitation to greater clarity of vision. Rather than see the year's cessation of work and the release of the land as dangerous, as threatening, as a source of fear, we are called to see them as the beginning of a process of great blessing. After all, if God asks us to step back from active work on the land, can we not anticipate some benefit—a year of relaxation, of attention to family, to study, to prayer, and to good works? Are we not asked in this observance to face up to social inequalities, to look squarely at how far we have allowed the gap to grow between the "haves" and the "have-nots"? Rather than paying attention to the growling in our bellies and the worries in our hearts, we are challenged to look for the good that these "rules and laws" may bring to all bellies, to all who hunger.

But without preparation, without a practice of attentiveness by which we can free ourselves of our habitual reactions, from the grasping of hunger, we will not likely be able to see the blessings before us. Rabbi Shaul Natansohn, a mid-nineteenth-century leader in the Ukraine, makes this very point.

> A righteous and upright *(tzadik veyashar)* person finds that what
> he needs is already prepared and set out before him. We learn

this from Hagar (expelled from her home, wandering blindly in the desert): "Then God opened her eyes and she saw a well of water" (Genesis 21:19). We see that the well was prepared there already, only that she had not seen it until this very moment. Similarly we find with Moses (immediately following the crossing of the Sea, when the people came to Marah, where the water was bitter): "Adonai showed him a piece of wood (by which he sweetened the water)" (Exodus 15:25). That is, the wood already was prepared and set out for him, yet he had to find it. But someone who is not worthy, whose faith is weak and whose trust is fleeting, like those who are always asking, "What shall we eat?"—for this person God has to command a blessing for them, to create something new.

(DIVREI SHAUL, CITED IN ITTUREI TORAH
ON LEVITICUS 25:21)

Although this selection does not present a clear "instruction manual" to overcome the blindness caused by hunger, it is suggestive. First, if we wish to find our needs "prepared and set out for" us, we need to be "righteous and upright." These two qualities suggest a way of living that prepares us to see clearly, and to control hunger. That is, to be righteous implies a generosity of spirit (*tzedakah*) that flows from justice (*tzedek*). One who understands that possessions are not prizes awarded to the deserving but rather wealth entrusted to partners by God will give willingly to others. For that person, caring for others' needs will not be seen as loss, but as fulfillment. At the same time, the righteous person also recognizes the limits of generosity, of the parallel obligations of home and community, and the legitimate right of individuals to control the use of their personal wealth. To be upright (*yashar*), as well, suggests a degree of transparency in a person's behavior. That is, there will be a consistency between values and behavior, between opinions and actions. Both of these qualities require attention to the state of one's heart and mind, to overcome the limiting darkness of ego needs.

Second, one who is righteous and upright will have prepared himself to see more clearly, to be open to the presence of God in his life. He will be more likely to appreciate the blessings already present in the world around him, as well as the opportunities to serve others, and so save himself. After all, that is what the examples offered in this text suggest. Both Hagar and Moses are responsible for others. Their dependents (Ishmael and the People of Israel) are thirsty; their lives are at risk. Hagar and Moses are helped by God to see what is already present before them so that they can provide for others. Generosity and transparency open our eyes to the fullness of Creation, and not its limits. Righteousness and uprightness are practices that can train us to trust in God, to overcome our habitual response of hunger.

The conclusion of this teaching is instructive as well. That is, all that we need is already present in the world. If we had sufficient trust, if only we could see clearly, we would find whatever we truly needed, not what our egos, our fears, our anxieties, and our selfishness lead us to think we needed. Lacking that trust—allowing our habitual responses to prompt us to ask "What shall we eat?"— requires a new Creation, an initiative on God's part to fill our perceived need. Yet the consequences of that new initiative are that it might lead us to want even more, or that, as we fill our "needs," we will come into conflict with others. Always needing, always expecting an extra blessing, we generate further suffering for us and for others. At the very least, depending on this new Creation to satisfy our hunger will reinforce our uncertainty, leaving our inclination to hunger intact and unchallenged. And we will live blind to the truth in darkness.

In fact, asking the question "what shall we eat," allowing our doubts and our hunger to close off our awareness of blessing and sufficiency, actually creates more confusion, more of a sense of need. This, in turn, makes it even harder for us to see clearly where blessing lies in our lives and in the world, as Rabbi Elimelekh of Lyzhensk teaches.

> When the Holy Blessed One created the world in His goodness, He established channels through which blessings could flow to provide for peoples' needs. The nature of the outpouring of these blessings was to be continuous and unchanging. But, when we lose our sense of place in the world and have no trust that the Blessed Creator faithfully looks out for us, providing copious sustenance ceaselessly, then our thoughts damage the divine realms and diminish the heavenly forces (of blessing). The consequence: the otherwise continuous blessings ebb, requiring the Holy Blessed One to command the outpouring to begin again in full, as at Creation.
>
> This is Scripture's intention: to teach us the importance of maintaining full trust in God. When we doubt saying, "what shall we eat," we create our own lack.
>
> (No'am Elimelekh, Behar, s.v. vekhi yomru ma nokhal
> bashanah, etc.; vetziviti et birkhati lakhem, etc.)

This text offers a close reading of the Torah. The author notes that for the most part the Torah does not explain the motivation for God's words or actions, but it here offers the introduction, "But, should you say, etc." He reads this to mean that there is something about the question that then requires God's response in "commanding My blessing for you." The question itself creates the circumstances demanding God's renewed action on our behalf. Our degree of trust—that is, our capacity to experience fullness even in the face of uncertainty, to incorporate the darkness into the light to create the whole oneness of a day—sustains the experience of acceptance and hope. Our lack of trust generates more doubt and distrust, more hunger and more grasping. Sensing ourselves whole, even when incomplete in some way, sustains our trust, our capacity to experience the fullness of Creation, and not just its limits.

Why is it that we don't see clearly?

> Rabbi Shimon ben Eleazar taught: In all of my days I never saw a deer picking figs, a lion carrying a load, or a fox tending shop—yet they all find a living without struggle. They, in turn, were only created to serve me. Yet, I was created to serve my Creator. If they, who were only created to serve me, can find a living without struggle, while I was created to serve my Creator, is it not right that I also should find my living without struggle? [It would be so,] but I have defiled my deeds and deprived myself of my sustenance.

(PARAPHRASE OF MISHNAH KIDDUSHIN 4:14,
CITED IN MA'OR VASHEMESH, ADDITIONS ON KIDDUSHIN 82A)

We don't see clearly because we get in our own way. How we behave and how we respond to the events of our lives stand in the way of experiencing God's abundant provisions.

The text above draws out two lessons from this passage in the Talmud. It suggests that we can learn to see more clearly by observing the behaviors of animals. How do these wild animals serve people? They model complete trust in God. In every instance, these animals (so far as we can see) find adequate sustenance for themselves and their young. We can learn to trust that just as God has provided sufficient provisions for the wild animals, so has God provided for us as well. In addition, we learn that even when we hear the animals crying—roaring in hunger, panting in thirst—whenever they do find food they are satisfied with what they have, and do not start looking for more for the next day, wondering, "What shall we eat?" "How much more so might we, who are graced by God with knowledge by which we can understand and analyze our lives, trust in God that He will provide us with sustenance tomorrow! Only when we start to devise 'how?' and 'by what means?' do we get into trouble" (*Ma'or Vashemesh,* ibid.).

Let us not pass over the context in which these lessons were taught. The authors of these texts did teach people who struggled to find sufficient food for each day. These lessons may have been intended to help calm the anxiety that rightly troubled them, that must have gnawed at their innards. Further, they were taught by the same leader who distributed charity to his followers and, if the tales of the hasidic masters are to be trusted, they often gave away even their last coin, leaving their own families hungry and poor. These teachings are not meant to justify poverty, or to legitimate hunger. They do not validate ongoing inequity, injustice, or suffering. These teachings, in their context, were meant to fortify those who truly hungered for sustenance, to help them keep their hearts balanced and overcome panic, so that they might continue, to give them strength to carry on.

That is not our problem, however. Living in a land of such wealth, in a community of such great resources, finding the next meal is not a regular concern for us. Or is it? When I worked in a congregation, I liked the fact that I could go home for lunch. I always knew what was in the fridge, and I never had to worry if I would find what I liked or wanted. But there were occasions when I could not get home: Ministerial Association meetings, appointments with congregants, overburdened schedules that preempted eating lunch. At those moments, I could feel my anxiety rising in me. Would the pastor providing lunch remember to offer a salad or a vegetarian alternative? Will the restaurant have something satisfying? Will I be able to get anything to eat before dinner? These concerns then expressed themselves in my behavior—I would often arrive late for those meetings and lunch appointments. I could sense my anxiety in my body: I felt more highly-strung, more nervous, a little cloudy in my thinking. Even when I found positive answers to my anxious questions, I continued to experience tension—by eating too quickly or by taking too much food, for example. It was only when I fully experienced those feelings, gained a degree of composure, and examined why I was behaving that way that I could begin to get control over my behavior. I could slow my eating, enjoy the food, look around to speak with my colleagues, to be fully present. Only then did I feel that the horizon of my vision expanded beyond the buffet or the menu; only then was I able to pay attention to the people around me, to conversation, to life.

I often joke that I suffer from what I call an "occupational illness": a compulsion to buy books. I don't know if I caught it in rabbinical school (or, perhaps, even in college), or if it is a genetic predisposition that was activated in the rabbinate. For years, there was not a book catalog that I could pass up, particularly if it offered a "sale." Every book looked interesting; each book might prove useful; everything touched on a subject I thought I ought to know about, I ought to master. I did not sense anything strange in my behavior, I did not feel any limit in terms of money expended, and I did not sense any incongruity between buying lots of books that I merely placed on my shelves and did not read. Living in a fairly remote area without access to a large Judaica library, I told myself that I needed one of my own. I reassured myself when, every year, I found one or two books on the shelf that helped me prepare a lesson or a course: "See, I really do need these books."

As time passed, however, I came to recognize a pattern in my book buying. Often my purchases coincided with times of stress or uncertainty in my life. When I was feeling vulnerable because of some problem in the congregation, threatened by a sense of inadequacy to the task at hand (teaching, leading, counseling), or simply passing through a time of self-doubt, I would respond by buying books. Deep inside I was saying to myself, "Now that I have this book, I will really know what I'm talking about. Now I will have an answer to this problem." But the books did not solve my problem, of course. I had to wait for them to arrive. And, I didn't read them right away. By the time I peeled off the shrink-wrap or cut the pages, the anxiety had usually passed or I had done something to resolve the issue.

But the books still came, and my library still grew. My anxiety expressed itself in hunger for books. I felt my disquiet as something lacking. Rather than acknowledging the root of my anxiety and trusting that the feeling would pass as I addressed the problem with honesty and clear vision, I responded to my hunger in an attempt to deflect the suffering. Having a "thing" to hold onto distracted me from the existential struggle of the moment, which I experienced as hunger. By externalizing the solution to my problem (buying a book), I avoided facing my own inner battle.

These two examples reflect two sides of hunger. One—my anxiety about lunch—is the projection of anxiety about the future. Both literally and figuratively I was worried about being "filled." I worried that I would not have enough—that my appetite (both physical and emotional) might not be filled, that my desires might not be met. It was not that I wanted more than anyone else, or that I wanted more of any one thing. I just worried that I would not get what I wanted, what I thought I needed. This hunger is the sense that we will not even have what others have, that we will have less than we expect. When I look at hunger in that light, when I experience it fully in my body, I realize that this sort of hunger is the other side of greed.

My book buying reflected a different sort of hunger: an expression of my anxiety in the moment. I was ill at ease, and I experienced that feeling as emptiness, as hunger. I satisfied it with buying books. I wanted to feel more confident, to sense power in the face of my fears. Having more books symbolically represented wisdom, knowledge, and power. When I stop to feel that uneasiness and look compassionately, but honestly, at my desires, I realize that this hunger is indeed greed.

In both the Torah ("What shall we eat?") and in my personal experience ("What will I eat?" and "I am not up to this challenge"), we see greed expressed as hunger. Even before the Israelites have entered the land and begun to work it, they are concerned that it will not support them. They worry before the fact, unable or unwilling to trust that the land will provide for them. I worried that I would not be able to eat lunch, even though I had not yet seen the buffet, and even though I would not, in the end, go hungry. And I was anxious that I lacked the skills or capacities to do my job, even though I had not yet started on the task, and even though I had succeeded in the past.

Mishnah Berakhot 4:4 teaches: "Rabbi Yehoshua taught: One who is walking in a dangerous place should recite a short prayer (substituting the short prayer for the longer *Amidah*), saying, 'Save, O Adonai, the remnant of Your people Israel. In all moments of crisis may their needs be before You. Praised are You, Adonai, who hears prayer.'" While it is not clear what constitutes a "moment of crisis," it seems from the discussion in the Talmud that it is when God might be angry at Israel. The implication is that in God's moment of anger, He might ignore Israel's needs or be blind to their concerns. The prayer is intended to remind God not to forget us. But, what is the nature of the "moment of crisis"? As noted, the Talmud assumes that the word for "crisis" here (*ibbur*) suggests a moment of God's anger (*evrah*), one that might result from Israel's transgressions *(averah)*. But, *ibbur* (related to pregnancy) might also suggest a time of transition from one state to another, a time when a new circumstance is about to emerge. In just such a situation it would make sense that Israel might be anxious, that we might be anxious: we worry if there will be enough for us, if our needs will be fulfilled in the new situation. In just that circumstance we pray not that our needs be fulfilled, but we rather confess our own fears and anxieties. We pray that God not lose sight of that truth, that God hold our neediness, our anxiety, and our uncertainty—even in this time of transition and fear—with compassion. And in that prayer, we are made aware of how God does always keep our needs in mind, how we are sustained always.

Often, in the midst of our moments of crisis, we lose sight of the truth: we are scared, we feel anxious. We then turn those simple feelings, our immediate reactions to crisis, into stories: we feel hungry, we are afraid that we will not have "enough," we resist the changes that transitions bring. In turn, we doubt God's presence and God's sustaining power. We find ourselves constricted, closing up inside, unable to give to others out of fear for ourselves. We grasp for something to fill us up, to reassure us that we will be sustained. In this way, we compound the difficulty of the critical moment, leaving ourselves more alone, more defensive, and more needy. The path to release and relief is to acknowledge the truth of our experience. In this short prayer from the Mishnah we acknowledge that we feel threatened; we sense the hunger that has arisen in response and we let go of it. We ask that God assess our needs, that God provide for us in that moment. By placing our needs before God, as it were, we acknowledge them to ourselves. When we hear our own confessions of need, we see the truth more clearly, and sense our hunger diminishing.

A parallel passage in the Talmud (Berakhot 29b) echoes this: "One who travels where there are herds of wild beasts or bandits should recite a short prayer. . . . Others taught (that this is the prayer): 'The needs of Your People Israel are great, but their understanding is constricted. May it be Your will, then, Lord our God, to give each and every one of them their sustenance, and each and every body according to what it lacks. Praised are You, who hears prayer.'" Our needs, indeed, are great, and in the end we are dependent on God to fulfill them. The problem that we face is that we often are not clear about what are our true needs, and what are the "hungers" that arise in our confused, "constricted" minds. Rashi, the great Talmud commentator, suggests that the phrase "their understanding is constricted" means that "they do not know how to lay out their needs." That is, we are confused by conflicting feelings, our minds are clouded by habitual responses to challenge and anxiety, and we are always hungry. In that light, we could paraphrase this prayer thus: "We are anxious, and so we are confused. You, God, know the truth of our situation; You understand the confusion in our hearts. Provide us with what we truly need. Sustain our bodies and our lives."

Is it possible for us to preempt this prayer, relying less on God to see our needs, and instead to see the truth ourselves, through our hearts and minds directly? There are two prayers that have been incorporated into normative Jewish practice that may help us in that regard. One appears at the beginning of the preliminary service, where there are a series of prayers called *Birkhot Hashaḥar,* the morning blessings. Their origins are in the Talmud (Berakhot 60b), where they are linked to various acts we do when waking up: When you hear the cock crow, when you open your eyes, when you sit up (in bed), when you dress, when you straighten up, when you stand on the ground, when you take a step, when you tie your shoe, when you tie your belt, when you put on your headdress, etc. Regarding the act of tying shoes, we are told to recite the blessing "Blessed are You, who provides for all my needs (*she'asah li kol tzorki*). What is the relationship of tying shoes to God providing for our needs? It may mean that we acknowledge the blessing of God's attention down to the very least detail—from the ground up. (The next two blessings touch the middle of the body and then the head.) Alternatively, it may express our awareness of God's blessing in the luxury of having shoes for our feet. (This was not a given in antiquity—that is why wearing leather sandals on Yom Kippur was considered a luxury and not in keeping with the obligation to afflict ourselves.)

This blessing echoes the prayers we examined above. In the short prayer of the "others" from the Talmud, we are led to recognize that often our perceived needs emerge from constricted understanding. What we think we need is frequently an expression of our deep hunger, our fear or anxiety, jealousy, or selfishness. In the blessing from *Birkhot Hashaḥar,* again, we are presented with this truth. We praise God for having provided us with "all of our needs" when we put on our shoes. But, shoes are already an "extra." After all, we have already found that we can straighten up and stand on our feet. We praise God for directing our steps—that is, for helping us walk. Is that not enough? What more do we want, in order to feel that *all* of our needs have been filled?

Perhaps this is how we ought to understand this blessing. When we acknowledge God for having provided for all of our needs, we are primarily testifying to the fact that we do, indeed, have needs. It is the first step in opening ourselves to the truth of our existence: we are mortal, we are finite. The nature of all living beings is that they need sustenance: they need to be able to transform nourishment into energy and substance, and they need to be able to expel wastes. In that sense, we start out at a deficit: we are neither self-contained nor self-sustaining. We are always in need. Nothing is complete in itself. Only in the totality of the cosmos and its ultimate equilibrium do we sense self-sufficiency and completeness (and this is a way of thinking about God). Within that system, living things have needs (and so, too, perhaps, do inanimate things, as they make their way toward entropy). To say, then, that God "provides for all our needs" is to express gratitude for our mere existence with—and perhaps even because of—our needs.

We can thank God for having actually created all our needs. That we have needs does not indicate that we are flawed, that we are diminished, that a mistake has been made in the cosmos, or that we have been intentionally denied our due or punished by having something withheld. This is simply the way of the world: we have needs. When we see this clearly, when we open our hearts and so quiet our grasping hunger, we can become aware that God has created us with our needs, simply in providing us with our existence. To have needs is to be alive. Yet we also have access to that which will satisfy our fundamental needs. Even in our "neediness" we can be whole. In this moment of awareness, in our capacity to acknowledge the truth at all, we know that God has "provided for all our needs" as well.

This brings us to the other blessing I mentioned above. It is to be recited after a light meal: "Blessed are You, Adonai our God, Ruler of the universe, who creates many creatures and their needs. For all that You have created to sustain the life of all living beings, Praised are You, who are the Life of the Universe." The most striking aspect of this blessing is that it states outright that God has created us as beings with needs. Lack is a fundamental, existential fact, built into the nature of Creation. When we recite this blessing we are invited to confess the truth of our existence: we need support. In that moment, when we see clearly that need is not a flaw in Creation or in our lives, we are less likely to respond to anxiety or fear with additional hunger. We will recognize our true needs— for sustenance, health, shelter, community, work, and sleep—and so we will be less likely to crave more. Rather, we will have some compassion for ourselves, and for others. We will see them as creatures, like us, whether they are our neighbors or people living in distant lands; whether they are our pets or animals on farms or in the wild. We will sense our shared dependence on the workings of Creation to provide us with our sustenance. More, we will sense God's life-force (the "Life of the Universe") flowing through us. We will see God's hand in the capacities of farmers to produce enough not only for themselves but for us as well. Our hearts will open and we will desire good for all other beings, and we will work to extend to them God's sustenance as well. When we recite this blessing, our perspective expands and we see ourselves and our situation differently. We can respond to the events of our lives with less fear, and we are less inclined to express our anxiety as hunger. We will be satisfied.

The problem is that people do go hungry. Not everyone finds sufficient sustenance, or shelter, or health. They may be aware that their lack is not a flaw in Creation but a flaw in society, and so, when they do eat, they might even recite this blessing. But is it not likely that they also pray for themselves, that they hope that their situation will be reversed, that their circumstances will change? Their hunger is real, and their needs are great—should we expect them to put aside their real hunger in order to open their perspectives, to see their hunger as a grasping for what is missing, as a response to anxiety, fear, selfishness, or jealousy? That would be as cruel as it would also be incorrect. Even though God has created sustenance for all beings, that does not mean that it has been distributed equitably, or that we have shared it fairly. When someone else is hungry, we cannot discharge our responsibilities simply by praying this prayer—and imagining that sustenance will eventually come to all of God's creatures. We must fill their needs. And then, our prayers will reflect reality. Our prayers will be answered—as will theirs.

This is one way of understanding of the verse, "He fulfills the desires (*ratzon*) of those who revere Him; He hears their cry and saves them" (Psalm 145:19). For some people this is a troubling verse, generating a sense of guilt or deficiency and so, also, anger at God. That is, I may consider myself to be one who reveres God, and yet my desires (even my most gracious wishes—for the health and well-being of my family and friends) may go unanswered. That will leave me with one of two responses (or both): I can be angry at God for not answering my prayers, or I can castigate myself for not being sufficiently reverent, devout, observant, or loving toward God to have my prayer answered. In either case, the result will be loss: loss of trust in God, or loss of trust in my capacity to evaluate my own life honestly. Nevertheless, this verse can also serve as an entry to a more mindful assessment of our circumstances and our lives.

Many hasidic teachers shared this assessment of our verse.

In this manner we can interpret the verse, "Open your hand to the poor and needy kinsman in your land" (Deuteronomy 15:11). That is, you must open a way, a gate, for your fellow by means of your truest desires and the willing gift of your heart. The Holy One "fulfills the desires of those who revere Him" and will therefore do good for your fellow, providing all his needs, by means of the way and the gate you open.

(OHEV YISRAEL, TERUMAH,
S.V. VE'AL DEREKH ZEH YESH LEFARESH GAM KEN PASUK)

This is the upright path for the one who seeks to walk wholeheartedly: that his desire and his intent are to see the good of his fellow, to rejoice in his deliverance and the good that comes his way by God's graciousness. This is what David meant in the psalm: "Many say, 'Who will show me good?' (But,) You put joy into my heart when their grain and wine show increase" (Psalm 4:7, 8). The essence of his joy was the good that came to others. . . . This is the meaning of the verse, "He fulfills the desires of those who revere Him; He hears their cry and saves them" (Psalm 145:19). That is, when the Holy One sees the strong desire of those who revere him to see good happen to their fellows, then the all-powerful Holy One combines all these wishes together to fulfill the requests of their hearts, that the others should have no lack.

(Tiferet Shelomo, Shabbat Naḥamu/15th Av,
s.v. o yomar lo hayu yamim tovim beyisrael ketu be'av, etc.)

In both of these texts the primary emphasis is on the desire of one person to see good for another. God acts to fulfill "the desires of those who revere Him," influenced by our willingness to look out for others. It is not that God will fulfill *our* will for *ourselves,* but that God will respond to our wishes on behalf of others. In that sense, we might read the verse from Psalm 145 as "the desires of those who truly revere God (caring only for the good of others) are fulfilled by God." In the first text above, not only are we commanded to open our hands and provide for the needy in our midst, but also to open a way for them to be blessed by God. It is not the physical act alone that will open the pathways of blessing to shower him with good. We are to open a gate, to clear a path by which this blessing can flow—and that is through our own hearts. If our hearts are locked shut, concerned only about our own needs, afraid to consider the want of others, then we will block blessing from reaching them. When our hunger arises out of fear, when we are plagued by worry over having enough or fear of not getting more, we are not able to take the needs of others into consideration.

But as the second text suggests, we might deliver ourselves from this trap. We can open our eyes, and see that God "creates many creatures and their needs." We are not alone in our sense of neediness. And feeling a deficit does not mean that we actually lack something, or that it will not ultimately be provided for us. Thus, we might actually find joy in the good that others receive— even when we do not receive it as well. When we experience that truth—feeling deeply in our hearts that our lacks are not flaws, that our needs are provided for on the most fundamental level, and that our deepest joys are experienced in the good that comes to others —then we will no longer clasp our own hands closed, but open them to share the whole of Creation with others.

The process is difficult. The fundamental truth of our being creatures that are dependent, that are subject to hungers and passions and needs, constantly renders us subject to cloudy vision. Every time that we respond out of habit, allowing hunger to arise as our chronic reaction to adversity or fear, we become blind to the needs of others, seeing only our own perceived lack. In the following text, we are given a hint for how we might break out of that prison and clear our eyes to see the truth. In this instance, we are told that the "desires of those who revere Him" are not only fulfilled, but actually generated by God.

> Consider the verse, "He fulfills the desires of those who revere Him" (Psalm 145:19). The Holy One generates wishes and desires in those who revere Him so that they will ask Him, in turn, for that good. Thus, when the Holy One wants to do a particular good for Israel, He sends that wish into them that they might ask. We learn, then, that there are two forms of goodness in this process: the first is that the Holy One sends the desire so that they will ask Him for it, and the second is the prayers they offer to request that good.
>
> (Kedushat Levi, Vayigash,
> s.v. o yevo'ar hakatuv unetatem ḥamishit lepharaoh)

Here, the whole orientation to "hunger" and "desires" shifts. That is, rather than see them as a distraction, as an impediment to seeing our lives clearly, they are gifts from God. It is not our uneasy hearts that generate hungry needs; it is God. But this is ultimately for our good. That is, when we sense that we have needs, that we are hungry, we are invited to see this as a boon, an opportunity to turn in prayer to God. In this instance, identifying a need is recognizing that we are in need of God's help. Our needs exist because we are human, and we are dependent. We are not complete in ourselves. When we turn to God, our prayers are our confessions and they serve as testimony to our needs.

We can understand the two moves in this teaching as mindfulness instructions. That is, first we have to recognize what is going on in our hearts. We need to be able to sense that need has arisen, that hunger is the expression of our anxieties, our fears, our jealousies. In that moment, when we discern that our sense of global, restless "hunger" is a manifestation of inner uncertainty, we are blessed. We are released from the grip of the hunger, since we find that it derives from God's creative initiative, and so it must be good. When we respond from a balanced heart, we will recognize these feelings as an invitation to see that in truth our basic needs are filled. This is indeed a blessing.

The second turn, in prayer to God, is the transformation of our previous hunger into acknowledgement of our dependence on the ultimate goodness of Creation, of God's presence even—and especially—in our lack. It is a movement out of ourselves, toward a more expansive perspective that can encompass another. We can let go of our self-concern and begin to look at the larger picture, at the needs of others. The freedom that we experience results from the compassion we express to ourselves in our dependence. In turn, we can turn in compassion to others. We can pray for—act for—their good, for the relief of their needs and suffering. Our prayer leads us back to the previous teachings, to an orientation toward the other.

There is yet a third way of reading the verse from Psalm 145. Where the first mode suggested that when we look out for other people God fulfills our own desires, and the second proposed that God inserts desires into us to prompt us to pray and to benefit others, a third approach returns the matter of wishes and desires to rest in God. So we can read the verse as follows: "regarding God's *ratzon* [will, desire, wish]: *yerei'av ya'aseh* [it will be fulfilled by those who revere Him]." This interpretation reminds us of two blessings used in daily prayer. The world exists as it is according to God's will. Included in that is our finitude, our dependent nature—that we have needs. One consequence of that truth is that we are constantly at risk—of starvation, of illness, of accident; ultimately, our very mortality flows from this truth. Our calling is to nevertheless live our lives fully, without shrinking from life's challenges, without being overcome by our hungers. When we see our lives clearly, when we experience the truth of our lives, we are released from our habitual responses so that we can fulfill God's will and desire: that all people should be free from suffering. This interpretation of the psalm invites us to shift our perspective from our limited selfish orientation to that of God, accepting all that is—in all its varied forms and manifestations—with all of its flaws and disappointments. God's ultimate *ratzon,* gracious and loving will and desire, is that this awareness might open our hearts in compassion—both to ourselves, and to others.

It may be possible to put ourselves in God's place and view the world through God's eyes. Knowing that in the end God's desire is for us to live fully despite our limits, to enjoy the world without denying each other life and happiness, our hearts open to a degree of equanimity and joy. Yet when we look at the world from God's place, we still see our family, friends, and neighbors suffering. We see hunger, homelessness, disease, ignorance, enmity, jealousy, and strife. That we stand in God's place does not mean that we then stand aloof from the rest of humanity and all Creation. We are still one of those whom God created, together with all of our own needs. We share in the life of the universe.

And, so, we cry out. Our hearts break in the face of the suffering of others around us. We know their pain. We ache for the extra suffering they experience when they add hunger and selfishness to their already difficult lives. We acknowledge the truth of existence to ourselves, and we hear our own cry. That moment of confession, that instant of truth-telling, is the beginning of our deliverance. Our capacity to stand in God's place is upheld by our willingness to witness over and over again the full truth of our human existence. Only when we are willing to see the pain, to feel it ourselves, and then to commit ourselves to doing everything in our power to ease the suffering of all beings, will we truly be free. We will be not be trapped by our habitual responses and we will not fall into false hunger. We will be able to act without hesitation. The proof of our deliverance will be our constant attention to looking for the signs of our closed hearts, the signals that there are harsh decrees from which we must pray for salvation. Our devotion to seeking the good of all others will be the sign of our freedom from selfish hunger. We will no longer be plagued by the question, "What are we to eat?"

When we understand that "there is nothing but God," we do not disappear. Instead, we become more fully present in the world. But as we come to see the truth of existence, to know our dependent nature and the pain that is its consequence, we face a choice: to react defensively, shutting our eyes to the truth and responding only with need, with hunger—or, to realize the offer of blessing in each moment. When we choose the latter, we are delivered from our habitual responses, our hearts are opened to others, we act to fill their needs and to ease their hunger, and we engage in the world to fully reveal ourselves as manifestations of God's loving will.

Chapter Ten

Mindfulness and Social Responsibility

*I*n the spring of the year 2000 several frightening events took place in California (where I then lived) that shook the Jewish community. Two synagogues in Sacramento were firebombed and a man shot several people, including children, in a Jewish Community Center in Granada Hills. With support of my neighbor rabbi, I called together a group of religious, civic, and political leaders to discuss how we should respond as a community. As we talked about these specific events, we realized that they were not unique. Although such attacks on Jews and Jewish institutions are very rare in the United States, and violent anti-Semitism is troubling for all people, these hate crimes fit a larger pattern.

The man who attacked the JCC in Granada Hills also killed a mail carrier specifically because he was Asian. The police identified suspects in the synagogue burnings, and connected them to the double murder of two gay men in Northern California. In Chicago, a man drove through several neighborhoods, shooting at observant Jews walking to synagogue and African-Americans simply enjoying the streets, killing a well-known and beloved basketball coach. Matthew Shephard was brutally beaten and left to die because he was gay. James Boyd, Jr., had been shackled to the back of a pick-up truck and dragged to his death because he was black. Hate, violence, mayhem, and murder seemed on the increase, affecting Jews and others, and we needed to respond.

We undertook, with the support of the local Commission on Human Rights, to create a Hate-Free Community. The goal was ambitious, perhaps messianic, but we all felt that the circumstances demanded that we address head-on what we were seeing: hatred acted out against others. We knew that we could not root out or change what was in the hearts of people, but we could at least remind each other that unopposed, hate speech and bigotry create the conditions in which hate violence becomes possible. We sought to make people mindful of their behavior, to make them conscious of the small, often unconscious ways that we communicate fear, intolerance, insensitivity, and being ill-at-ease in the presence of people who are different from us. Our goal was to remind people that they could, without insulting someone else, express their unwillingness to allow bias and bigotry to go unchallenged. Our hope was that through the efforts of businesses, civic groups, neighborhood groups, religious congregations, government agencies, and non-profit organizations, we could generate a climate of tolerance, even of love, in our community.

I liked to use as a teaching tool a report from the "Newshour with Jim Lehrer," a follow-up to the murder of James Boyd, Jr. The small town of Jasper, Texas, where Byrd lived, is fully integrated. The children attend school together, and the leadership of the school district has been African-American. The heads of other local agencies have been African-Americans, as well. There had been no recent acts of racial violence. The community at large was shocked by the murder, the white folks incredulous that such a thing could happen in their community. Then, their black neighbors began to describe the ways that they still felt excluded, dismissed, and belittled by their white neighbors. One woman spoke of her embarrassment when the clerk at the grocery store returned the change to the white customers by placing it in their hands, while she received her change on the counter, left for her to pick up. The clerk, she surmised, did not want to touch her hand. That was her experience. Small, seemingly insignificant actions create responses in other people, communicating much more than we may think or intend.

The white folks were surprised to find that there was still prejudice and bias in their community. They felt that they had worked hard and succeeded in creating a unified community. But there were other small, seemingly inconsequential moments that the black folks recounted to their neighbors—not out of anger, but out of frustration. The black folks held up to them a mirror that reflected back more than they had been able to see before. The producer of the "Newshour" report used the following as the symbolic central image for the story: although the town had been integrated, seemingly successfully, no one had thought before this event to take down the wrought-iron fence that separated the white half from the black half of the local cemetery. As blatant and obvious as that was as an expression of ongoing separation, it was so much a part of the community, so "natural," that no one had even seen it as an insult, as a barrier to mutual understanding, full equality, and social integration. Habit, ignorance, and fear often prevent us from seeing what is right before us.

Habit, ignorance, and fear often prevent us from seeing the truth of our lives. Mindfulness practice can help us overcome those constraints so that we can see more clearly, respond more truthfully, and act more lovingly. Our hope is not only to do so in the small interactions of the day-to-day, important as they are for creating a life of heartfelt ease and compassion. We want to be awake to the whole of our lives, to clearly see our place in the larger workings of our communities and the world. Indeed, as we have seen, mindfulness practice and Judaism both turn us from concern for our own lives and personal experiences to concern for the well-being of others. We can take that concern from the immediate context of our daily interactions with family, friends, and co-workers and apply it as well to our interactions with the whole world. We can bring our mindful capacities to bear on the larger forces at work in the world as we engage in political action for the good of our communities and beyond.

The hasidic tradition emphasized the presence of divine sparks in all things, reminding us that "there is no place devoid of God." There are social and practical implications to this orientation, as this text suggests.

I heard the following interpretation from the Baal Shem Tov on the verse, "The steps of a man are made firm by Adonai, but he delights in his way" (Psalm 37:23). He construed this verse to refer to those people who travel to distant places to engage in business, as well as others who find themselves traveling far away. The Holy One's thoughts are not theirs: they think that all of their endeavors on the way to the distant place are for the sake of earning money in return for the business they do, and it is for this reason that they set out on their journey. In truth, this is not the Holy One's intention, for God can accomplish even more than they. That is, sometimes, in that far-away place, there is a loaf of bread that is tied to the businessman's root-soul, and he must eat of that very loaf in that very place at that very time (to connect his soul with the divine sparks in it). [There is an image in Jewish mystical thought that conceives of the souls of all people having their origins in particular locations in the body of the original Adam. Souls from the same location are related and seek each other out.] Similarly, he may have to drink his fill of water there. It is for this purpose that "the steps of man are made firm" to travel several hundred miles away—to connect his soul (to its related sparks), in consuming that bread or drinking that water.

Sometimes this mission does not apply to him, but rather to one of his workers. Perhaps this other person is required to eat some bread or drink some water, but does not have the means to get there himself. The boss chooses to send him on this business trip to fulfill this mission . . . for thus had the Holy One decreed, so that he might fulfill his soul in this manner. These are both instances of God's ways.

This is what the verse suggests: "The steps of a man are made firm by Adonai," he sets out on one or another business trip to some distant place at the instance of the Blessed One, as decreed by His wisdom to fulfill his soul in one of these ways known to the Holy One. Still, this person does not see it this way, rather "he delights in *his* way," as if he were just on a business trip, forgetting God in his heart.

(OR HAME'IR, TZAV, S.V. VA'ANI AMARTI
MA DE'ITA ETZEL SHMUEL HARAMATI)

When reading this text, we can imagine the community to whom this sermon was directed, one of small businessmen and tradesmen, bent on making money to support family and community. These two motivations are worthy, but they can overtake and obscure our spiritual sensitivities. We see our successes in the field, we enjoy the benefits of the work of our hands. We focus more and more on ourselves, and forget about God's place in our lives, in our successes. There is nothing wrong with earning a living, making money, or being successful. In fact, it is our duty to strive to do so. There is a problem, however, when we disconnect our work from our spirituality. Remember the teaching from Pirkei Avot: "Rabbi Eleazar Hakappar taught: Jealousy, desire, and honor remove one from the world" (Avot 4:23). When we decide that making a living is the primary guide to our actions, we cloud our vision and thus miss the opportunity to experience divine sparks, even in the workplace.

There are two messages in this teaching. One is a reminder that no action is without importance. The other is that mindfulness applies in every situation; not to be mindful in any circumstance is likely to lead to unhappiness. The first message is expressed in the images of root-souls and the presence of divine sparks in everything, even things as mundane and simple as bread and water. Not only are there sparks in everything, divine energy trapped in husks that needs to be identified and raised up in consciousness and holiness. These sparks also have a connection to other sparks. According to one view, the links among sparks reflect their original positions in the cosmic order, before the initial "shattering" that scattered them in the physical world. Sparks that derive from the "space," that have the same root-soul, are connected and related one to the other. Thus, it is possible that we are related not only to our own family, but also to people we do not know—both contemporaneous with us and before and after our time—as well as to material objects. We are connected to sparks found in all of Creation, and it is our duty to connect with them and to try to raise them up. No occurrence or interaction, then, is simply "by chance," and nothing that we do is solely for the sake of our own personal goals. Everything that happens is for the sake of connecting sparks from common root-souls, to raise them up for the good of the whole.

There was once an ad campaign aimed at reducing gasoline consumption. Its tag line was, "Is this trip really necessary?" The implication was that it may very well not be, and often that is the case. We can consolidate errands, put off unnecessary travel, choose the days and times in which we travel to limit idling, etc. But in the end, we will set out in our cars to do something. We can still ask the question: Is this trip really necessary? That is, what are the implications of our setting out now to do this work, to complete this errand, to visit this friend? How will our decision to use the car, to leave home, to spend time, affect us, our families, and the world? We cannot know the ultimate answers to these questions. Everything we do has repercussions, echoing in time and space in ways beyond our ken. When we consider that this trip may be to discover and raise up some spark that is not now in our hands or under our control, we are likely to become more intentional in our travels. We will pay greater attention to all that we do.

This leads us to the second message in this text. The businessmen who travel to close a deal and make more money, oblivious to the true agenda God has for them, wind up forgetting God in their hearts. This is bad, not only as an affront to God, but because it is dangerous to focus only on personal success or failure. The tragedy in Arthur Miller's "Death of a Salesman" derives from the blindness of Willy Loman to the love of his family, even as he struggles and fails to earn the love and respect of his bosses and clients. When we make our work our lives, when we base our self-esteem on our success in business, we obscure the true root of our worth and the truth of our lives.

When we learn to see in our travels for business (and for pleasure) that we are on a mission intended by God to bring us to a certain circumstance so that we might redeem a holy spark, our attention will no longer be solely on our work, or even on our particular, personal plans. Everything around us will come alive with possibility. Everything we eat will reveal itself as a source not only of sustenance but also of joy. Every interaction with another person will challenge us to look carefully and deeply not at the end that they might serve in our lives, but to discern the holy spark within them, and to raise that spark (and them) up. Such an attitude may relieve us of the stress and anxiety that accompany our work and travel—or at least help us to put it into perspective. It will remind us that our business success or failure is not the final outcome of this trip. We will be able to allow events to unfold without forcing them to fit our expectations, since we will see that each moment, each exchange, and each interaction reveals another moment of holiness.

This teaching might lead us to think that consumption is the only means to redeem sparks. There is a stream of hasidic thought that suggests that it is indeed through our use and consumption of minerals, plants, and animals that we free and redeem the sparks in them. But there is also an awareness of a limit, that we have an obligation to preserve things for others as well.

> "The Torah is concerned with not wasting Jews' money" (cf. Ḥullin 49b). Why is this so? This is the way it is: When a person wears or eats something or even uses a tool or implement, he benefits from the vital force that is in that thing. Indeed, except for that spiritual force these things could not exist at all. Now, in each of these items are found divine sparks that are connected to his root-soul, and when he uses this thing or eats it or wears it, even if it is only for his physical well-being, he can repair these sparks. This comes about because afterward, by virtue of the comfort of the clothing he wears or the strength he gains through the food he has eaten and so on, he will work to serve the Holy One, and in this manner the sparks will be repaired.
>
> In this same respect, at some time he may lose this thing. That happens when he has completed repairing those sparks in it that are connected to his root-soul, and the Holy One takes the implement from him to give it to someone else whose root-soul is linked to the sparks that remain in the tool. . . .
>
> Therefore, we have to concern ourselves with our belongings and whatever might be in our possession, because of the sparks that are in those things, in order then to better take care of the holy sparks.
>
> (Likkutim Yekarim, No. 177)

This text sets off from the premise that the Torah is concerned with sparing the money of Jews. In the Talmud, it means that the rabbis framed laws seeking to limit undue expense in their implementation. Here, the author suggests that the concern of Torah is to preserve our things (not only money) *in their existence,* so that we will have the opportunity to use them fully—thereby repairing all of the sparks to which we are linked.

This teaching suggests that things cannot be "used up." Although the concept of "recycling" may not have existed in earlier times, the adage "waste not, want not" certainly did. Clothing, tools, building materials, books, papers of all sorts were regularly mended and "handed down," repaired, reused, and used again. Old papers were bound into the covers of new books. What was no longer useful in its own right was refashioned to serve a new purpose—swords into plowshares, or tools into candleholders. The original impetus for this practice might have been practical—the savings in the cost of replacement, the difficulty in procuring needed materials. But in this teaching we are led in a new direction. We are encouraged to think of things not as items useful to us, but of ourselves as actors useful in the repair and redemption of things.

This orientation stands opposed to the values of our materialistic culture. The great engine of modern consumer capitalism is disposability. It saves labor and time for the consumer, but requires greater and greater consumption. From cars to diapers, computers to ballpoint pens, this drives our economy: planned obsolescence, new-and-improved, use it and throw it away. What our text suggests is that this approach to "things" sunders the connection between God and all of Creation. When we view food, clothing, shelter, tools, implements, and appliances merely as disposable "things," we close ourselves off from a deeper experience of our place in the world. We hide from our neediness. Since there will always be something new to take its place, we can hide from our dependence on any given object. We have come to rely on "things" to make us feel comfortable. When they break we get angry, and we perceive our lack as hardship. In response, we lash out at the inanimate object, tossing it aside, demonstrating that we are not dependent by replacing it with another. Where we need to recognize the value of all things, filled as they are with divine sparks, for "there is no place devoid of God," we instead create whole realms of things that are merely dispensable, of value only to the degree that they serve us.

But in this text we are taught that food, clothing, and tools are not merely "things" that I use for my own benefit. They are part of the divine expression brought under my sway, into my domain, so that I might repair them and then integrate them more fully into the divine realm. Even when I no longer "need" some item, even when I have repaired all of the sparks that share my root-soul, the item has not lost its utility. Its value is not dependent on my personal, particular situation. Apparently there is more than one spark to be redeemed, more than one way that an item can be used. It is not in our hands to "dispose" of anything. Rather, while we are free to use it, we are also called to engage with it, delight in its utility and its helpfulness, and find its divine quality. When we are done with it, we are to pass it along.

On the other hand, there are teachings that differ from this one, alternatively suggesting that once a spark has been repaired, what is left is mere refuse. The primary example of this is, in fact, the consumption of food. We take in something that is recognizable in its original form—vegetables and fruits, bread that we have shaped from wheat, meat that has been taken from an animal. We digest it, absorbing the divine "energy" in it, using the spiritual vitality in the food to give us strength to more fully serve God, and then we expel the waste.

Now we can understand the teaching of our sages in the Mishnah, "Who is wealthy? One who rejoices in his portion" (Avot 4:1). That is, he does not make his heart rejoice in filling his belly with delights, nor is he a stranger to his heart's desires, as it is said, "Of rejoicing [I asked], 'What is that?'" (Ecclesiastes 2:2). Rather, the basis of his joy is to rejoice in the portion of goodness that is clothed in the letters that comprise the food on his table, and in raising them up to their sources, by means of removing everything extraneous from the food and expelling the waste. [If that is the true source of joy,] why would he eat more than necessary? After all, "The righteous person eats to his heart's content *(lesova nafsho)*" (Proverbs 13:25). The verse actually means that he eats to satisfy his soul *(nafsho)*, to rejoice in that part of the food that touches it, raising up that portion so that it can vitalize his soul to rise even higher. This is the meaning of the statement from Avot above.

But, we also have the teaching, "Who is wealthy? One who has his privy nearby to his table" (Shabbat 25b). What this means is: when he is eating at his table, he gives his attention only to the portion of goodness in the food that touches his soul, the rest remaining waste to be expelled. Why would he eat more than his portion, then? It is that portion of good that arouses his intention to eat in holiness and purity, and so he can be satisfied with only a little food, since in the end he will expel what is left into the privy.

These two teachings really point to one message: be wise when eating and do not add on non-essentials; rejoice in your portion (as explained above). In the same vein, when the "privy is nearby to his table": his fervent intention during his meal is to gain strength from the food to sustain him when he goes to the study hall, there to speak words (made up of divine letters) and to engage in the study of Torah and in doing *mitzvot*.

(Or Hame'ir, Counting the Omer, s.v. umei'atah
tavin asher shanu haḥakhamim bamishnah)

This text reminds us that we cannot evade the fundamental laws of nature, that both energy and matter must be preserved. We do indeed ingest food to use its energy and nutrients to sustain us, and in the end we also produce waste. And in general, the nature of things is that they are impermanent; ultimately they wear out. Not everything can be mended, reused, recycled, or handed down. In the end, we must throw some things away. Does this free us from responsibility for how we how we consume—literally and figuratively—for how we use our "things"? That this text (and much of Jewish tradition) looked with a negative eye on waste, excrement, that which is left over after we have lifted up all of the sparks, does not mean that we can act mindlessly. We cannot avoid waste. Our capacity to "use" things is made meaningful—and in a spiritual sense is "successful"—only when we are discriminating in our use of things and devote that use to holy purposes. In that manner we will become more accountable for our waste.

"Is this trip really necessary?" When we ask that now, we can follow with these questions: "Is my use of the car today going to increase my compassion and express a deeper justice toward other people? Will I be using the energy, the divine sparks, in the gasoline that is actually tied to my root-soul, or will I further estrange it from the one(s) who need to redeem and repair those sparks? Can I accept full responsibility for the pollution this trip will produce?" When we sit down to eat a meal, we might consider these questions: "Is the joy that I take in this food from a sense of wealth and possession, or is it from gratitude and awareness of responsibility? Have I done what I could to make sure that I have not wasted food in the preparation of the meal, and will I not waste what is left over? Have I minimized the impact my waste will have on the environment? Have I done what I could to make sure that others are eating as well, that no one lacks for physical or spiritual nourishment? Will I use the energy I derive to serve God and others?"

When we consider purchasing a new object for use we might ask these questions: "Was this object created because there is a clear need for it, or has it been produced with the hope of creating a market? Will my possession of this thing help me to improve my life and the lives of those around me, or will it go largely unused? Is my inclination to buy a response to a deep movement of my soul in response to the sparks in this thing, or has my alienation from God created a 'need' that I hope this thing will satisfy?"

These are not merely rhetorical examples. They are how we might actually think about our lives, about our actions. Not only do we respond out of habit to the actions and words of other people, but our inner lives lead us to react to the physical world around us, as well. Each one of these questions creates for us a moment of pause before acting, an instant in which we step back from the ongoing flow of our lives to consider what we are doing. We like and dislike, we are attracted to and repelled by, we engage with and reject things around us—food, clothing, commodities, buildings, neighborhoods, and so on. Only when we are aware of our reactions will we be able to make wise decisions as consumers. We know that we will not hurt the feelings of brussels sprouts if we refuse to eat them; after all, they have no feelings. But we should not let that fact lead us to think that their repugnance is innate. It is our response to them, and we are responsible for that, just as we are responsible for our reactions to other people. In the same way that mindfulness practice helps us to create a moment in which we can observe our reactions, step back, and consider what is true, we can do this in response to the physical, inanimate world as well.

The significance of making this space in our hearts and minds is that out of it we will be wiser in our decision-making. The capacity to choose between good and evil, between holy and profane, between pure and impure, between necessary and contingent, is the mark of our humanity. It is our exercise of that capacity that makes our *avodah*, service of God, meaningful. The more aware we are of the forces at work in our decision-making, the more likely we are to make good decisions. We are more likely to do what is "right," what is in line with the truth. The following text from *No'am Elimelekh* sets forth the significance of how we choose to act, in determining how our deeds become *avodah*.

Moses' intention when he prayed, "Give us joy equal to the days You have afflicted us" (Psalm 90:15), was to say: cause us to rejoice in Your holiness as in the years that You have afflicted us by the *yetzer hara*, whose power and attraction we are required to resist. "For the years we have suffered misfortune" (ibid.), that is, all the years that we watched and observed how we were attracted to our mindless desires, and yet were vigilant and careful not to follow them. By this means, "Let Your deeds be seen by Your servants" (ibid.), please consider it as if we have fulfilled all of Your commandments and deeds; working so hard to recognize the attractions of the *yetzer hara* and suffering in the process, let it be considered as if in this manner we have done all of Your commandments.

In this vein we can understand the verses, "You have granted him the desire of his heart" (21:3), in that You have given us the capacity to make choices according to our desires; "You have not denied the request of his lips" (ibid.), and You have not prevented us from speaking however we will. All this You have done for our good. "You have proffered him blessings of good" (ibid.): we have the capacity to choose our way, yet we are easily distracted, and so we often follow our *yetzer hara.* When we overcome our habitual reactions and do what is right, the Holy One extends us blessings and great reward.

(NO'AM ELIMELEKH, VAYEḤI,
S.V. O YOMAR VAYEḤI YA'AKOV, ETC.)

It is difficult to do what is right. It is hard to resist the pushes and pulls of the heart when we cannot see the forces at work within it, when we are blind to our passions. We suffer when we experience those forces and cannot see them as the sources of our own suffering; when we are blind to our own neediness, our own grasping for immortality and permanence. We externalize these forces, as if we were being buffeted about by something other than our own hearts, and we call it the *yetzer hara.*

Rather than see the *yetzer hara* as an independent actor, however, we can understand it to be the forces at work when we are not paying attention. It is not that there is a force for good and another one for bad battling in our hearts. Rather, when we pay close attention to our lives, we are more likely to do what is good for us, good for others, and good in the eyes of God. Our mindful responses to others in speech and deed, our attentive use and manipulation of the physical world, is the expression of the *yetzer hatov.* When we are heedless of the truth of the moment—when we get caught up in the seduction of things, in the yearnings of our neediness, in the passions of the moment—we are more likely to act in ways that are harmful to us and to others, which are not pleasing to God. That is the *yetzer hara.* Our capacity to exercise our will in a mindful manner is the determinant of our ultimate happiness, as well as that of those around us, and the world in general.

Mindfulness practice helps us to see more clearly the truth of the moment. We are able to discern when we are reacting to outside forces; we create space around the passion of the moment, so that we can choose proper behavior. We are then able to see what serves the good, and what reflects our commitment to compassion and justice for ourselves and others. We become better able to resist the seductions of things, recognizing that they will not quell our fear of loss and annihilation. We will be better able to control our appetites, committing ourselves to consuming that which is truly for our benefit, not wasteful, and can sustain us without depriving others.

How can we keep our hearts open toward other people? What will prevent us from allowing our passions to override our inclination toward compassion and justice? That human beings are created in the image of God can motivate us toward this goal. In a sense, when we look at another person, we are looking at a representative of God, a reminder of God's presence everywhere. When we are made mindful of God's presence in all things, we respond with reverence and love. We are reminded of how easily we are frightened, how quickly we allow our hungers and needs to determine our actions, and we step back to reconsider our behavior and our actions, to be more present before God's image.

The mystical tradition reinforced this idea of the divine image when it visualized the pattern of the emanations of the *sefirot* as if they were tied to parts of the human body. That is, the first *sefirah, Keter,* the crown, is tied to the very top of the human head, followed by the pair, *Hokhmah* and *Binah,* in the center of the head below that. The next set, *Hesed, Gevurah,* and *Tiferet,* represent the right and left arms and the heart. Below them are *Netzah, Hod,* and *Yesod,* the right and left legs and the phallus. From *Yesod* divine blessings flow into the world, represented by *Malkhut.* Although there are a number of other ways of depicting and relating these qualities one to another, this one is particularly potent—and challenging.

When we look at this image, our first impression is that we are facing another person, with their left hand opposite our right. That is the way our minds process the image of someone standing opposite us, since that is the case when we stand face-to-face with another person. But that is not how this depiction of the *sefirot* works. When we look at it we are asked to see the side in front of our right hand as the right side of the opposing body. The body facing us is like a mirror image, in that when we move our right hand, the hand opposite it moves in the mirror, and this hand is also the right hand. There is no "being" whom we can face whose right hand will also face our right hand, other than God before us. When we look at the image of God depicted in the schema of the *sefirot*, and when we consider that this "image" of God is imprinted on the person facing us, it is as if we are also looking at ourselves in the mirror. Levi Yitzhak makes this very point.

> The Baal Shem Tov taught regarding the verse, "Adonai is your shadow" (Psalm 121:5): a person stands next to his shadow, and just as he moves so does the shadow. So, too, is it with the Holy One. Just as we behave on this plane, the Holy One acts toward us in the divine realms, as it were. Thus, if we behave with lovingkindness (*hesed*) toward other people, then God will act toward us with *hesed.* That being so, shouldn't we always behave with love toward others? (Not only will they benefit, but) we will draw down *hesed* and it will go well for us.
>
> This seems also to be what the sages intended when they taught (Ketubot 111b): "And you who cleave (to Adonai your God are all alive today)" [Deuteronomy 4:4]. This means that you should cleave to God's qualities. Just as He is merciful, so you, too should be merciful. That is, if we behave with the quality of *hesed,* an outflow of *hesed* will pour down on us from above. In this manner there will be communion, which is to cleave.
>
> (KEDUSHAT LEVI, ḤANUKKAH, S.V. BAGEMARA KOL HANEVI'IM
> NITNAB'U BEKHOH UMOSHE NITNABEI BAZEH, ETC.)

This text reminds us that we are mirror images of God. The qualities of God's right hand are mapped on our right sides as well. Whoever looks at us can see the divine image, as if looking at the mystical schema of the divine qualities. But God also mirrors our actions—shadows us, as it were. Our movements generate a response on the divine level. Our actions on behalf of others—our love for others, our compassion for others, our gratitude, our justice—energize the flow of divine energy into this world as well. We benefit others and, in turn, God benefits us. What we do on behalf of the image of God before us in another person—mirroring God's qualities—is then mirrored by God toward us.

When I see the *sefirot* aligned in me as they are in the divine image, I recognize that they are at work in me as well. I embody these qualities, and it is my duty to utilize them in a manner that honors their divine source. When we are mindful, when a passion arises in us, we step back from our immediate response of selfish enjoyment, of fear, of compulsion to possess, of revulsion. We try to examine the truth of our reactions, the substantiality of our feelings, and to respond with compassion for ourselves and for others. We are invited to recognize the truth of the moment, the divine origin of all things, the divine spark that may be present that only we can redeem or repair. In this process we can transform each moment, devoting everything to the service of God. When I see the image of God imprinted on every other person, I recognize that they too are called to serve God, to redeem sparks, to help me see the truth. They are not my mirror image; they are God's. Facing each other, we realize that our individuality does not dissolve and we are not simply replications of the other. But we recognize that God is between us, and that we are each reflections of the Divine. Others are not here to serve me, and I am not permitted to use them. But together, in mutual attention to the truth, we may serve God more fully.

There is another way that the Jewish tradition has conceptualized the idea of human beings embodying the image of God. We are not only physical reminders to one another that there is a God in the world, but we actually become emissaries, effectuating God's will in the world. To the extent that we behave in Godly ways, we represent God in the world.

> "To walk in His ways" (Deuteronomy 11:22). These are the ways of the Holy One: "Adonai is compassionate and gracious" (Exodus 34:6). Scripture says, "All who call upon the name of Adonai" (Joel 3:5). How is it possible for a human being to say the name of the Holy One? The Holy One is called "compassionate," so you, too, should be compassionate. The Holy One is called "gracious," so you, too, should be gracious. It says in Scripture, "Gracious and compassionate is Adonai" (Psalm 145:8), providing for all as a gift.
>
> (SIFRE DEUTERONOMY,
> EKEV 49, FINKELSTEIN, P. 114)

Our behavior can be like God's, and in that manner we can embody God's image. How we act, how we present ourselves in the world, the very words we use—all these things bring God's virtues and God's attributes into the world. We can control our behavior and hope to live up to God's expectations of us, to be like God. Our intention to behave this way does not determine how we will view others. That is, our reactions to others may differ from how we actually come to act. How, then, can we come also to view others with compassion and grace?

The previous text refers to verses from Exodus 34, following the incident of the Golden Calf. Moses pleads for the good of the people, for God's mercy, and for God's ongoing presence among them. Then,

> He said, "Oh, let me behold Your presence!" And He answered, "I will make all My goodness pass before you, and I will proclaim

before you the name Adonai, and the grace that I grant and the compassion that I show. But," He said, "you cannot see My face, for man may not see Me and live." And Adonai said, "See, there is a place near Me. Station yourself on the rock and, as My presence passes by, I will put you in the cleft of the rock and shield you with My hand until I have passed by. Then I will take My hand away and you will see My back; but My face must not be seen."

(Exodus 33:18–23)

This eventually comes to pass.

Adonai came down in a cloud; He stood with him there, and proclaimed the name Adonai. Adonai passed before him and proclaimed: "Adonai! Adonai! a God compassionate and gracious, slow to anger, abounding in kindness to the thousandth generation, forgiving iniquity, transgression, and sin; yet, He does not remit all punishment, but visits the iniquity of parents upon children and children's children, upon the third and fourth generations."

(Exodus 34:5–7)

This scene was brought into Jewish theology and liturgy, and is recalled in times of distress as the model for petition and supplication. Indeed, the rabbis abbreviated God's declaration, ending this speech with the declaration that God remits punishment. The rabbis teach that God is instructing Moses in His qualities of mercy and compassion, thirteen in all, to be employed in seeking God's mercy and forgiveness (Rosh Hashanah 17b).

We learn in this episode that people cannot view the face of God. Oddly, however, we can see God's back. Rabbi Jeff Roth, one of my teachers, once interpreted this passage as follows: He imagined Moses in the cleft of the rock, hidden under God's hand.

Then his eyes are uncovered and he looks, but his vision is altered. He realizes that he is looking at the world, as it were, through the back of God's head, through God's eyes. What he sees, how he sees it, is shaped by God's dramatic annunciation of thirteen qualities of mercy. He sees the world as God sees it, with mercy and compassion.

The implication of this interpretation is that we may not be able to see God's face directly, but we can see the world through God's eyes. In this manner, we can shape the nature of our responses to other people. Not only will we act with compassion and grace when we set out to do good, but we will be able to respond to others when—in the natural course of events—they challenge us, scare us, or puff us up. We will look out and remember to see the world through God's eyes. Again, we are invited to respond mindfully, with compassion and grace toward others.

In the following text these two aspects of the image of God and the thirteen attributes of mercy are brought together. The idea that emerges here is one that both leads us to honor other people as the embodiment of these qualities of God, and also inspires us to actuate those qualities in ourselves, so that we may come to see the world through God's eyes.

> There are thirteen attributes of God, which are also called the thirteen qualities of the beard. These attributes are "Adonai! Adonai! God, compassionate and gracious, etc." They are the glory and splendor of the Holy Blessed One, similar to (yet, different in thousands of thousands, even infinite, ways from any comparison to material existence) a man, whose actual beard brings glory to his face. In a very distant way, this is how in supernal spiritual realms God's attributes might be called "qualities of the beard," since it is through them that God directs the world and its creatures, and is thereby glorified and exalted.

Now, human beings are a microcosm, their physical beings reflecting their supernal spiritual beings. The divine attributes descending down to the physical world become present in people so that they might glorify, exalt, and honor the Holy Blessed One by cleaving to the good that is in these attributes. In the descent of these attributes from their source to their endpoint in people, they become mixed with both negative and positive qualities, for "God made both the one and the other" (Ecclesiastes 7:14). But this is the origin of the obligation to make choices. Just as there is a positive quality to the attributes, so there is a negative quality, which is its opposite. . . . It is the role of a Jewish person to cleave to the good in the attributes, for it is by means of the attributes that he can cleave to the Blessed Creator at all, and that is the point of all *avodah.* So the sages taught: "'Cleave to Him' (Deuteronomy 10:20): Is it possible to cleave to the Holy Blessed One? Is He not a devouring fire? Rather, cleave to His attributes. Just as He is compassionate, you, too, must be compassionate." We must use these attributes in all of our endeavors, so that all of our actions will be by means of these (divine) attributes.

(Me'or Einayim, Ḥayyei Sarah,
s.v. lehavin ha'inyan denoda msharz"l)

This text works on two levels. We are to see other people and recognize in them the qualities of God, the image of God. The beard on the face of a man reminds us of the mystical image of God, whose "beard" is the means by which divine blessings of mercy and compassion flow. This association leads us to honor that other person—bearded or not, male or not, Jewish or not—and to extend to him mercy and compassion. Seeing God's image in the face of the Other leads us to act like God. We are God's mirror image, enacting God's actions. But, we are also reminded that we are a "microcosm," that we are a whole world in ourselves. We embody the divine attributes. When we discern between good and evil, separating out the good in each thing, knowing what is merciful and compassionate in each moment, we enact the divine intent. Our actions are like God's actions; our movements, like God's movements. The love and glory that are God's qualities, and which are identified with God's right side, are on our right sides as well. We are the image of God, and we are God's emissaries in the world: our actions are God's actions.

All of these images can lead us to a more mindful response to the world around us. Each of them disrupts our accustomed ways of viewing the world. By trying to hold the mirror image of God between us and another person, by trying to see God's attributes in others and in ourselves, by trying to see through God's eyes, we find that we cannot rely on our sense perceptions alone. We are forced to distinguish between what our eyes register and what we really know about what we see. We are led to the question, over and over, "What is really true here?" As we strip away superficial appearances, and as we become conscious of our habitual responses and personal biases, we come to see in the person before us the image of God, a microcosm in which the divine attributes abide. When we quiet our minds and hearts, calming ourselves in a moment of repose in "the cleft of the rock," protected by "God's hand," we find that we are more able to see through God's eyes, to view the world with mercy and compassion. We recognize that there is no moment in which we are not responsible for the world. Our choices, for good or for evil, for more mindful and informed action or for habitual reaction, affect others. When we know this in our hearts, we become calmer and the world becomes more peaceful, so we are more able to choose to exemplify and live out God's qualities in our own lives.

When I approached business owners to invite them to participate in the Hate Free Community Project in California, one of the arguments I used in support of the program was that it made good business sense. That is, whatever they might feel about anyone else in the community—due to race, sexual orientation, ethnicity, etc.—their self-interest demanded that they create a community in which everyone was made to feel welcome and safe. The more that was true on the streets of the city, the more that was felt in their stores and those of their neighbors, the more likely people would feel comfortable entering and taking advantage of what the business had to offer. Without denying the need to be safe from vandals, shop-lifters, and other miscreants, it would still be to the business owners' advantage in increased sales and profits to be welcoming, accommodating, and knowledgeable of the various interests, tastes, inclinations, and predilections of all possible clientele, and to provide for that as much as possible.

The teachings of the hasidic tradition share an element of that view. That is, when we are fully mindful of the world around us, we will see divine sparks in all people and things. We will sense that every interaction with another person, that every use we make of some tool, every experience, is for the sake of redeeming or repairing a spark. We will be interested in people and things because they help to reveal to us sparks related to our root-souls. The more sparks we can find and repair, the more we are fully engaged in redeeming sparks from our root-souls, the more we will have fulfilled our tasks in this life. We will, ourselves, be more complete. Our positive interest in all that happens to us, and to all people and things, is in that way self-serving. Our actions have an element of self-interest.

In both cases, however, the immediate self-interest gives way, in the end, to a greater good. In the case of the businessperson, not only will his or her business thrive, but the well-being of the community will improve. There will be less crime, property values will rise, the capacity of schoolchildren to learn will increase, creating a more talented and able workforce—"quality of life" in general will improve. Among those who will enjoy this improved life will not only be the businessperson and his or her family, but all other people living in the community. What had been done out of self-interest will ultimately serve the larger interest.

The presence of self-interest in doing good does not demean the good that is done. The ultimate issue is if the good gets done. Nevertheless, we recognize that there is a danger if we remain solely on the plane of self-interest: we might never see the good that is actually done. We might never learn that we can actually commit to doing good simply because it is the right thing to do, regardless of our own interest. In addition, there is the danger that once we close our business, or if we suffer a setback, we will define our self-interest differently, and stop doing what we had originally set out to do. So, self-interest is only a starting point.

In other community organizing work that I did with religious congregations, I found that there was another sort of argument that often motivated participation: noblesse oblige. Members of the participating congregations recognized that there were social and political inequities in the larger community. They could see that there were neighborhoods and communities within the city who were not being served. And they were willing to participate in an organizing project to help "those people." Separated from those other folks geographically, economically, and socially, however, the congregants did not see their own problems as related to those of the other participants in the organization. The congregants were accustomed to having power—political, economic, social—and did not see that participation in an organizing project would increase their power or well-being. But for the sake of others they were prepared to participate in the endeavor. The result, in the end, was half-hearted, wavering involvement, and ultimate disengagement from the organizing project.

The problem with this approach to action is that it lacks personal urgency. There is no self-interest except, perhaps, the fear of what other people might think. That, for all its pain, is not a good way to motivate people to give of their time, energy, and substance. Indeed, fear is just as likely to generate resentment and anger, emotions that undermine selfless action. Moreover, the sense that one can or must respond out of noblesse oblige creates a gap between oneself and other people. One can feel magnanimous, generous, and helpful, yet never really get involved in the lives of others. This, then, is also an insufficient source of motivation for involvement in working with other people.

The texts presented earlier in this chapter offer us another way of understanding our place in the world and among other people. There are divine sparks scattered throughout Creation. They are found not only in the mineral and animal kingdoms, but they are also present in people. Our individual charge is to locate, repair, and redeem those sparks related to us in our root-souls wherever we may find them. To find them we must be looking, and we must never exclude anything or anyone from our search. Thus, everyone is important to us. To accomplish our goals, we must engage with as many people as we can, in whatever contexts we may. This is not to say that we must become social butterflies or never establish friendships or maintain long-term, intimate relationships. Rather, it is to remind us that when an opportunity arises that challenges us to step out of our accustomed milieu, to interact and work with people who are different from us, we are being invited to seek out new sparks to redeem. That can only come about through honest interest and mutual involvement with other people.

The reverse is also true. We bear sparks of which we are unaware, but which are connected to other people in their root-souls. When we refrain from interaction with others, holding back communication and resisting engagement, we prevent those sparks from being repaired in us. Those sparks hidden in us that remain undiscovered might actually become more deeply obscured and harder to repair at a later time by another person. Without laying ourselves bare, giving up all sense of personal space or privacy, we can still strive to remain open to other people. We can treat each interaction as another divine revelation—if not to us, then to the other person.

The idea of the presence of sparks in other people as well as in us may help us to attain more open hearts. It will still require work on our part. Mindfulness of our situations, awareness of our inner lives, will help us to maintain a degree of openness. We will have to pay attention to the sensations of our reactions to other people. That is, when we sense our bodies holding back, tensing up, turning away from other people, we will at least be in a position to ask ourselves why. This will begin a process in which we will be able to see more clearly how we close ourselves off out of fear, guilt, fatigue, or insecurity. As we work through the layers of our responses, as we become aware of pieces of our past and present that cause us pain or that we have closed off out of anger or frustration, we offer ourselves compassion. These moments are not meant to generate guilt, for there is nothing to feel guilty about. These are our feelings; they are merely present in our hearts. When we recognize their presence, when we truly feel them, our hearts break open in awareness at our own suffering and the suffering we might cause others. When we treat ourselves with compassion in response, we will want to do so for others as well. In this manner we will learn to see what holds us back from offering ourselves to others, and what keeps us from giving of ourselves for others. Our eyes will open with our hearts, and we will offer ourselves to redeeming the world.

Recall this text:

The Exodus from Egypt was for the purpose of bringing the awareness of God out of exile. That is, even though today we still experience our exile, nevertheless the awareness of God is not in exile—except among those who absolutely deny God's existence in any form or manner. But for most everyone, it is God's qualities that are in exile—that is Love, Fear, Beauty, and the other attributes of God. Everyone acknowledges God's existence, each according to his way and ability, but God's qualities are dressed in exile—in false desires and groundless fears, whenever one of God's attributes is used contrary to the Blessed Creator's will: that they be employed only in the service of the Holy One. Therefore the Torah reminds us over and over, "Remember the day you came out of Egypt" (cf. Exodus 13:3), "So that you will remember" (Deuteronomy 16:3), and the like. These adjurations are instructions for bringing the attributes of God out of exile. For if each of us were to remember that awareness has already come out of Egypt, and we each acknowledged God's existence and being, then certainly it would be easy for us to redeem God's attributes from their negative applications and bring them to the good.

(ME'OR EINAYIM, SHEMOT, S.V. VEHINEI AḤAR YETZIAT
MITZRAYIM SHEHOTZIU HADA'AT MEHAGALUT)

The awareness of God that has come out of Egypt is the knowledge that it is possible to live a balanced, meaningful life. Our attempt to see clearly, to know the truth of the moment, is how we return over and over to that awareness of God. Although that truth is not hidden, we have to remember it all the time. When we do, we are able to make good choices, to seek the good for ourselves and for all others. We turn our love from things to people; we transform our fear of life's losses into reverence for all life. Our deepest desire is to liberate ourselves from the darkness of habitual responses, so that we might exercise our free will in concert with the awesome unfolding of all Creation. To live in that manner we must redeem our awareness in every moment, and we must extend our love and concern to all beings, as this text illustrates.

[The Mishnah (Berakhot 1:5) and the Passover Haggadah record a debate between Ben Zoma and the sages.] Ben Zoma interpreted the verse "that you may remember the day of your departure from the land of Egypt all the days of your life" (Deuteronomy 16:3) in this manner: "the days of your life," this refers to daytime; "all the days of you life," this refers to nighttime.

The quality of "day" applies to the time when the mind is clear, for then certainly the mind is spontaneously conscious of the awareness of God's existence and being. But, even during the times of darkness that are called "night," if we recall our capacity to know that there is a great, awesome God who created something from Nothing and who holds all things in His power, then certainly also night will become as bright as day, and we will depart from the darkness. Awareness of God's being will repair everything, and we will be able to bring all of God's attributes into the realm of the good.

The sages and Ben Zoma are actually not in conflict in their interpretations of this verse. Ben Zoma addressed the situation of an individual person, and the sages focus on the general principle. They interpret the phrase "the days of your life" to mean this world, for when we remember God's existence and being even in this world, which is one of exile, we are strengthened in our capacity to bring all of the rest of God's attributes to the realm of the good. . . .

[The Baal Shem Tov taught that] every person who serves the Blessed Creator in truth must bring to this service that aspect of the Messiah that is his . . . raising up his portion to be included in the complete reconstitution of the primordial unity. This is accomplished by means of the quality of "all," by unifying heaven and earth, fulfilling the instruction "know Him in all of your ways" (Proverbs 3:6), even in the mundane and material realm. This, then, points us to the sages' interpretation, that "all the days of your life" leads us to the days of the Messiah: by uniting "all" we connect that portion of the Messiah that is ours to the perfection of the world.

(ME'OR EINAYIM, SHEMOT,
S.V. VEHAKHAMIM UVEN ZOMA LO PLIGEI)

In this text I hear a reminder that not only for our own sake are we to strive to maintain an awareness of God's presence in the world, that is, the possibility of living a balanced, meaningful life. Our endeavors over and over to see the truth of the moment and to respond in compassion actually contribute to the redemption of humankind and of the world. This text couches this in terms of the bringing of the Messiah, which is dependent on *tikkun olam,* repairing the world. Every one of us has a place in the primordial, original form of Creation, the original cosmic Adam. Our endeavor to repair and redeem sparks returns them to their original place in that form, a place that we share and yet is unique to us. In our attempts to repair the world by returning sparks to their primordial position in the perfect cosmic Adam, we also find our place in that mythical body. As well, we learn that we are connected to all other people and their sparks. In that, our work and our lives—devoted to *tikkun olam*—let us play a role in bringing about the coming of the Messiah.

Each of us plays a role in the appearance of the Messiah. Each of us has a unique place in the body of the Messiah, and bringing our sparks to that position helps to build the completed and perfected Creation. Every act of *tikkun olam,* redeeming sparks and returning them to their roots, can contribute to the coming of the Messiah. The necessary condition out of which we do that work is awareness of God's existence and being, that is, mindful awareness. When our minds are clouded by fear, anger, jealousy, greed, pride, or doubt, we respond to our circumstances out of habit. Our reactions to challenge, to the unknown, to loss, will tend to be resistance, deflection, possessiveness. When we create space in our minds and hearts, seeing through our immediate reactions to recognize the deeper issues, we can transform our responses. We can welcome challenge—even though we will not be able to determine the outcome. We can open ourselves to the unknown—not without caution, but without fear. We can accept loss—without giving up on loving and holding.

There were many people who resisted participating in the Hate Free Community Project. Some thought that the whole enterprise was unnecessary, since they didn't hate anyone, and could not imagine that anyone they knew hated other people. Others were concerned that we would institute a form of "thought police" or otherwise limit the exercise of free speech. Still others thought that the problem was misdirected, since the prevention and prosecution of "hate crimes" belonged to the police and other legal authorities. Most of those who did not participate or who did not support the Project thought that it was not practical. They did not believe that it is possible to address the human heart, much less to change it. The whole endeavor, in their eyes, was messianic, and therefore not in our hands to accomplish.

The mindful practice of Judaism leads us to see the world differently. We have been created in the image of God, and so must have the capacity to fulfill the role of God's emissaries or representatives. We have been given the ability to choose between good and evil, and so we can bring more good into the world. There is nothing but God, and we are charged to make that more evident. But we are also material beings, subject to the pushes and pulls of our physical bodies. We love, and so we also get jealous; are devoted, so we also become defensive; need sustenance, and so we become gluttonous and possessive. These behaviors and others obscure God's presence from us, and cloud our hearts to other people. To fulfill our obligations to God, others, and ourselves, we need to learn how to open our hearts and minds, to see clearly, and to respond from the awareness of the truth of the moment.

Openness of heart and mind is the awareness that that whole world is filled with God, that there is nothing but God, that there is no place devoid of God. We seek to return to that awareness over and over, throughout our lives, since it is then that we truly come to know joy and peace. When the heart is darkened by fear or sadness, by doubt or anger, we lose the capacity to see clearly and so to make free choices in our responses to circumstances. We return to exile. When we remember our capacity to see clearly, to open our hearts to the blessing of each moment, we come out of exile and repair one more aspect of Creation, add one more component to the body of the Messiah. We are able to bring the Messiah into each moment, to transform our hearts so that we can act with compassion and justice toward all people. When we liberate ourselves from the exile of a closed heart, we acquire the capacity to liberate others with us. Mindfulness practice helps us to free our hearts and liberate others from their suffering. Jewish life and practice help us to bring the Messiah.

Section Five

Teshuvah

Chapter Eleven

Mindfulness and the Way of Return

*J*udaism is a spiritual discipline, a practice that leads us to an awakened awareness of God's being and existence. That awareness moves us to seek God in all things and places, in all of our activities, and in all the happenings of the world. The more we are able to perceive God's presence—the more we are moved to serve God, to celebrate God's compassion, to walk in God's ways, and to cleave to God. This endeavor demands that we pay attention all the time, to be as aware as possible of our actions as well as our intentions. We seek to bring our capacity for *kavanah,* for awareness and directed action, into everything we do. When we see most clearly, when we recognize the truth of the moment and what it demands of us, we then sense the necessary obligation of response; we are commanded. There is no moment in which we are free from paying attention, in which there is no spark of divine light to be discovered, celebrated, and raised up in thanks to God.

Yet we are human beings. From the moment of birth we are dependent—on parents and family, on teachers, on our community; on breath, on water and sustenance; on shelter and garments; on God. Our needs generate urges, passions, hungers. Our bodies respond spontaneously to our surroundings—helping us to avoid dangers and generating energy for both fight and flight, but also leading us into temptation. Our capacity to see clearly is constantly challenged by our natural, but difficult, responses to the vicissitudes of life. Our egos—our sense of a separate self, different from God, cut off from God, in competition with all others and with God—cloud our vision and close our hearts. We feel alone; we experience loss and pain; we suffer.

Mindful Jewish practice helps us to wake up to the truth of the moment, to see the truth of our lives in the whole of Creation. We grow in our ability to identify each moment as a gift from God, to rejoice in our existence, and to offer our unique capacities to others and to God. We develop the skills to apply our intention to be compassionate and just, to prevent our spontaneous and habitual reactions from creating more suffering for us and for others. Our attempts to maintain open hearts and willing responses to all of life make us aware of how strongly we desire to do what is right and how much we regret having done what was hurtful or destructive. Our compassion for our own flaws and failures strengthens our resolve to make up for what we have done, and then to remain as awake as possible to avoid repeating our mistakes. The joy that we feel when we realize that we have the capacity to atone for injuries we have inflicted moves us to help other people find ease and joy in their lives as well.

This practice does not take place in segregated moments, special times of day, or holy seasons. It is constant. With each and every breath we are reminded of the blessing of the moment, and we are invited to renew our lives. Mindfulness is an approach to life, an awareness that shapes how we view each moment of life, how we respond to every incident and accident. The desire to wake up and remain awake in our lives must be applied to each and every interaction, every thought, always. We do not become mindful once and for all. We return over and over to our intention, and we wake up again and again.

This is the way of *teshuvah,* of return to the ways of God. No moment is the same as the one before, and the one that follows will be different as well. In each instance, we are called to remain awake to the truth and to act with compassion and justice. When we fail, when our habitual reactions lead us astray, when we are overtaken by passion or fear, we are still charged with waking up to the truth. When we create a moment of calm in our hearts, we realize the truth and we seek to make amends. We change our ways, and we set out on a different path. This is the way of *teshuvah.*

The capacity to change, to make our lives different, is an important counter-balance for our God-given freedom of choice. If we can choose wrongly, then there must also be a mechanism to right the wrong. That mechanism is the way of repentance, a path of transformation. This, too, is *teshuvah.* The potential that mistakes may be made and yet also amended lies behind the rabbinic teaching: "Seven things were created before the world was created, and they are: Torah, repentance, the Garden of Eden, Gehenna, the Throne of Glory, the Temple, and the name of the Messiah" (Pesaḥim 54a). The possibility of change, the potential of repairing what has been damaged, must precede the creation of humankind if people are to be given freedom of choice, since they may choose poorly. Otherwise, they will not survive their first transgression.

> "Adonai God (made earth and heaven)" (Genesis 2:4). This may be compared to a king who had some empty glasses. He said, "If I pour hot water into them, they will burst; if cold, they will contract [and snap]." What then did the king do? He mixed hot and cold water and poured it into them, and so they remained [unbroken]. Even so, the Holy One said, "If I create the world on the basis of mercy alone, its sins will be great; if on the basis of

judgment alone, the world cannot exist. Let Me create it on the basis of judgment and of mercy, and then may it survive!"

(Genesis Rabbah 12:15)

The balance of God's mercy and God's judgment must exist at the time of Creation if the world is to survive. It is only in the context of this dynamic tension that *teshuvah* can exist, and it is also because of this careful balance in the nature of existence that it is necessary.

The world survives in that constant balance—moving back and forth between failure and success, inattention and clear-sightedness, obfuscation and honesty. All of us, individually and collectively, move from one pole to the other. We wake up to the truth of the moment, and then we are startled, frightened, seduced into blind action again. That we seem to be incapable of maintaining our integrity and honesty for long may be frustrating. We cannot let that frustration prevent us from fulfilling our intentions and desires to attain to the truth. In the face of frustration we offer ourselves compassion, and we renew our commitment to living honestly before God. This commitment actually inclines the collective balance toward greater clarity, toward a preponderance of good. Our actions—renewed intention, revived awareness, improved behavior—make a difference.

Mindfulness can be developed and supported by the practice of meditation. Often, as we have seen, that practice begins with focusing our attention on the breath. The regular cycle of inhalation and exhalation provides both a dependable point for our focus and also a metaphor for our experience. That is, each breath rises and falls away. We cannot inhale and never release our breath. There is never—at least in health, at least before we die—a moment in which one half of the breath exists without the other.

The breath returns over and over, reviving us, sustaining us, reminding us that it is possible to renew each moment and to be renewed in it. This is also the process of *teshuvah*, the constant practice of return to our highest desires, our deepest intentions—to live mindfully, in devotion to the God of truth, as we read in *Kedushat Levi*.

"Take us back, O Adonai, to Yourself, and we shall return; renew our days as of old!" (Lamentations 5:21).

What is the meaning of the word *k'kedem* (as of old)? We can clarify this according to the rabbinic teaching on the verse, "And now, O Israel, what does Adonai your God demand of you? Only this: to fear Adonai your God" (Deuteronomy 10:12). The sages teach, "The word *ve'atah* (and now) suggest a moment of *teshuvah*" (Genesis Rabbah 21:6).

This is what it means: Each and every Jew must believe with complete trust that in each and every moment he is revived and sustained by the Holy Creator. This is what the sages taught on the verse, "Let all that has breath praise Adonai" (Psalm 150:6): "with each and every breath praise Adonai" (Genesis Rabbah 14:11). Each moment the vital force seeks to leave the body, yet each moment the Holy One sends renewed vigor. From this we can understand that every person has the capacity to experience *teshuvah*. In the moment that a person transforms himself through *teshuvah* he also comes to believe that he has become a new creation. On that basis the Holy One, in His great mercy, does not recall his earlier transgressions. But, if a person does not believe (that he is made new each moment), then his *teshuvah* is ineffective.

This, then, explains the teaching that "and now" means *teshuvah*. When we believe that we are made new each moment, each "now," our *teshuvah* will be effective. Further, this explains the verse from Lamentations. "Take us back, O Adonai, to Yourself, and we shall return." How shall we return? "Renew our days as of old."

(KEDUSHAT LEVI, LAMENTATIONS, S.V. O YEVO'AR HASHIVEINU
H' EILEKHA VENASHUVAH ḤADESH YAMEINU K'KEDEM)

This text calls our attention to each breath. As we attend to our breath, we realize that each inhalation is a gift. With each breath we are renewed, our bodies refreshed with oxygen. The unconscious, unspoken fear that we may not breathe again is relieved and we reclaim our place in the world. That experience in itself can be transforming: with each breath I am renewed, I am made new. How inspiring and commanding an awareness that is! With each breath, then, in each moment, we can wake up to the truth of our lives and change how we respond, how we engage with the world. We are not trapped in habitual reactions. We can be born again into a new sense of who we are, of what our stories truly are. We can be released from the bonds of compulsion and passion, of hunger and fear, into a new life.

"And now" means *teshuvah*. And now. And now. And now. Over and over we are offered another moment in which we can transform our hearts, our intentions, our lives. What are the conditions under which we will be able to awaken to God's presence in the world? How will we attain a balanced, meaningful life? One step on that path is to develop the awareness that each new moment can be one of renewal; that, in fact, we are made new each day. The promise that even "now" we can be released from our own personal bondage, that we can be redeemed from exile, is heartening. It is possible to transform ourselves and our lives, since we are made new each day.

What is it like to experience a moment of *teshuvah*? How does it feel to be made new? It is to feel a great relief, freed of the need to maintain a façade, to sustain a public persona. Once we recognize our habits of mind and heart and see the moment clearly, we are released from the bonds of fear or greediness that prevented us from doing the right thing, whether for ourselves or for others. When we see the truth—that this moment will pass and what we feel in the moment is not all that is happening; that we are not bound to respond reflexively, but we can choose compassionately what to do—we are set free, redeemed from exile. When we step back from our habitual responses, we give ourselves the space to see an alternative way of behaving. We experience the possibility of becoming someone new.

This new person comes into being in that very moment. The awareness creates not only the potential but makes real the new way of behaving. Our habits are strong and comforting, however, so there is always the possibility that we may lose sight of our new being and respond out of old habits and well-worn patterns of behavior. And even if we succeed in changing our responses in this moment, we will be faced by other challenges in the future, and we may not be as successful then. Nevertheless, with every next breath, in every next moment, we might see clearly again and be released from bondage. We are renewed over and over, and the possibility of doing *teshuvah* is always at hand. Consider this teaching in *Me'or Einayim.*

> The sages taught that a man who engages a woman on the condition that he is a righteous man, and is then found not to be so, is nevertheless married, since he may have done *teshuvah* in his thoughts (Kiddushin 49b). From this we learn that merely in thinking of *teshuvah* he was transformed fully into a righteous person, in the very moment the thought arose in him.
>
> This is the explanation. *Teshuvah* preceded Creation (Pesaḥim 54a), which was brought about through Ten Utterances (cf. Avot

5:1). From this we learn that all the worlds of Creation, and all that is in them, came about through speech. That which preceded Creation, therefore, also preceded speech; it existed merely in thought. For this reason, *teshuvah* is dependent on thought alone, since it is superior to the letters of speech. Thought returns to a source above even all of the worlds of Creation. . . .

Now, this world is bound up in time. But, before Creation there was no time at all. Therefore, there is no aspect of time connected with *teshuvah;* it can happen in a moment, since it derives from a realm beyond time. In that manner, we can repair our lives in the blink of an eye; we do not have to wait a long time. Those who argue that *teshuvah* is dependent on the passage of time cannot be talking about real *teshuvah.* We have to believe with full trust that our lives can be repaired in an instant.

This is the meaning of Hillel's teaching, "If not now, when?" (Avot 1:14). If you were to think that you cannot change things now, since thoughts themselves are ineffective and it takes a long time to put right what you have made wrong, then when would you ever be able to make things right? Waiting and working will never bring it about. Whatever you accomplish will not really be *teshuvah* since you will not really believe that it is beyond the realm of time, and that you can repair your life and your actions in a moment.

(Me'or Einayim, Likkutim, Shir Hashirim,
s.v. ketiv bekhol derakhekha da'ehu)

Do not mistake the claim in this text. It is not that over the course of our lives—that is, from year to year, from day to day, from moment to moment—we do not have the responsibility to consider our behavior and to try to change for the better. That is indeed our challenge and our duty. This is the work of growth and maturity, of self-awareness and other-awareness. It points us toward recognition of God's existence and being, of the potential to be fully awake in our lives, to see the truth of each moment. It is the practice and discipline of ritual and of mindfulness. It takes time to develop the skills to see each moment clearly. And even when we acquire that capacity, we are still subject to the accidents of human existence, and we may become scared or zealous in self-protection, needing to regain our composure, our clarity of vision. But that work is not *teshuvah* itself in its fullest sense.

Still, that work is the ground from which full *teshuvah* springs. Mindfulness practice prepares us for the moment of liberation—or, perhaps, moments of liberation. Over and over we will respond mindfully to our circumstances and realize that that which challenges us is actually transient. It will not last. What moves us to act without compassion for ourselves or for others is seen as fleeting. We are then released from the compulsion of contentious engagement, and we see beyond the moment. We see that no place and no event is devoid of God. Everything takes place in God; all things happening are manifestations of the divine expression. When we see this, our intention to reveal and redeem the divine sparks in that moment connects us to God, and to God's timelessness. We participate in a realm beyond time. This is full *teshuvah*.

This form of *teshuvah* liberates us from the mundane course of our lives. We are not freed of our bodies, and we do not transcend the norms of social conduct. But we learn that it is possible to return, over and over, in every moment, to an awareness that is timeless. In these moments, we are free to choose how to respond. When we offer ourselves compassion for our own suffering, for our own mistakes, we are released from guilt and self-recrimination, so that we might act differently in the future. The compassion we experience then is like the great love and compassion of God for us, bringing us closer to God's presence, helping us to walk more closely in Godly ways. Blessed with God's love, freed from our self-concern, we are able to turn with compassion toward other people. Transformed in each moment, redeemed through *teshuvah,* we relate differently toward other people, offering them the possibility of redemption as well.

While the personal transformation that comes about with *teshuvah* is powerful and redeeming, we do not appear different to others; the course of our daily lives does not change. But the inner experience of liberation in the face of the truth of our existence redeems each moment and makes us different. The power of this aspect of *teshuvah* is illustrated in the following text from *Me'or Einayim.*

> For example, the sages taught in the Talmud, "'[Happy are they who act justly,] who do right at all times' (Psalm 106:3). [Is it possible to do right at all times? Rather this is what our teachers at Yavneh, and some say Rabbi Eliezer taught:] This refers to one who feeds and sustains his minor children, etc." (Ketubot 50a; cf. M. Ketubot 4:6). That is, the father (who, according to the rabbis, is otherwise not responsible for their upkeep) realizes that there is also a portion of the divine in them, and that the Holy One has appointed him as an administrator of these divine portions, to support them. If this is his intention, then his endeavors on their behalf are divine service. But if he acts mindlessly (inattentive of the Divine), then, even though he supports them, his work is not considered *avodah.*
>
> Similarly, the Talmud teaches, "This is like two people who roasted their Passover offerings [one of whom ate his for the sake of the commandment, while the other one ate his out of gluttony]. Regarding the one who ate his for the sake of the commandment, Scripture says, "[The paths of Adonai are smooth;] the righteous walk in them" (Hosea 14:10); of the one who ate his out of gluttony, it says, "Sinners stumble on them" (ibid.).

From this we can see that in one and the same act, two people can do the same thing, but according to their intention and their awareness, they are not equal. One will bring himself closer to the Holy One, and the other will distance himself. In all cases, the most important thing is the awareness, the degree of *kavanah*, as it says, "Know Him in all of your ways" (Proverbs 3:6).

(ME'OR EINAYIM, ḤUKKAT,
S.V. ZOT HATORAH ADAM KI YAMUT BA'OHEL)

All people walk the same path. We human beings are all born dependent. We need help from parents and others to raise us, to sustain and protect us. We seek comfort, cherishing those who care for us, fighting against those who threaten us, shunning those whom we fear may disrupt our comfort. We strive to be creative and productive, we scheme and build, gather and save. We fear loss and we work hard to prevent it. We love, seek companionship, support others. We age, suffer illness, and die—some of us among family and friends, others alone. In this way, our lives are filled with suffering.

Throughout our lives we are challenged by these accidents of existence. In every instance there exists the possibility of responding with wisdom or with foolishness. We can act in ways that are compassionate and just, increasing peace within ourselves and among others. Or we can behave selfishly, blindly, causing more suffering to ourselves and others. The difference between one act and the other may be subtle, indiscernible outside of our hearts. But the consequences will become known.

For many years I thought that the print on my wall was of a tightrope walker. The original painting by Graciella Rodo-Boulanger depicts a man, straining, his face turned upward, wild hair blowing in the wind, carrying a long stick. At either end of this pole there are three birds: at one end, two are perched on the top and one hangs from the bottom, and at the other it is the other way around—one on top and two on the bottom. The pole seems balanced, but only just so. The birds seem to be agitated, their wings flapping, their heads in motion. The man, in turn, seems also to be in motion, just lifting his right foot to take a step. Very subtly, merely suggested in the composition of the background, there appears to be a line under the man's feet, the rope on which he was making his precarious, careful way.

Recently I have learned that the artist called the painting "Bird Vendor." What I had seen as a rope under the man's feet is merely the road he is walking. Now, his pace seems even, his steps easy. The birds do not threaten to throw him over; they are merely part of his baggage. He carries them lightly, the pole appearing to support itself in his hands. His upturned face is not twisted in a grimace of fear or terror, but in joy, inviting customers to come take a look. Whereas in my imagination the painting had closed inward, bringing my attention to the "rope" in the center of the image, I now perceived a movement outward, the background spreading out to the edge of the canvas and beyond.

The same painting, two different perceptions. And so it is with our lives. We all walk the same paths from birth to death, we face the same struggles, and we suffer the same challenges. On either side of us there are distractions, challenges—forces moving in opposing directions, pushes and pulls on our hearts and minds, like birds on a pole. We may feel, as we make our way, that we are constantly on a tightrope, always at risk of toppling. When we bring our full attention to our lives in any moment, however, we find that we can establish a sense of balance in our hearts, and in our lives. We sense that the forces that push and pull at us are the play of life, the ups and downs, the flights of fancy, the soaring elation, the diving terror of our fluttering emotions and thoughts. From tense focus on our feet, overly concentrated attention to each and every wobble and bump, we turn our hearts and minds outward to take in the fullness of the present moment. We find balance in the simple process of moving through each step, each moment, with clarity of intention and openness to what is and what may be. The tightrope walker is walking through the same painting as the bird vendor, yet, he is tense, fearful, and constrained in his motion. "He who is wise will consider these words; he who is prudent will take note of them. For the paths of Adonai are smooth; the righteous can walk on them, while sinners stumble on them" (Hosea 14:10). The bird vendor finds his way at ease, even as he works to move forward.

The Talmud asks: Is it possible to do charity, justice, righteousness all the time? Our teachers suggest that it is, if we direct our hearts to charity, justice, and righteousness. Everything depends on the purity of our intentions, the clarity of our vision, the depth of our awareness. Over and over we are challenged to see clearly and to respond out of the truth of the experience: to transcend our immediate fears and passions, to break free of our habits, to touch the infinite, to enter into the Oneness that is God. We return to this task over and over, with each breath. Mindful Jewish practice—*avodah* in all of its forms, in its highest form—is the ongoing, never-ending, ultimate work of *teshuvah*. In every moment we stand on a tightrope that may become a broad path, having to choose how to respond and what to do, in order to clarify our inner responses. We can choose to do what is compassionate and just, or what is constraining and selfish. The choice is in our hands. The consequences of our choices will affect us and all other people from that moment on. Our experience of the consequences will, in turn, affect how we make our next choice, and the one after that, and the one after that. Mindful attention to the truth of each moment may lead us on a way that is smoother, that we are more able to walk. Inattention may cause us to stumble.

The Torah and Jewish living help us to live our lives without denying death, and without embracing it, but by living fully with awareness of our mortality and celebrating our full humanity. We are created in the image of God, and we have it in our power to cleave to God, thereby bringing God's love into the world. In devoting our lives to serving God, to *avodah*, we commit ourselves to finding God's presence in every thing, in each moment. For this, we return to our intention, our *kavanah*, over and over. Whenever we succeed in overcoming our habitual reactions, responding instead with compassion and righteousness, we help to repair the world and move Creation toward its completion, toward the Messianic Era. We are not saved from death; we are redeemed instead in God's eternity, in the wonder and power of fully experiencing the truth of each moment.

This is mindful Jewish living. We move from moment to moment, from breath to breath, experiencing over and over the possibility of being created anew, of being reborn in *teshuvah*. We do not become mindful once and for all, and we do not finish serving God with any one act. We set out over and over again on our way, striving to open our hearts in compassion for ourselves, and for others. In moments we fail, caught in the snares of our own hearts and minds. And, in moments we succeed, redeemed from the exile of our own making. From moment to moment we walk the same path—aware sometimes, blind sometimes—but always making our way through life. "He who is wise will consider these words; he who is prudent will take note of them. For the paths of Adonai are smooth; the righteous can walk on them, while sinners stumble on them." Mindful attention to the truth of each moment, the truth of our lives, the truth of human existence, offers us the way to wisdom. We may still stumble, but we will always know that there is yet a smooth path under our feet, only to be found again with our next step, with our next breath.

Appendix

This is the Torah: Man

Mindfulness as *Deveikut*

Throughout this book I have used selections from various texts to illustrate how traditional Jewish sources express a mindful awareness of God's presence, and offer practices by which we might experience that from moment to moment. The following text presents many of the concepts and terms that we have encountered in this book in one connected, unified message, allowing us to see the interaction of values and concepts in the unfolding of one teacher's lesson.

> "This is the Torah: when a person dies in a tent" (Numbers 19:14). Our sages taught, "The Torah is sustained only by one who kills himself for its sake" (Berakhot 63b).
>
> There are 600,000 letters in the Torah, against which there are also 600,000 root-souls, even though today there may be more or less that number of Jews. Nevertheless, the essential idea is that there are 600,000 root-souls, and the multiplicity of people results from the splitting of the divine sparks. Therefore, each Jew is connected to one letter in the Torah. The Torah and the Holy One are a complete unity, and each letter then represents the divine element in each person. It is actually the very letter from which his soul derives. It is this letter that pours forth divine blessings and holy vital force.
>
> Now, consider that letters dwell in the human mouth, and each letter actually is made up of all of the Torah itself. In this way,

the whole of the Torah is found in our mouths. In addition, is it not also true that a Torah scroll that is missing one letter is unfit for use? Indeed, it is not even considered a Torah, since each and every letter is considered a Torah, connecting with the others to make a complete unity.

Now the essence of divine service is connected to these points. Our work is to bring ourselves close to our root-soul, which is the Torah, which is itself a complete unity, made up of 613 commandments. We are all also composed of 248 limbs and 365 sinews (similar to the 613 commandments of the Torah). Now if one letter is missing from the Torah it is not complete, which led the sages to teach, "One who destroys one Jewish soul is like one who destroys the whole world, and also the opposite: one who sustains a single Jewish soul is like one who has sustained the whole world" (M. Sanhedrin 4:5).

For this reason we say each morning before we pray, "I hereby take on myself the positive commandment of 'Love your neighbor as yourself'" (Leviticus 19:18). All Creation is a complete unity, like the Torah, which can only be called a Torah when all of its letters are present and united. Therefore, even if we see something wicked in our fellow we should only hate that wickedness in him, but the holy element in him we must love like ourselves. The Baal Shem Tov (may his soul rest in supernal repose) said that a fully righteous person who has no wickedness in himself sees no wickedness in anyone else. Further, anyone who sees something wrong in his fellow is like someone looking in a mirror: if his face is dirty that is how it will appear in the mirror, but if his face is clean then he sees no blemish. Just as he is, that is how he will appear.

This is what it means to "love your neighbor as yourself": as [you relate to] yourself. If we see something unfavorable in ourselves, we do not hate ourselves but only that unfavorable thing.

This is how we should relate to our fellow. In the end, we are all one. Does not our fellow have a divine portion and a letter in the Torah, just as we have? But, the gentiles' souls have their source in the husks, and therefore their speech also has the character of the husks. Most of what they have to say is foulmouthed and the like.

But, we might ask, how do the husks have power to give gentiles the capacity to speak? The source of that power is from the *leshon hara* (gossip and evil speech) that Jews speak, or their idle talk. It is for this reason that the sin of *leshon hara* is as weighty as the three transgressions (for which one should die rather than trespass): idolatry, illicit sexual relations, and murder. This act *(leshon hara)* powers the speech of the gentiles who themselves are idolaters, engage in illicit sexual relations, and commit murder. For this reason Scripture says, "Who is the one who desires life, loving life, seeing good?" (Psalm 34:13). And not evil? That person should be like the righteous one we spoke of before, who does not see the flaws in his neighbor. Further, "Guard your tongue from evil (and your lips from speaking guile), turn from evil," and then "do good" (ibid., verses 14–15). The essential element is to turn from evil, that is, forsaking evil ways with a full heart and contrition. In this vein the sages taught, "One who marries a woman on the condition that he is a righteous person but is found to be a scoundrel is still married, since we suspect that perhaps he had thoughts of *teshuvah* in the meantime" (Kiddushin 49b). And, the intention alone is sufficient to make him sufficiently righteous (to fulfill his condition).

How is this so? "Every sin creates a prosecuting attorney" (Avot 4:11). How is it created? Someone who commits a sin first thinks about it, which generates the soul of a husk. When he commits the sin, he creates the body. When later he thinks of doing *teshuvah*, these thoughts repair his earlier thoughts, removing the vital force from the husk, which then remains like a lifeless stone.

Why is leaving off from committing a sin in the heart called contrition (*ḥarata*)? This term derives from the phrase, "human script (*ḥeret enosh*)" (Isaiah 8:1). Truly, in changing one's behavior, it is verbal confession that is most effective, and it should flow from the heart. One who spoils (his life) and sins erases the letter that is his root-soul (as it were) and cuts himself off from holiness. And, when later he speaks his confession, his words are drawn from his root-letter. In this manner he renews his letter and writes afresh that which he had erased. The most important thing is that his confession should flow from the heart, just as a stylus or pen will not work if you do not dip it first in ink: in this way we understand the verse, "[my tongue is the] pen of an expert scribe" (Psalm 45:2). For this writing to be effective we must connect our hearts. Then we can "do good," and not again turn away from it.

There are words that we have to speak, like those necessary to conduct business, but even they can be a form of divine service. This is like one who writes a Torah scroll. First he has to prepare the parchment from some material substance, from animal hides, to create something on which the letters can abide. (Similarly, we are physical beings, and therefore we need something material on which the divine holiness may abide.) The scribe must then prepare staves for the Torah scroll, which are called "Trees of Life" from the verse, "It is a tree of life to all who hold fast to it" (Proverbs 3:18), since by them we can hold fast to the letters of the Torah. Similarly, we who serve the Holy One must create a vessel in every entity, whether in our work or in any other obligatory worldly endeavor. In this manner these activities are called "those who hold fast to it," since through them we are able to observe the Torah, as the sages said, "If there is no flour, then there is no Torah" (Avot 3:17). Everything must be for the sake of serving the Holy One, not for our own sake (like the deluded and wicked ones).

For example, the sages taught in the Talmud, "'[Happy are they who act justly,] who do right at all times' (Psalm 106:3). [Is it possible to do right at all times? Rather this is what our teachers at Yavneh, and some say Rabbi Eliezer, taught:] This refers to one who feeds and sustains his minor children, etc." (Ketubot 50a, cf. M. Ketubot 4:6). That is, the father (who, according to the rabbis, is otherwise not responsible for their upkeep) realizes that there is also a portion of the Divine in them, and that the Holy One has appointed him as an administrator of these divine portions, to support them. If this is his intention, then his endeavors on their behalf is divine service. But if he does not think so, then, even though he supports them, his work is considered *avodah.*

Similarly, the Talmud teaches, "This is like two people who roasted their Passover offerings [one of whom ate his for the sake of the commandment, while the other one ate his out of gluttony]. Regarding the one who ate his for the sake of the commandment, Scripture says, "[The paths of Adonai are smooth;] the righteous walk in them" (Hosea 14:10); regarding the one who ate his out of gluttony, it says, "Sinners stumble on them" (ibid.).

From this we can see that in one and the same act, two people can do the same thing, but according to their intention and their awareness, they are not equal. One will bring himself closer to the Holy One, and the other will distance himself. In all cases, the most important thing is the awareness, the degree of *kavanah,* as it says, "Know Him in all of your ways" (Proverbs 3:6).

This is the meaning then of the verse, "This is the Torah: when a person dies in a tent." That which makes us human beings is the divine portion in us, which is the letter from the Torah. But "the Torah is sustained only by one who kills his 'self' for its sake": specifically "his self," so that his intention is never for his own sake. He kills the thought that anything happens for his sake, that his ego never be remembered or noted, but everything be for the sake of serving the Holy One.

(Me'or Einayim, Ḥukkat,
s.v. zot hatorah adam ki yamut ba'ohel)

Annotated Bibliography of Sources Cited

Hasidic Sources

Avodat Yisrael Hashalem. Jerusalem: Siftei Tzadikim, 5759/1999.
> Written by Rabbi Yisrael, Maggid of Koznitz (1733–1814). He was one of the first propagators of Hasidism in Congress Poland. His teachers were Shemuel Shmelke Horowitz of Nikolsburg, Dov Baer (the Maggid of Mezritch), Elimelekh of Lyzhensk, and Levi Yitzhak of Berdichev, with whom he was on friendly terms. This work was published around 1832.

Degel Mahaneh Efraim Hashalem. Jerusalem: Mir Publishing, 5755/1995.
> Written by Rabbi Moshe Hayim Efraim of Sudylkow (c. 1740–1800?), grandson of Yisrael ben Eliezer, the Baal Shem Tov. In this work he frequently reports teachings of his grandfather.

Divrei Moshe. Bnei Brak: Institute for the Dispersion of the Teachings of Hasidut "Nahalat Tzvi", 5762/2002.
> Written by Rabbi Moshe Shoham ben Dan of Dolina, a student of the Baal Shem Tov. In this work (first published in Polonnoye in 1801), he quotes teachings of his teacher, as well as the notable hasidic master Yehiel Mikhel of Zlotzhov.

Divrei Shaul. Brooklyn, NY: R. Sh. Sharf, 1985.
> Written by Rabbi Yosef Shaul Natansohn (1817–1878), a leading talmudist in Lvov, Ukraine (once Poland), where he also erved as the chief rabbi. His legal works include *Sho'eil Umeishiv* and *Yam Shel*

Shelomo, and *Magen Giborim* and *Me'irat Einayim* with his brother-in-law Rabbi Mordecai Ze'ev Itinge. His interpretive commentaries on Scriptures and rabbinic works include *Divrei Shaul* on the Torah, on the Haftarah (prophetic readings), on the Passover Haggadah, etc.

Hanhagot Tzadikim. 6 vols; ed. Ḥayim Shelomo Halevi Rothenburg. Jerusalem, 5748/1998.

A collection of personal practices *(hanhagot)* includes that of Tzvi Elimelekh of Dinov (1785–1841), which appear in the first volume. He is the author of *Bnei Yissakhar,* and the disciple of Tzvi Hirsch of Zhidachov, Yaakov Yitzḥak "Haḥozeh" of Lublin, and Rabbi Yisrael, the Maggid of Koznitz.

Itturei Torah. Ed. Aharon Yaakov Greenberg; Tel Aviv: Yavneh Publishing, 1993.

The editor was active in Palestine and in the early years of the State of Israel. He served in the first five sessions of the Knesset, as vice-chairman of the session for the last three before his death in 1963. His background was in the world of Hasidism, and was the son-in-law of Rabbi Yitzḥak Zelig Morgenstern, the rebbe of Sokolov (of the Kotzk school). He served in the leadership of the Torah Va'avodah movement in Israel. The teachings in this collection first appeared as weekly lessons in the Israeli weekly *HaTzofeh* and in the New York weekly *HaDoar.*

Kedushat Levi Hashalem. 2 vols; ed. Michael Derbaremdiger. Brooklyn, NY: Machon Kedushat Levi, 1995)

Written by Rabbi Levi Yitzḥak of Berdichev (c. 1740–1810). He was a distinguished pupil of Rabbi Dov Baer, the Maggid of Mezritch, to whom he came through the offices of Rabbi Shemuel Shmelke Horowitz of Nikolsburg. He worked to expand the influence of Hasidism in Poland. His teachings were published first in Slavuta (1798) and then again in 1811, with additional material included from manuscripts by his sons.

Keter Shem Tov. Brooklyn, NY: Kehot Publications Society, 2001.

A collection of teachings of the Baal Shem Tov, taken from the works of Rabbi Yaakov Yosef of Polonnoye by Rabbi Aaron Cohen of Apta. First published in 1794.

Likkutim Yekarim. Jerusalem: Mosdot Toldot Avraham Yitzḥak, 5758/1998.
Written by by Rabbi Meshullam Feivush Heller of Zbarazh (died c. 1796). He was a student of early hasidic teachers, particularly Rabbi Yeḥiel Mikhel of Zlotzhov and Rabbi Dov Baer, the Maggid of Mezritch. While there is some question as to the authenticity of this claim, Rabbi Meshullam Feivush presents the teachings in his book (first published in 1792) as those of his teachers

Magid Devarav Leyaakov (Likkutei Amarim). Jerusalem: Mosdot Toldot Avraham Yitzhak, 5758/1998.
This is a collection of the teachings of Rabbi Dov Baer, the Maggid of Mezritch, the leading disciple of the Baal Shem Tov. This collection was published by his student Rabbi Shelomo of Lutsk in 1781, and is one of the primary sources for understanding the theology and practice of this central figure in the development of Hasidism.

Me'or Einayim. 2 vols. New Square, NY: Machon Me'or Torah, 1997.
Written by Rabbi Menaḥem Naḥum of Chernobyl (1730–1897). He was born into a rabbinic family and received a traditional rabbinic education, at which he excelled. He was introduced to the Baal Shem Tov and became one of his disciples, subsequently following the Maggid of Mezritch after the former's death. This work was published in Slavuta in 1797, after the death of the author.

Me'or Vashemesh Hashalem Hamefo'ar. 2 vols. Jerusalem: Even Israel, 5752/1992.
Written by Rabbi Kalonymus Kalman Halevi Epstein (1751–1823). He was a disciple of Rabbi Elimelekh of Lyzhensk and Yaakov Yitzḥak "Haḥozeh" of Lublin. This work, pubished in 1842, is one of the fundamental works of Hasidism, and includes information on the activities and the personalities of other popular teachers and leaders.

No'am Elimelekh Hamefo'ar. Jerusalem: Mesamḥei Lev, 5759/1999.

Written by Rabbi Elimelekh of Lyzhensk (1717–1887). He was an important student of Rabbi Dov Baer, the Maggid of Mezritch, who developed his thought in terms of the practical role of the "tzadik," the perfect master whose spiritual devotion mediated between heaven and earth, raising up and redeeming his followers with his efforts. He was one of the founders of Hasidism in Galicia.

Ohev Yisrael Hamefo'ar. Jerusalem, 5756/1996.

Written by Rabbi Avraham Yehoshua Heschel of Apt (d. 1825). He was a disciple of Rabbi Elimelekh of Lyzhensk, and possibly also of Rabbi Yeḥiel Mikhel of Zlotzhov. He carried forward the teachings of his master regarding the role of the tzadik, and was known for his devotion to his followers. This book was first published in Zhitomir in 1863.

Or Haḥokhmah Hamefo'ar. 2 vols; ed. Yisrael Ephraim Fischel Landau. Brooklyn, NY: Gefen Publishing, 5761/2001.

Written by Rabbi Uri Feivel of Dubenka (c. 1730–1898). He was a student of the Baal Shem Tov, and subsequently of his disciples Rabbi Kehat Hakohen of Varish and Rabbi Leib ben Sarah. This book was published in Lashtzov in 1815.

Or Hame'ir. 2 vols; ed. Yisroel Yaakov Vidovsky. Jerusalem: Even Israel, 5755/1995.

Written by Rabbi Ze'ev Wolf of Zhitomer (d. 1800). He was a student of Rabbi Dov Baer, the Maggid of Mezritch. This text, first published in Koretz in 1787, contains significant material reflecting the early history of Hasidism and the teachings of its early founders.

Or Torah. Brooklyn, NY: Kehot Publication Society, 1972.

This is a collection of teachings of Rabbi Dov Baer, the Maggid of Mezritch, published by Rabbi Yeshayahu of Donovich (Koretz, 1804).

Sefat Emet. Jerusalem, Pe'eir Hatorah, 5731/1971.

Written by Rabbi Yehudah Aryeh Leib Alter of Ger (1847–1805). The descendant of a distinguished family of scholars and hasidic leaders, he succeeded his grandfather as the head of the Polish hasidic community centered in the town of Gora Klawaria (also known as Gur or Ger). This work comprises his Sabbath teachings through the more than thirty years he served as head of the community (1871–1805)

Teshuot Ḥen. Bnei Brak: Hasifriyah Hahasidit, 5759/1999.

Written by Rabbi Gedaliah ben Isaac of Lunietz (d. 1785). He was a student of both Rabbi Dov Baer, the Maggid of Mezritch, and Rabbi Yaakov Yosef of Polonnoye. This book was first published in Berdichev in 1816.

Tiferet Shelomo. 2 vols. Jerusalem, 5752/1992.

Written by Rabbi Shelomo Hakohen Rabinowich of Radomsk (1803–1866). He was associated with the emerging school of Polish Hasidism as a student of Rabbi Meir of Apta. This work appeared between 1867 and 1869.

Tikkunei Zohar. Tel Aviv: Mosad Harav Kook, 5709/1949.

This text is considered popularly to be a part of the larger work called the Zohar, yet modern scholars see it as a later addition to that work. It appeared in the generation or so following the death of Moses de Leon, considered by many to be the main author of the Zohar itself. It is an esoteric work, offering commentary on the first word of the Torah as a means of entering into mystical discussions.

Toldot Yaakov Yosef. 2 vols. Jerusalem: Vielepoli Association, 5733/1973.

Written by Rabbi Yaakov Yosef Hakohen of Polonnoye (died c. 1782). In 1741 he came under the influence of the Baal Shem Tov and became one of his prominent followers. This work, published in Koretz in 1780, is the first book to appear relating the fundamental teachings of Ḥasidism, containing many citations of lessons from his teacher.

Yismaḥ Moshe. 2 vols; ed. Shmiel Teitlebaum. Brooklyn, NY, 1997.

Written by Rabbi Moshe Teitlebaum (1759–1841), who was a student of Rabbi Yaakov Yitzḥak "Haḥozeh" of Lublin and among the first to spreaed Hasidism into northern and central Hungary. This book was first published in Lemberg, 1848–1861.

Rabbinic Works

Mekhilta D'Rabbi Yishmael, ed. Ḥayyim Shaul Horowitz and Israel Abraham Rabin. Jerusalem: Sifrei Wahrman, 5730/1970.

Sifrei al Sefer Devarim, ed. Eliezer Aryeh Finkelstein. New York, NY: The Rabbinical Assembly, 5729/1969.

Other Works

Bauby, Jean-Dominique. *The Diving Bell and the Butterfly.* Translated by Jeremy Leggatt. New York: Knopf, 1997.

Buber, Martin. *Tales of the Hasidim* (2 vols.). Translated by Olga Marx. New York: Schocken Books, 1947.

Fischer, Norman. *Opening to You: Zen-Inspired Translations of the Psalms.* New York: Viking Compass, 2002.

Pinsky, Robert. *Jersey Rain.* New York: Farrar, Straus and Giroux, 2000.

Salzberg, Sharon. *Lovingkindness: The Revolutionary Art of Happiness.* Boston: Shambhala Press, 2002.

Sarna, Nahum. *The JPS Torah Commentary: Exodus.* Philadelphia, PA: Jewish Publication Society, 1991.

Sarna, Nahum. *The JPS Torah Commentary: Genesis.* Philadelphia, PA: Jewish Publication Society, 1989.